EARLY SPANISH FLORIDA

FLORIDA HUMANITIES PARTNERSHIP PUBLICATIONS

UNIVERSITY PRESS OF FLORIDA

Florida A&M University, Tallahassee
Florida Atlantic University, Boca Raton
Florida Gulf Coast University, Ft. Myers
Florida International University, Miami
Florida State University, Tallahassee
New College of Florida, Sarasota
University of Central Florida, Orlando
University of Florida, Gainesville
University of North Florida, Jacksonville
University of South Florida, Tampa
University of West Florida, Pensacola

University Press of Florida
Gainesville/Tallahassee/Tampa/Boca Raton
Pensacola/Orlando/Miami/Jacksonville/Ft. Myers/Sarasota

Judith A. Bense

EARLY SPANISH FLORIDA

Unearthing the History of America's Oldest Colony

COVER ART *front cover, clockwise from top*, Spanish artifacts found at Fort San Anton, courtesy of the Florida Museum of Natural History—Historical Archaeology Collections; rendering of Doña Maria Melendez, art by William Celander, courtesy of the Florida Museum of Natural History—Historical Archaeology Collections; burned Spanish soldier's house at Fort San Joan, 1566–1568, courtesy of the Museum of Anthropological Archaeology, University of Michigan; a Southeastern Indian being sold into slavery, courtesy of Granger Historical Archive. *spine* Spanish ceramic artifact from Presidio Santa María, courtesy of the Archaeology Institute, University of West Florida.
COVER DESIGN Mindy Basinger Hill

Funding for this publication was provided through a grant from Florida Humanities with funds from the National Endowment for the Humanities. Any views, findings, conclusions, or recommendations expressed in this publication do not necessarily represent those of Florida Humanities or the National Endowment for the Humanities. As the nonprofit, state affiliate of the National Endowment for the Humanities, Florida Humanities supports programs and resources that explore the history and culture of Florida and encourage a lifelong appreciation of literature, literacy, and learning.

Published in the United States of America

31 30 29 28 27 26 6 5 4 3 2 1

A record of cataloging-in-publication information is available from the Library of Congress.

ISBN 978-0-8130-8148-9

The University Press of Florida is the scholarly publishing agency for the State University System of Florida, comprising Florida A&M University, Florida Atlantic University, Florida Gulf Coast University, Florida International University, Florida State University, New College of Florida, University of Central Florida, University of Florida, University of North Florida, University of South Florida, and University of West Florida.

University Press of Florida
2046 NE Waldo Road
Suite 2100
Gainesville, FL 32609
floridapress.org

GPSR EU Authorized Representative: Mare Nostrum Group B.V., Mauritskade 21D, 1091 GC Amsterdam, The Netherlands, gpsr@mare-nostrum.co.uk

THIS BOOK IS DEDICATED

TO THE PEOPLE OF FLORIDA,

BOTH PAST AND PRESENT.

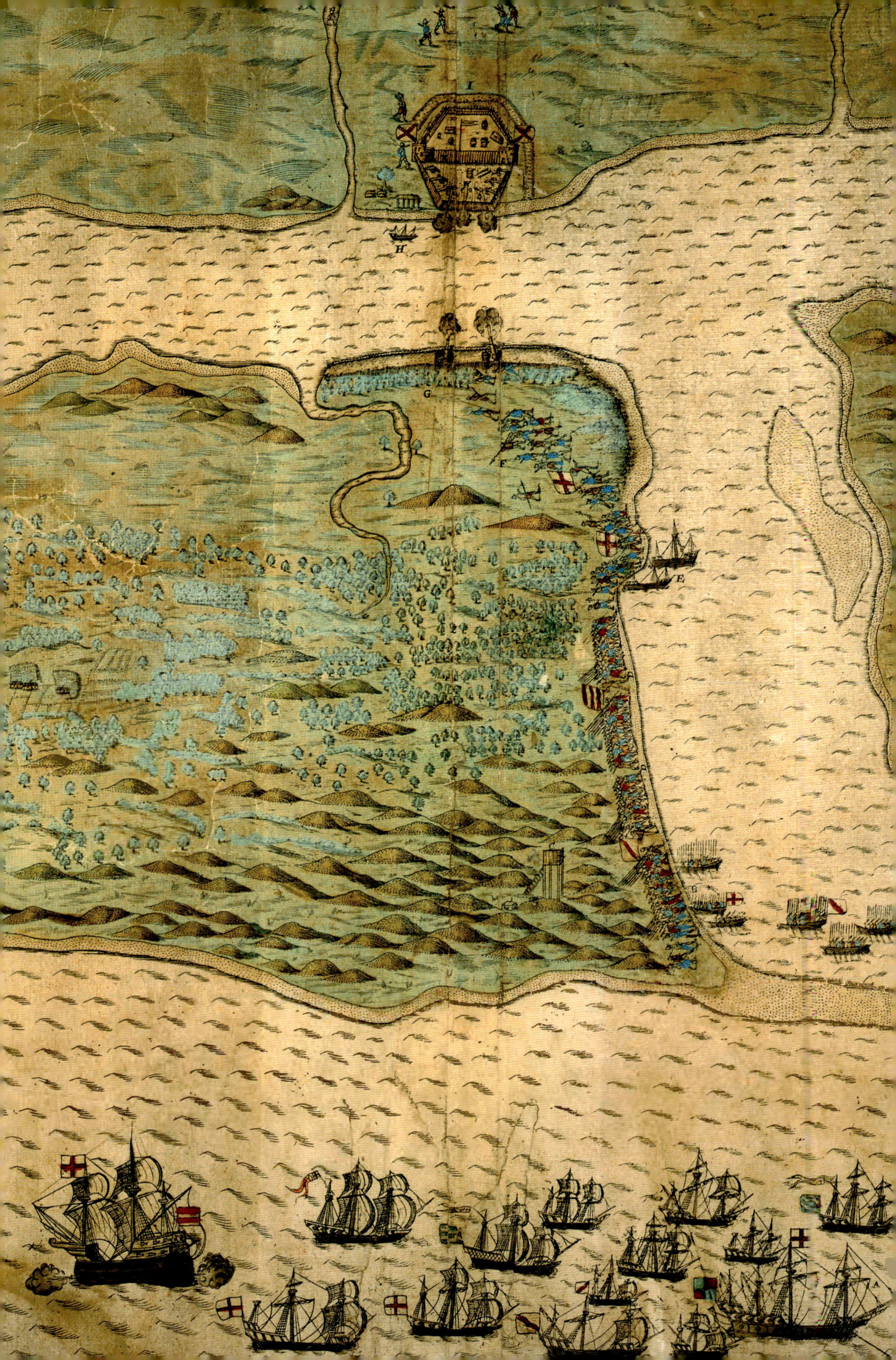

CONTENTS

PREFACE

For as long as I can remember, I wanted to be an archaeologist. Growing up on a small dairy farm near Panama City in northwest Florida, I was exposed to *National Geographic* magazine at home and the *Weekly Reader* in the small country elementary school I attended, where I learned about exciting discoveries in Africa and new dating methods using radiocarbon. I also had an inspiring ancient history teacher in high school who explained that the past is knowable despite the passage of time. I read everything I could find about archaeology and history, went to two universities, and at the age of twenty-seven, earned my PhD in anthropology/archaeology. I have never looked back. I have practiced archaeology for almost fifty years, except for nine years when I had the privilege of being the president of the University of West Florida in Pensacola. That's where I have spent virtually all my career, where I am still an emerita president and professor, and where I wrote this book.

This is my sixth book, the second explicitly written for lay readers. I have written and published more than fifty academic journal articles, reports, and books covering a variety of topics in archaeology. I also have always felt a responsibility to share with the public what I and other archaeologists have discovered through the media that people regularly watch, read, or listen to, including radio, TV, newspapers, magazines, and public talks. This book was written for people who are curious about Florida's history and archaeology. Florida is a unique state with a surprising story. One thing you will notice about this book is that there are more than 150 illustrations, most of which are in color. I believe in the adage that "a picture is worth a thousand words," and I want you to "see" the archaeology and history as well as read about it.

The story of *Early Spanish Florida* begins in 1513 with the Spanish invasion of the Florida peninsula by Ponce de León and ends in 1763 when Spain lost its Florida colony to the British. Spanish Florida initially extended north to what is now South Carolina and west to the Mississippi River, an area where hundreds of thousands of Indigenous people lived. There are three versions of the story of what happened in the first 250 years the Spanish owned Florida: the Spanish, the Native American, and the African. Each group had a different experience, goals, successes, and failures. I tried to present each point of view in the interweaving of archaeology and history of the Florida we know today, from the first encounters between Natives and Spaniards to massive Spanish armies marching through the region to failed colonies, Catholic missions, and finally, the British invasion and commercial Indian slave trade. This narrative includes the latest discoveries of archaeologists and historians who have unearthed incredible information about the people and their experiences in Early Spanish Florida. I think you will be surprised and intrigued by many things that happened in the first 250 years of Florida's colonial past. I certainly am. I hope you enjoy the journey into Early Spanish Florida.

EARLY SPANISH FLORIDA

31BK22
STR 1
6/20/08

ONE
INTRODUCTION

If you know little or nothing about Florida's archaeology and history and would like to know something about it—but not more than you really want to know—this book was written for you! It is not a textbook but more like a *National Geographic* magazine, with many illustrations and maps to guide you along the way. This book summarizes what is now known about the first 250 years of the Spanish occupation of the province of La Florida. There is much more information available in books, websites, and places to visit, which are listed at the end of each chapter. So, relax now and enjoy the little-known story based on the latest research on the history and archaeology of Early Spanish Florida.

Many people think that Florida's history began in earnest in the late 1800s when the railroads and hotels from the Northeast reached Florida's east coast. Others think of it beginning with the land booms of the 1920s or with World War II. However, Native Floridians, the first Floridians, had lived in Florida for more than twelve thousand years before the Spanish arrived in the early 1500s. Florida has the *oldest* recorded history in the United States. By the time Jamestown was founded in 1607, a third generation of Euro-Americans was already growing up in St. Augustine, founded in 1565. When the Pilgrims came ashore at Plymouth in 1620, St. Augustine was due for urban renewal. It was a town with a fort, church, seminary, hospital, fish market, and about 120 shops and houses. In what is now the United States, La Florida saw the first European explorations, colonization attempts, settlements, conversions to Christianity, churches, enslaved people, mixed-race marriages, and much more. We also have shipwrecks from this Early Spanish era, including three ships of a 1559 Spanish fleet that sank in Pensacola Bay.

We will begin the story of Early Spanish Florida with the arrival of Ponce de León, who thought the landmass was an island when he claimed it for Spain in 1513, and we will end it when the Spanish lost Florida to the British in 1763. There are many surprises in the Early Spanish occupation of Florida. For starters, the first capital was founded on Parris Island, South Carolina, in 1566, and (on paper at least) the province of La Florida included almost *all* of

FIGURE 1.1.
A typical sixteenth-century Spanish army.

what is now the Southeastern United States. But by 1763, the occupied area of Spanish Florida had shrunk to only two small areas around St. Augustine and Pensacola.

This book is an illustrated synopsis of what happened in Early Spanish Florida based on what we now know from historians and archaeologists. The story is not a particularly pretty one. It was a classic clash of cultures: well-armed invaders at first literally waged war on resident Native Americans and tried to take them and their land by force. Five hundred years ago, that is how Europeans fought each other. In warring against the Native Americans, the Spanish military had superior weapons of metal, armored soldiers on huge war horses, and attacking war dogs; with those advantages, they thought they could defeat any Native American force (figure 1.1). The truth is that while the Spanish armies won many battles against the Native people, they lost the war and were driven out of the Natives' homelands.

This story of Early Spanish Florida is organized by time. Each chapter reflects a distinct period during which the Spanish tried a different method and approach to settle and hold on to their colonial province. It starts with the Spaniards who first found Florida while raiding to capture Indians to sell to their colonists in the Caribbean as slave laborers (figure 1.2). We will follow the first Spanish military campaigns as they explored the region, waging war on the Native Americans in their path. When the Spanish realized they could not conquer Florida's Indigenous people, they pivoted to a peaceful approach toward Native people and traditional colonialism. After that failed, the Spanish turned to using religious conversion and a mission system to pacify and suppress the Indians (figure 1.3). When this approach also failed, we will see that Spain's European rivals, France and Britain, swooped in and took almost all the Southeast. With little Spanish resistance, the French and British reduced Spanish Florida to the area around St. Augustine and the peninsula. The Spaniards' last attempt to keep their rivals from taking more land was to fortify and occupy Pensacola Bay, the only deepwater port on the northern Gulf of Mexico. But this was too little too late, and though West Florida successfully held the line, Spain finally handed over its entire Florida colony to Britain in 1763 in a treaty ending a European war.

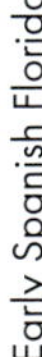

FIGURE 1.2.
Spaniards branding captured Indians about 1530.

FIGURE 1.3.
Apalachee Indians raising a cross at Mission San Luis.

I have been a historical archaeologist specializing in the Early Spanish period for more than thirty years. When I started my research, I focused on West Florida because little was known of what occurred there during the first Spanish occupation. We have learned that what happened there was both different and similar to what happened in East Florida, and the military colonists there had quite unusual experiences. Just as it is today, West Florida was different from the rest of Florida, and the experiences of the people there provide the "rest of the story" of Early Spanish Florida.

Our Florida is a land of swaying palms, beachfront condos, interstates,

FIGURE 1.4. Example of a typical Spanish colonial document (*legajo*).

and entertainment destinations. But five centuries ago, other people lived here, people whose ancestors had their own cultures, religions, and ways of life. They hunted, fished, and farmed, living in villages, towns, and rural hamlets. This book will tell the story of how new people with a different culture—Spanish Europeans—arrived and, over the next two and a half centuries, instigated changes that transformed both the Natives and Spaniards forever. This is the most intriguing and least understood time of Florida's three hundred years as a European colony. It is the very beginning, and it shaped what would become "our" Florida.

A key reason why we know so much about Early Spanish Florida is that the Spanish were incredible recordkeepers. They usually wrote in triplicate, sending copies of reports, letters, military orders, inventories, shipping documents, and much more to the Spanish colonial government in Seville and the colonial administrative centers of Mexico City and Havana (figure 1.4). Historians have long studied the meticulous documents from Early Spanish Florida preserved in archives. Over the past two centuries, they have written scores of books and other publications. Historians caution us to remember

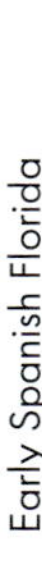

that the writers of historical documents (priests, military officers, designated scribes, clerks, accountants) had personal and professional agendas behind what they wrote. In other words, the writers of documents about early Florida began with a bias. They were only writing their interpretations of what they saw (while portraying their actions in the best possible light), and the documents were intended for their superiors, who often had never been to Florida. As we know today, multiple eyewitnesses can have quite different and even conflicting accounts of past events. We also must remember that only a small sample of the existing Spanish documents have been found and studied.

Archaeologists also have their biases. For example, it is only in the last few decades that there has been a strong interest in the archaeology of Spanish Florida. On the other hand, British and early American sites such as Jamestown, Mount Vernon, and Williamsburg have long drawn a great deal of archaeological interest and research, and much is known about how people lived in the British colonies. This British bias resulted in a paucity of knowledge about the archaeology of Spanish Florida and the people who lived here in the past. But much has changed in the last sixty years.

FIGURE 1.5. Archaeological excavations in Plaza Ferdinand, downtown historic Pensacola.

A relatively new branch of research, *historical archaeology,* has developed, which combines both the written and unwritten records of people in the past. It blends what people wrote about what they witnessed, thought, and did (history) with the materials left behind from what they did (archaeology) (figure 1.5). This partnership has produced a more accurate and robust picture of what happened in the past compared to those studies that use only one source of information. This book is a product of historical archaeology. The narrative you are about to read brings together information from scores of research projects that used history, archaeology, geography, cartography, shipwrecks, climatology, chemistry, and many other fields to understand Early Spanish Florida.

All the people living in Spanish Florida adjusted and adapted during the 250 years of colonization. They would be shocked that their struggling former colony is now a flourishing state of the United States, with more than twenty-two million people, 27 percent of whom have some Spanish heritage, and where today, Spanish is considered a second language. The story of what happened so long ago in Florida is fascinating, and much more is known today than ever.

TWO

DISCOVERY AND FIRST ENCOUNTERS

Violence between the Spanish and Natives in a vast swath of land, the former La Florida, marked the first seventy years after Spanish discovery. However, this story began long before Columbus, in the eighth century, when Muslim Moors from northern Africa invaded and took over Spain. A seven-hundred-year religious civil war followed that finally drove the Moors out in 1492. Within a few months after the victory, Queen Isabella sponsored Columbus's fateful voyage in search of a shortcut to Asia and its riches. Although he thought he had found islands off the coast of Asia, he had in fact discovered a "New World" that he claimed for Spain. The first encounters between Europeans and Native Americans shocked both groups, and they reacted predictably. The Spanish attacked, and the Natives resisted. The Spanish quickly realized they had superior weapons and experience in conquest, and the Natives promptly discovered that they vastly outnumbered the Spanish, who were vulnerable to ambush attacks.

Following the traditional medieval approach to encountering foreign lands, the Spanish attacked the Indigenous people they found in the Caribbean and soon mercilessly enslaved them on their plantations, ranches, and mines. The Indian populations on the islands soon collapsed, and the Spanish went in search of more Indigenous slaves, finding the Florida peninsula. However, Natives attacked them everywhere they went. Word had spread among Native groups spread over hundreds of miles that the Spanish were an enemy to be resisted at all costs. The Spanish made three efforts to explore and colonize Florida: expeditions led by Ponce de León, Pánfilo de Narváez, and Hernando de Soto. Hostilities between the Spanish and Native peoples characterized each expedition. De Soto's four-year expedition between 1539 and 1543 defined the size of the Florida province for the Crown: from the Gulf of Mexico north to today's South Carolina, from the Atlantic west to Arkansas, and south down the Mississippi River. His army

FIGURE 2.1. Provinces of Spain in 1492.

spread disease and violence everywhere they went on their four-thousand-mile trek through the Southeast.

The most significant result of the three exploratory expeditions was the realization that there were no deposits of gold or silver in the region, nor were there large agricultural populations. The Native Americans violently resisted the invasion of their homelands, and their relentless resistance drove each of the Spanish armies out of their territory. As a result, the Spanish implemented a new policy in which the Natives would be treated peacefully, and colonies of settlers would be established and protected by a military force. Tristán de Luna led the first such peaceful colonization attempt, but it was devastated by a hurricane soon after landing on the shores of Pensacola Bay. Overall, the clash of cultures during these seven decades was severe and significantly changed both the Natives and the Spanish.

The Spanish *Reconquista*

In 711, Muslim Moors from northern Africa invaded and quickly conquered Iberia—present-day Spain and Portugal. Spanish Catholic armies slowly retook Iberia in a seven-hundred-year-long civil war called the Reconquista (Reconquest). By the early fifteenth century, Iberia had two large, powerful provinces: Castile and Aragon. In 1469, the heirs to both these provinces

Ferdinand and Isabella, married, uniting about 85 percent of Iberia. They immediately turned their attention to finishing the Reconquista, which they did in 1492 (figure 2.1).

For those seven hundred years, it was private armies that executed the Reconquista. Wealthy aristocrats called *adelantados* supported large armies to wage military campaigns that were approved by the monarchs. In return, the aristocratic sponsors were awarded the territories they conquered, and they enslaved the Muslim people living there. Other private armies also fought in the Reconquista, funded by wealthy minor nobility called *hidalgos*. Hidalgos had contracts with the Crown to seize and defend Muslim lands and share in the looted plunder they found. The perspective of the adelantados and hidalgos was typical of the medieval period: defeat the Moors, take their land and resources, and subjugate or enslave the people. Seven centuries of war developed a strong warrior culture in Spain. By the time the Moors were driven out of Spain in January 1492, the social, economic, and ideological systems were securely in place for new and profitable military conquests by the adelantados and hidalgos.

The Spanish Caribbean

Florida's story began when Columbus landed in the Bahama and Caribbean Islands in 1492 en route to Asia. The goal of Columbus's expedition was a monetary one: to find a shorter, cheaper route from Europe to Southeast Asia and India for easier access to their valuable trade goods. At the time, there was only one way to reach China: the dangerous, four-thousand-mile-long Silk Road, which was a four-year round-trip trek. Marco Polo's book, published in 1300, described his long journey from Europe to China and its riches. Inspired by Polo, Columbus was determined to find a more efficient way to reach Asia by traveling west from Europe by sea, and he had a copy of Polo's book with him. The risk he took was believing the earth was round, not flat. At the time, almost everyone thought that the world was flat and that Columbus's fleet would fall off its edge into an abyss. Of course, Columbus did not fall off the edge of a flat earth, proving that it was round. Instead of Asia, Columbus found a new and unexpected huge hemisphere of land, the Americas, populated by millions of people and with its own fourteen-thousand-year-long history.

One of the newly united Spanish Crown's first ventures of exploration, then, was sponsoring Columbus's expedition to Asia to find a shorter trade

FIGURE 2.2.
Portrait of Christopher Columbus.

route (figure 2.2). Columbus was promised 10 percent of whatever riches he found, a noble title, and the governorship of any lands he should encounter. Queen Isabella personally funded two-thirds of the costs of the voyage, and Columbus supplied the rest.

Columbus first landed on the Bahama Islands and soon explored nearby Caribbean islands. Because he was convinced the islands he found were off India, he called the Native people "Indians," which became the Spaniards' term for all the Indigenous people they encountered, a term that endures today. On Christmas Eve 1492, however, his flagship ran aground near the coast of Hispaniola (figure 2.3). Unable to onboard the crew in his two remaining small ships, they unloaded the cargo and supplies with the help of a village of local Taíno/Arawak people. He named the settlement La Navidad (Christmas) and directed the men to build a fort and search for gold while he was gone. Columbus returned to Spain with his remaining two ships to share the good news with his Spanish royal sponsors.

When Columbus returned to Spain, the news of his discoveries shocked the European world, and both Spain and Portugal claimed ownership of the newly discovered lands. Pope Alexander VI settled the issue in May 1493 with the Treaty of Tordesillas. Under the treaty, the pope drew a dividing line in the Atlantic Ocean from pole to pole, designating the rights to acquire and explore new lands west of the line to Spain and east of the line to Portugal. Unsurprisingly, other European nations ignored the treaty, but for the first seventy years, the Spanish had exclusive access to almost all of the Americas.

Columbus returned to Hispaniola a few months later with a large group of people to

INDIGENOUS PEOPLE

Indigenous people are distinct social and cultural groups that shared ancestral ties to New World lands and natural resources *before* colonization. They have distinct cultures, languages, beliefs, and knowledge sets. In this book, I also refer to the Indigenous people in Early Spanish Florida as Natives, Native Americans, and Indians, and the terms are used interchangeably.

FIGURE 2.3. Map of the locations of early Spanish landings.

start a colony. On arrival, he found his fort burned, all his men dead, and their supplies spread among the local Indigenous people, the Taíno or Arawaks. This led to a deadly war between the invading Spanish and the resistant Natives. Columbus successfully colonized Hispaniola, defeated the local Taíno people, and enslaved them to work in Spanish mines, plantations, and ranches on the island. The Taíno/Arawak population quickly collapsed from disease, overwork, abuse, and food shortages. Now dependent on Indian slave labor, the Spanish began attacking and capturing Indigenous people on other islands for enslavement on the Hispaniola colony. They raided the nearby Bahama Islands next and took thousands of Indigenous Lucayan people to their settlements on Hispaniola and Cuba, completely depopulating those islands. Soon, Spanish slave raids depopulated all the nearby islands. In need of more and more enslaved Indians for their expanding colonies, the Spanish began an ever-widening circle of slave-raiding voyages. Some of these expeditions probably reached the nearby Florida peninsula by the turn of the sixteenth century. Everywhere the Spanish went, they were met by intense hostility from local Natives. Word quickly spread from Native

FIGURE 2.4. Painting of Ponce de León.

people in the islands to the Florida peninsula that the Spanish were a deadly enemy, and the Spanish encountered severe resistance or flight wherever they landed.

Early Colonizing Attempts

Ponce de León was a top military official in the colonial government of Hispaniola. He had helped crush a Taíno/Arawak rebellion in the Caribbean, and the Crown rewarded him with an appointment as the first governor of Puerto Rico in 1509. He became wealthy from his plantations and mines, but that did not help him politically; he lost his governorship to Columbus's son. The king encouraged him to explore more of the Caribbean. By contract with the king (although at his own expense), de León was to explore new islands, govern any lands he found, and take a portion of any gold, Native Americans, and resources he encountered. On April 2, 1513, he landed on what is now the east coast of Florida, claiming the land for Spain (figure 2.4). Thinking it was a large island, he named it La Florida because he landed at Eastertime, a time of flowers. Local Natives were well aware of how the Spanish operated, and as de León explored the coast, everywhere they stopped local Natives either viciously attacked them or had already fled. Spanish documents state that the expedition explored the southern peninsula, probably landing at the Lake Worth Inlet, Jupiter Inlet, Biscayne Bay, and Estero Bay.

In 1519, Alonso Álvarez de Pineda discovered that Florida was not an island but part of a vast continent. After returning to Puerto Rico briefly, de León ventured back to Florida in 1521 with two hundred colonists, establishing the first intentional Spanish settlement in Florida. Although there is no evidence to support this conjecture, experts think he landed in San Carlos Bay near Cape Coral, where he had encountered and was driven off by the Calusa people in 1513 (figure 2.5). As before, the Calusa attacked the colonists immediately and continuously as the Spanish tried to build structures and plant crops. When an arrow wounded de León, he ordered the colony to be abandoned, and the fearful colonists fled to Cuba, where de León died from an infection of his wound. The Spanish began to view the Florida Indians as

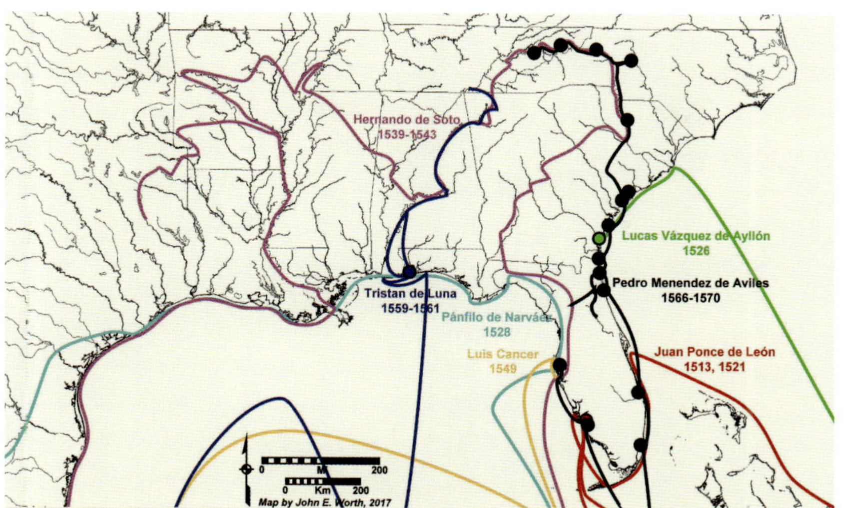

Early exploration routes and colonization attempts in La Florida.

FLORIDA'S EARLY SPANISH ENCOUNTERS

Between 1513 and 1570, Spanish explorers conducted a series of slave raids and short-lived colonization attempts, mostly following the Atlantic and Gulf Coasts.

1513	Juan Ponce de León's landing on the Florida peninsula
1514–1516	Pedro de Salazar's slaving trip to the lower Atlantic Coast
1516	Diego de Miruelo's slaving trip to the Florida Gulf Coast
1519	Alonso Álvarez de Pineda's exploration and mapping of the Gulf Coast
1521	Juan Ponce de León's colonization attempt near Fort Myers
1526	Lucas Vázquez de Ayllón's colonization attempt on Sapelo Sound
1528	Pánfilo de Narváez's attempt to explore and settle the Gulf Coast
1539–1543	Hernando de Soto's military expedition through the Southeast
1546	Friar Luis Cáncer's attempt to establish a religious settlement on Florida's Gulf Coast
1559–1561	Tristán de Luna's colonization attempt on Pensacola Bay

FIGURE 2.5. Calusa Indians driving off Ponce de León, 1513.

a problem since they all had resisted capture and attacked settlers.

Many of Florida's Indigenous peoples had successfully resisted Spanish attempts to capture them for enslavement and to take their lands. Unlike in the Caribbean, Florida Natives had been warned of what the Spanish wanted and how they would try to get it. Their consistent and coordinated resistance efforts across the southern peninsula indicate sophisticated channels of communication between local groups over hundreds of miles.

The demand for slaves for the Spanish Caribbean mines, plantations, and ranches continued, however, and historians feel sure that there were many unrecorded slave raids along the Atlantic Coast both before and after de León's failed attempts. One of the enslaved Indians from near today's Myrtle Beach, South Carolina, wound up in the court of Lucas Vázquez de Ayllón, a royal judge in Hispaniola. Named Francisco de Chicora, he painted a picture of his homeland that was almost too good to be true (and was exactly what the Spanish wanted to hear): gold, silver, good land, and friendly people. Ayllón quickly received a charter to settle Chicora's land and, in 1526, sailed there with some six hundred colonists, their families, friars, African slaves, and Francisco. They founded a colony they named San Miguel de Gualdape, probably on present-day Sapelo Island (figure 2.6). Ayllón died there soon after the colony was established, and the entire enterprise fell apart within

FIGURE 2.6. First encounter locations.

FIGURE 2.7. Pánfilo de Narváez.

weeks due to famine, disease, mutiny of the Spaniards, and escape of the enslaved Africans. Of the original six hundred to seven hundred people in the Ayllón expedition, only 150 survived and returned to Hispaniola.

Military Explorations and Conquest Attempts

Two years after Ayllón's colony failed, Pánfilo de Narváez, a soldier and conquistador, was granted a license to settle and govern the Gulf Coast from the Florida peninsula to New Spain (Mexico) and inland as far as he could control (figure 2.7). He was also instructed to establish two settlements. Narváez's expedition is thought to have landed in Tampa Bay in April 1528 with three hundred men and forty horses, and he began to explore the coastal area from there. Supply ships were sent ahead to meet him at another harbor on the Gulf Coast, but they disappeared and Narváez never saw them again. The expedition left Tampa Bay after the local Tocobaga people told Narváez that the Apalachee to

FIGURE 2.8. Early Spanish explorers of Florida.

the north had abundant food (figure 2.8). When the entrada (expedition) reached Tallahassee, they found a village comprised of about forty houses, but the men were absent. Narváez captured the village, took their stored food, and made hostages of the women, the children, and the chief. Upon their return, the furious Apalachee men positioned themselves on the outskirts of the village and used their exceptional archery skills to attack the Spanish for more than a month. Under this pressure, the Spanish retreated south to a village named Aute, but discovered the Natives had already set it on fire. Tired of losing his men, sick, hungry, and without any gold or food, Narváez became convinced they would never find the missing supply ships. He decided to halt the expedition, walk to the Gulf, build rafts, and sail along the coast to New Spain. They built escape rafts in a protected inlet on Apalachee Bay (figure 2.9) using makeshift bellows to melt down all their iron—such as stirrups, pikes, crossbows, and spurs—to make nails, saws, axes, and other tools. They fashioned planks for the rafts from the abundant pine trees and used pine pitch for caulking. They slaughtered horses for food, making rope from the animals' manes and tails and water containers from their hides. The men sewed their shirts together to make sails. By September, they had made five rough rafts, and the remaining 240 men set out for New Spain.

From the Apalachee perspective, they had driven off a Spanish army of three hundred armed men, including cavalry. They had conducted a successful monthlong siege of their village, occupied by the Spanish, by continuously ambushing and harassing them when they ventured out to find water or food, wounding and killing soldiers and their horses. Their primary weapon was the long bow, which was as tall as a person. Their arrows are said to have been accurate up to two hundred yards, to go through trees as thick as a man's leg, and to easily penetrate Spanish armor. The Apalachee continued harassing the Spanish as they retreated to the coast. So far, Florida Indians had beaten the Spanish in their attempts to defeat, capture, and enslave them or to establish colonies. They forced a well-armed militia of three hundred men to retreat. However, Native people were less successful elsewhere, such as on the coast of South Carolina, where the Spanish enticed about sixty Indians on board with gifts, took them to the Caribbean, and sold them into enslavement.

Narváez's retreating army got as far as the Texas coast before a storm capsized their rafts. Only eighty men survived, and Narváez was among those who perished. Local Indians attacked and killed some of the survivors. Only fifteen people lived to see the following spring, when they started walking toward New Spain. All told, only four of the original three hundred men sur-

FIGURE 2.9. Narváez's men building escape rafts near St. Marks, Florida, on Apalachee Bay.

FIGURE 2.10.
Hernando de Soto.

vived, completing what turned out to be an eight-year, two-thousand-mile journey that took them to the Pacific, down the west coast of New Spain, and eventually, to safety in Mexico City in 1536.

Álvar Núñez Cabeza de Vaca, the expedition's treasurer, was one of the four survivors of the Narváez expedition. In 1542 he published a narrative of the expedition. The account contains invaluable eyewitness accounts of the many Native groups they encountered, the terrain, their struggles and experiences, and how they managed to survive. It is a fascinating story, and de Vaca's book is still in print today. Several documentaries and productions have reenacted the incredible journey of the expedition and how the four men survived.

Undeterred by Narváez's misfortunes and determined to find and claim any valuable resources, eleven years later the Spanish sent another military expedition into Florida, led by Hernando de Soto (figure 2.10). Ruthless and ambitious, de Soto had learned the grim art of subjugation when he had accompanied Francisco Pizarro during the Inca military conquest in 1532–1535. In Central America, de Soto became rich by plundering precious minerals and slave trading in local Natives.

As with Ayllón and Narváez, the Crown made de Soto an adelantado and gave him four years to explore, subjugate the Indigenous people, find suitable places for a new colony, and search for precious metals and gems. He spent his fortune forming an army of six hundred soldiers, various servants and slaves, packs of war dogs, hundreds of horses, and a herd of pigs. Despite his official orders, de Soto's goal was to accumulate personal wealth by finding gold and gems, as Pizarro had done in South America. He expected to conquer and govern a portion of the New World comparable in size to New Spain or Peru. He had no qualms about subjecting people to mutilation, torture, and horrible death to get what he wanted.

De Soto landed on the eastern shore of Tampa Bay, near the mouth of the Little Manatee River, in May 1539. Immediately after landing, groups of soldiers were sent to find and capture local Indians, who in turn harassed the Spanish invaders. The local Natives were skilled archers and formidable fighters, especially against Spanish foot soldiers. Indians also burned their own villages and food to keep them from the Spanish. They fled into

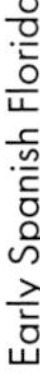

the woods and ambushed groups of soldiers from there.

FIGURE 2.11. Rescue of Juan Ortiz.

Surprisingly, a Spaniard, Juan Ortiz, had been left behind by an expedition sent from Cuba to find the Narváez expedition eleven years earlier. He had been captured by the local Indians and lived with them, learning their language. Rescued by de Soto's troops, Ortiz joined the expedition and became a critical interpreter and guide (figure 2.11). The army left Tampa Bay, marching up the peninsula past present-day Zephyrhills, Dade City, the Withlacoochee River, Inverness, Ocala, Leesburg, Gainesville, and Lake City. Natives harassed the army with hit-and-run ambushes, especially when the invaders were in thick woods or swamps, shooting them with arrows tipped with crab claws, fish bones, and stone points. Because the Indians' arrows could penetrate Spanish armor, soldiers wore three to four inches of quilted fabric beneath their metal armor. (Imagine how uncomfortable it must have been to wear all that in the Florida heat!)

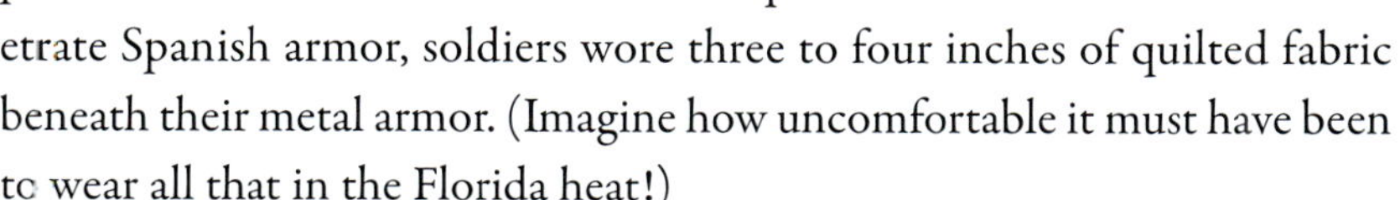

De Soto's frequent strategy was to meet with chiefs under the guise of peace then suddenly take the chief and other elite leaders hostage, often putting them in iron collars, shackles, and chains. Threatening to kill and often mutilating the hostages, he then demanded food and servants from the hostages' followers while the army rested. When they departed, de Soto used the hostages as a shield until they reached the next village. In this way, hundreds of Native men and women were forced to be porters, servants, and slaves, who were chained together when marching (figure 2.12). This was how the vastly outnumbered Spanish army safely traveled through hostile territories, and the strategy was repeated throughout the four-thousand-mile trek through numerous chiefdoms in the Southeast. De Soto's army was the largest, best equipped, and most experienced in the New World at the time, and they waged relentless war on the Native people. However, when it suited his needs, de Soto was also prepared to give gifts and make alliances with Indian groups.

Reaching the Tallahassee area, they found Anhaica, the abandoned main

FIGURE 2.12.
De Soto's army marching through Florida.

town of the Apalachee chiefdom. Since there were 250 houses available, as well as stored food, de Soto took it for the army's winter camp. They added a stockade for protection from attacks by Apalachee archers, which were ongoing for the five months the army lived there. De Soto sent a scouting unit south to Apalachee Bay, where, interestingly, they found bones of the horses killed by Narváez's crew as they built their escape rafts eleven years earlier. De Soto sent a unit back to Tampa Bay to tell his supply fleet waiting there to sail to Pensacola Bay, where he planned to meet them and camp for the next winter.

After five months of constant harassment by the Apalachee at Anhaica, and having found no gold nor any hint of its existence in the Florida peninsula or Apalachee, de Soto was anxious to move on. When two captives, named Marcos and Perico, told de Soto of a wealthy chiefdom to the northeast named Cofitachequi, whose dense agricultural population mined and processed gold, silver, pearls, and precious gems, the entrada left Tallahassee to find it, with the two captives serving as guides. After quickly marching five hundred miles in two months, the expedition found the town of Cofitachequi near present-day Camden, South Carolina. In his first meeting

WHAT DID INDIANS WANT FROM THE EUROPEANS?

Several types of European goods were new to Southeastern Indians, especially items made of metal, glass, and cloth. Native groups quickly made use of tools made of iron, such as axes and hoes, in everyday activities. They desired other items, such as chisels and horseshoes, which could be reworked into various cutting and scraping tools. Native people valued other European goods for personal ornaments, such as little brass bells and colorful glass beads. They also valued clothing items such as hats, jackets, and blankets, which they viewed as a sign of high status. The Spanish gave these and other trade items as gifts to elite Natives in exchange for food or animal skins. Native Floridians also salvaged metal from abandoned Spanish sites and shipwrecks, where they found gold and silver that they usually reworked into personal ornaments. Leaders of Native groups often exchanged trade goods among themselves as high-status gifts that circulated in a wide area.

with the paramount chieftainess, the Lady of Cofitachequi, de Soto asked about the gold, silver, precious gems, and pearls. While she did have chests of pearls, she said there was no gold or silver. To the soldiers' surprise, the Cofitachequi people already had some Spanish trade artifacts—such as glass beads, rosaries, and iron axes—which were undoubtedly from Ayllón's failed colony on the Atlantic Coast four years earlier. The Native leadership highly valued these Spanish artifacts and stored them in their most important temple. Although Cofitachequi had good agricultural soil that could support a future colony, there was none of the gold, silver, or precious gems the captives had promised, so the army moved on to the interior.

Historians and archaeologists have long been intrigued by the search for the places where the Narváez and de Soto armies camped. Historians first determined the general path of their routes from their study of the documents the survivors of the expeditions produced. Archaeologists then searched for sites along the proposed routes that matched the distances and landscapes described in the accounts and that contained mid-sixteenth-century Spanish artifacts. The artifacts that the armies carried were specific types of ceramics; metal artifacts such as horseshoes, crossbow tips, wrought-iron nails, and

FIGURE 2.13.
Map of de Soto and Narváez sites in Florida.

spikes; and the remains of European domestic animals the armies brought for food and warfare (pigs, dogs, horses). Narváez and de Soto followed similar routes in today's state of Florida, and it is not easy to distinguish the two entradas from the artifacts they left behind: The expeditions were only eleven years apart, and they brought essentially the same materials and animals.

Seven archaeological sites have been found in Florida containing sixteenth-century artifacts from the Narváez or de Soto expeditions (figure 2.13). Almost four and a half centuries after de Soto left, in 1987, archaeologist B. Calvin Jones discovered the remains of the army's 1539–1540 winter encampment in Tallahassee. Excavations led by Jones and Charles Ewen in the Martin Site, once a large Apalachee village, recovered many artifacts that are characteristic of the early sixteenth century (figure 2.14). These artifacts include five Maravedis coins (two minted between 1505 and 1517), crossbow tips, chain-mail links, key Spanish ceramics, and very early glass trade beads (figure 2.15). Questions remain, though. Could both Narváez and de Soto have stayed in the same Apalachee town? Did the Apalachee obtain the Spanish artifacts through trade and not from a resident army? These are the

FIGURE 2.14. Archaeologist Calvin Jones at the Martin Site.

kinds of questions historical archaeologists grapple with, but experts agree that the Martin Site was de Soto's winter encampment.

Archaeologists and historians base their conclusion that the Martin Site was de Soto's winter campsite on several facts. First, most Spanish artifacts at the Martin Site are ordinary utilitarian items found in everyday contexts, such as in trash pits and on house floors or the ground surface, indicating they were lost or discarded. The items specifically traded to and between Native people were different, special artifacts such as glass beads, small brass bells, and iron trade axes and chisels. Second, Spanish trade items were a symbol of high status; elite Native Americans were usually buried with these trade items and did not discard them in the trash, as was done at the Martin Site. Finally, the setting of the Martin Site matches the place described in the expedition chronicles—a large Indian village with 250 houses on a hill or ridgetop. Plus, the distance from it to the Narváez raft-building site on Apalachee Bay, where de Soto found the horse bones, matches de Vaca's recollection. Thus, there is strong archaeological, historical, and geographical evidence that the Martin Site is where the de Soto army camped.

South of Tallahassee, near Apalachee Bay, there are two Native American

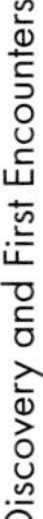

FIGURE 2.15. Spanish artifacts from de Soto's presumed 1539–1540 winter encampment in Tallahassee: *top row:* crossbow tips; *second row (l to r)*: two Native ceramics, Native flint projectile point or knife, decorated Native ceramic; *third row (l to r):* Spanish ceramic piece, pieces of Spanish chain mail, *upper*—possible Spanish metal coin, *lower*—metal disk, *upper*—crossbow tip, *middle*—glass Spanish trade beads, Spanish iron nails, decorated Native pottery; *bottom row:* both sides of a four Maravedi Spanish coin that dates to the early sixteenth century.

sites with Native burials and mid-sixteenth-century artifacts: Marsh Island Mound and St. Marks Cemetery. At Marsh Island, Natives were buried with scissors and other iron tools, glass beads, brass bells, and bracelets. At the St. Marks Cemetery site, eight hundred small silver disk beads were found in the graves. These beads are made of 99.9 percent pure silver, which, according to careful analysis, was mined in South America. Also found there were many perforated disks of brass, gold, and silver, along with a few pendants of copper or brass and silver, a brass scale weight, and several small brass bells. Unfortunately, the St. Marks Cemetery was excavated without modern scientific rigor, but most of the artifacts are available in museums. Researchers' consensus is that Natives fashioned the silver beads from silver salvaged from Spanish shipwrecks and then exchanged them with other Indigenous groups. Other trade items included traditional trade gifts mentioned above from the Narváez and de Soto expeditions.

There are three archaeological sites in West-Central Florida with early sixteenth-century Spanish trade goods: the Weeki Wachee, Ruth Smith, and Tatham Burial Mounds. The Tatham Mound in Citrus County, Florida, is the best-studied site containing materials from the de Soto expedition. In 1985 and 1986, archaeologist Jerald Milanich from the University of Florida directed excavations of the Tatham Mound, led by his then–doctoral student Jeffrey Mitchem. The site was a burial mound used before and after the de Soto army arrived. The funerary tradition of the local groups was to store the dead in a special building called a charnel house (similar to our mausoleum) until a significant person died; then all the stored remains were placed on a mound with the leader and covered with a layer of sand. However, in the upper layer of Tatham Mound was a mass grave of about 110 people of all ages and both sexes who had *not* been stored in a charnel house and had no signs of trauma. They were placed on their backs on the mound, and on top of and in between these individuals were loose bones from about a dozen people with wounds produced by *metal* weapons, undoubtedly axes and swords wielded by de Soto's men.

Mitchem explains the sequence of events as follows: After a battle between local Natives and de Soto's army, the Natives placed the bodies of those killed in the charnel house. Later, a large group of Natives must have died in a wave of European diseases introduced by de Soto's men when they returned to Tampa Bay from Tallahassee to direct the supply fleet to Pensacola Bay. They would have followed the trail the army made a few months earlier, bringing them back to the village where they had previously battled. On this second trip, the soldiers traded distinctive glass beads to the villagers. They also unintentionally infected the Natives with a European disease to which they had no immunity, starting a fatal epidemic. The disease victims were immediately placed in a mass grave on the mound, along with the remains of those previously killed in battle, who had been stored in the charnel house. The Natives placed many Spanish artifacts in the mass grave, in particular glass, gold, and silver beads; an iron chisel; and an iron spike. All the remains were then covered with a layer of sand. Many shell dippers and broken pottery containers were found on the mound's surface, indicating special ceremonies had been performed there, after which the mound was abandoned for good.

POWERFUL GLASS BEADS

Columbus first introduced colorful glass beads to Natives of the New World in 1492. The Spanish used them as gifts of friendship and traded them for a variety of Native goods and services. Most Natives valued glass beads, using them for jewelry and to decorate clothing, footwear, and personal items. Little did anyone back then know that the tiny glass beads would be used as time markers by archaeologists. Like everything else people make, glass bead manufacturing changed through time in Europe. Glass beads make perfect time markers because (1) literally millions were traded throughout the New World for centuries, (2) they were easily dropped and lost, and (3) they do not deteriorate. Because we can document when changes in their production were made at the glass factories in Europe, we can use beads to identify, date, and track the paths of the earliest explorers.

Sixteenth-century glass trade beads.

Glass trade beads.

De Soto was planning to spend the winter of 1540–1541 at Pensacola Bay. He intended to leave Cofitachequi, in today's central South Carolina, make a loop into the western North Carolina and eastern Tennessee mountains, then travel south through Alabama to Pensacola Bay. Following river valleys, the army passed near Embreeville, Tennessee, and Asheville, North Carolina. The first large Native town they reached, on June 3, 1540, was called Chiaha, near Warrensburg, Tennessee. De Soto again took the chief, his family, and other elites hostage, forcing their followers to provide food, shelter, labor, and women. After he determined that there was no gold, silver, or gems in the chiefdom, and the army had rested, he forced hundreds of Natives to move the army to the next chiefdom, with the hostages and porters usually chained together in iron collars.

FIGURE 2.16. Illustration of Tascaluza and de Soto.

On the southern leg of their route, near Montgomery, Alabama, de Soto's army entered the chiefdom of the Tuscaluza. He took the chief, Tascaluza, hostage, but this time things were different (figure 2.16). While Tascaluza met the Spanish demand for four hundred porters, he delayed their demand for one hundred women until they reached a town named Mabila, on the Alabama River (near today's Selma, Alabama), where he claimed the women were gathered. De Soto and his advance guard with Tascaluza reached Mabila ahead of his army, who were pillaging as they traveled. Mabila had a fort with a reinforced stockade wall and many bastions (wall projections where soldiers could fight), enclosing about eighty buildings. The stockade walls were covered with a hardened mixture of mud and straw on both sides. In addition, the area outside the fort walls had been cleared, and Coosa warriors had been conducting military exercises and skirmishes there. They also had built small huts in the cleared area for de Soto's army.

On October 18, 1540, despite receiving intelligence of an imminent attack, de Soto's guard entered the fort with their captive, Chief Tascaluza, unloading their baggage, including weapons, in a building provided to them. The

FIGURE 2.17.
Battle of Mabila, 1540.

local chief gave de Soto gifts, food, and evening entertainment; during this time, Tascaluza slipped into one of the other houses and would not come out. When a Spaniard was sent to force Tascaluza out, the unsuspecting conquistador barged into the building, found it full of armed warriors, and the battle began. About five thousand warriors hidden in houses suddenly attacked the Spaniards, blocking the gates and trapping them inside the fort. The warriors released thousands of arrows, but these could not penetrate Spanish armor. Nevertheless, they killed several Spanish soldiers and wounded de Soto. Most of the remaining Spaniards fought their way outside the town walls, but they had to abandon their stored weapons, which the Natives then used against them. Coosa warriors spilled out of the gates and immediately began attacking the tethered horses. At the last minute, de Soto's main army arrived with their horsemen and war dogs and defeated the Native warriors on the open field. The Spanish then attacked and set fire to the fort walls and all the buildings inside, killing the Coosa warriors as they fled the flames (figure 2.17). Native warriors fought with extreme ferocity and desperation, but they were unable to contend with the armor, weapons, horsemen, and war dogs of the Spanish. Fearing they would be captured, tortured, and enslaved, many warriors and women committed suicide.

The 1540 battle at Mabila badly took a heavy toll on both the Coosa

and the Spaniards. The Indians suffered a terrible loss of life, estimated to be about three thousand, not counting the hundreds that were wounded and later died. The Coosa had severely underestimated the advantage of the Spanish defensive armor, metal weapons, dogs, and horses, and overestimated the strength of their palisade. The Spanish lost 102 men, seven horses, their medical supplies, food, clothing, and most of their weapons; 148 men were wounded.

Just before the battle, de Soto heard that his resupply fleet had arrived at Pensacola Bay. He had planned to establish a colony on Pensacola Bay as a haven for Spanish ships, but the loss of men, weapons, and supplies in the Mabila battle caused widespread demoralization among the troops, and they were becoming mutinous. The ferocity with which the Native men fought at Mabila made it clear to de Soto that it would be impossible to conquer and subdue them; they would rather die than be captured and enslaved. When the soldiers heard their resupply ships were at Pensacola Bay, there was widespread talk of leaving the expedition and taking the ships home. De Soto realized that if his men knew how close they were to Pensacola Bay, only 140 miles to the south, his army would fall apart and he would be ruined.

This near mutiny changed everything for de Soto. Historians agree that his plans were falling apart, he was angry at his men, and he feared being a failure. From this point onward, accounts describe him as a changed and embittered man. Some say he had lost hope. Somehow, he rallied his army, and only two weeks after the costly Mabila battle, they marched northwest following the Black Warrior River, pillaging as they went. They stopped at several villages, taking chiefs hostage, taking the Natives' food, pillaging the area, then forcing hostages to serve as interpreters and guides as they moved on. Near present-day Columbus, Mississippi, on the Tombigbee River, they found an abandoned village named Chicaza, where they spent the winter of 1540–1541, stealing food from the surrounding villages and hamlets. However, the Chicaza people continually raided and terrorized the Spanish camp. In the early spring, de Soto demanded two hundred porters from the hostage chief, but he was refused. The Chicaza then attacked the Spaniards, who put up a lackluster defense, killing only one of the attackers. The Chicaza burned the army camp to the ground, killing twelve Spaniards and severely burning two others. The Spanish lost most of their weapons, saddles, and shields, as well as almost all their horses and pigs. Having lost all their clothes in the baggage at Mabila, and with no weapons or shelter, the Spaniards were thoroughly demoralized. But they soon took a nearby village, Chicazilla, where they made new weapons and saddles, and the cavalry raided and pillaged the surrounding area, stealing food and leaving no one alive for a radius of about fourteen miles.

The battle at Mabila also was a turning point for the Native Americans. No longer were they just harassing or fleeing from the Spanish army. At Mabila, they built a fort and trained for battle, and despite their losses, they continued to fight the Spaniards. This aggressive resistance continued all winter, and they drove the Spanish out of their homeland. The increased Native resistance and attacks throughout his trek made de Soto realize that despite his large, well-equipped army, he could not conquer the Southeastern Natives, take their land, and enslave them. The tide had turned for the Native Americans, who would rather fight and die than be conquered and become slaves. While almost all the Native groups the army encountered resisted with ambushes, deceptions, and snipers, it was at Mabila that they prepared for and fought a full-scale battle. Tascaluza had anticipated the arrival of the Spanish army, formed a plan to deceive de Soto, trapped him in the Coosa fort, and launched a surprise attack. The wounded Spanish army, with its dwindling number of horses, was in disarray, without their weapons, and was retreating. Word must have quickly spread through Native groups that the Spanish were vulnerable and could be damaged. In the battle at Chicaza, the Natives almost defeated the Spanish, and historians think that if the Chicazas had returned the next day, they could have finished off de Soto's army.

For the next two years, de Soto and his steadily shrinking army wandered from one Native town to another, using the same tactics of taking hostages, pillaging the countryside, and terrorizing Native people as they moved through the landscape. After the devastating battle at Mabila, historians describe de Soto's path through what was then northwest Spanish Florida (today's west Tennessee, Arkansas, and east Texas) as an aimless wandering in search of an Inca-like civilization rich in gold, silver, and gems. De Soto is described as increasingly reckless and careless of the lives of his army, constantly moving from place to place, searching for something that he realized did not exist. De Soto died suddenly of disease in May 1542 and was buried in the Mississippi River.

Luis de Moscoso Alvarado, de Soto's second in command, immediately realized the army was surrounded by enemies on both sides of the river, and they needed to escape to New Spain. They first tried to walk there, but the amount of food available to steal was diminishing in arid eastern Texas due to the lack of agriculture there. So, the army turned back to the Mississippi River where, like the Narváez crew, they built boats and floated down the Mississippi, while hostile Native groups often attacked from the riverbanks. When they reached the Gulf, they followed the coast westward, reaching the Spanish settlement of Pánuco (Tampico), New Spain, in September 1543.

Overall, de Soto's story is a difficult one. He was a contentious and self-centered leader of a vast army that bullied its way through the interior of La Florida for four years and four thousand miles, claiming all of Southeastern North America for Spain. De Soto's strategy of hostage-taking, brutality, and terrorizing by a mounted, well-equipped army had limited success and ignited increasingly violent resistance from Native American groups, who learned how to drive the Spanish out of their territories. His army was the first to encounter scores of Indigenous groups, their chiefdoms, and the interior landscape. This was a unique "first" encounter, and four eyewitness accounts of de Soto's expedition were written, providing our first glimpse of the Native people living there and their lands. Skilled ethnohistorians, paleographers, historians, and historical archaeologists such as Charles Hudson, John Worth, Robbie Ethridge, and Vernon James Knight have gleaned valuable information from these accounts in their study of the written and archaeological records of this expedition.

The de Soto expedition substantially affected many people in La Florida. Dozens of chiefdoms, overstressed and often humiliated by de Soto, soon declined or collapsed. The military defeats and tremendous losses of fighting-age men destabilized the balanced hostilities that had previously existed between chiefdoms. Traditional enemies of defeated chiefdoms could and did easily mount heavier attacks on them than previously. Moreover, the invaders released an invisible killer on the region: germs and viruses of Old World diseases such as smallpox, measles, and typhoid fever, to which Native peoples lacked immunity. While the invasion of microbial diseases had begun many years before in peninsular Florida with Spanish slavers and earlier explorers, de Soto's men spread them over four thousand miles through the interior of Florida. Combined, the diseases and defeats the Native peoples suffered started a long decline of Native Americans in the Southeast. It was the beginning of the end of their previous cultural world and the beginning of a new way of life that continues today.

For the Spanish, the de Soto expedition also had negative aftereffects. One problem was that the de Soto entrada defined and claimed an expansive Spanish Florida province for Spain, encompassing virtually all of Southeast-

FIGURE 2.18.
Map of Spanish shipping lanes.

ern North America. This vast size concerned the Spanish Crown because of the long-term cost of settling and controlling such a region. It was one thing to discover and claim territory in the New World but another to occupy and keep it. In 1543, after three major expeditions by de León, Ayllón, and de Soto in thirty years, there still was not a single Spanish settlement in La Florida.

Soon after the de Soto expedition, the richest silver deposits in the New World were discovered in Peru (1545) and northern New Spain (1546). While thrilled at the discoveries of untold riches, the Spanish became concerned that their silver mines in New Spain were vulnerable to their rivals by both land and sea (figure 2.18).

After the three expeditions through La Florida between 1513 and 1543, it was clear to the Spanish government that the Natives living in their expansive province would not be subjugated by force, and there were no deposits of gold or silver or large agricultural populations to be found. These realizations caused an important change in Spanish colonial policy in 1542 that abolished Indian enslavement and ended military attacks on them. Natives' cooperation with the Spanish was vital to the success of their Florida province. Now, the Spanish were to approach them peacefully and make requests for support, not demands. The resistance of the Natives ended the Spanish military war on them. It could be said that, in this sense, Native people won

Peaceful Colonization Attempts

The Spanish first implemented this new, peaceful approach to Native American interaction after the de Soto entrada. In 1549, the Dominican friar Luis Cáncer de Barbastro, who was appalled at the brutality the expeditionary armies had inflicted on Native people, became determined to win the friendship of Florida Natives by peaceful means. Sailing in an unarmed vessel from Veracruz along with three other friars, including a Spanish lay brother and a captured Florida Native American, Fray Cáncer gave strict orders to the ship's pilot to avoid all harbors where the Spanish had previously landed and harmed Native people. However, they arrived at Tampa Bay, where both Narváez and de Soto had murdered and terrorized the Indigenous people; as we might expect, almost immediately, the Spanish party was all killed.

In 1557, King Philip II of Spain ordered the Viceroy of New Spain, Luis de Velasco, to find a way to protect the treasure fleets and colonize the Florida province. Velasco developed a plan to start with a new port town on Pensacola Bay, which would be the supply port for future settlements and a means to protect the treasure fleets. Velasco selected an army colonel, Tristán de Luna y Arellano, to lead the effort in La Florida (figure 2.19). Another new port town was to be established at Port Royal on the Atlantic Coast. The treasure fleet could avoid the pirates and marine hazards of the long Atlantic Coast by sailing in the relatively protected Gulf of Mexico from Havana to Pensacola Bay. The bullion would be offloaded and carried overland to Port Royal on the Atlantic. The treasure would then be put on ships to sail across the Atlantic to Spain. Another settlement was to be built in the interior at Coosa in today's northwest Georgia. The plan was for new roads to connect the three settlements and continue to the silver mines in central New Spain. Later, Spanish settlements would be established along these roads. One of the flaws in the plan was a gross underestimation of the east-west distances involved because longitude could not be calculated yet, and these distances were merely guesswork.

FIGURE 2.19.
Tristán de Luna.

FIGURE 2.20.
Painting of Luna's fleet arriving in Pensacola Bay.

The Luna enterprise was the largest and most expensive colonizing effort in Florida to date, and it included a series of "firsts." It was the first to be substantially financed by the Spanish royal treasury and completely staged in New Spain. It was the first colonial venture to consist primarily of mixed-race people from New Spain as colonists and Aztec warriors as part of the army. It was the first colonization effort required to treat Native people peacefully and without violence. The Crown constructed four new ships for the expedition and purchased or leased eight more. About 1,500 people were assembled for the expedition, which included an army of 500 infantry and cavalry soldiers and 200 Aztec warriors, 240 horses, and about 500 colonists with their families, servants, slaves, and craftsmen. They carried more than a million pounds of food to last for a year while the colonists cleared land, planted and harvested crops, and constructed buildings for the settlement.

The fleet arrived in Pensacola Bay (then named Ochuse Bay) on August 9, 1559, and soon selected a location for the settlement on a high bluff overlooking the bay (figure 2.20). They promptly unloaded people and equipment but kept the food on the ships since they did not yet have warehouses for storing it. The settlement was named Santa María de Ochuse, and in accordance with Spanish town-planning regulations, it was to have a central plaza bordered by public buildings and surrounded by a grid pattern of residential blocks. During the first few weeks of construction, Luna sent the first of several military units to explore the inland area, where they encountered small groups of hostile Natives. Five weeks after landing, on September 19, a massive hurricane struck the settlement, tearing the ships loose from their anchors and driving six into the seabed, breaking them to pieces; one was thrown on land. Only three boats remained afloat. There was significant loss of life, and almost all the food stored on the ships was destroyed. As there were no Native settlements in the area to provide food, the large group of people quickly began to suffer from hunger.

One of the surviving ships was quickly sent to New Spain with the bad news and a request for relief. Luna also sent a second military unit of 150 to 200 men into the interior to search for Native populations to provide food, and a delegation was sent to Havana for provisions. It took three months for the first relief ships to arrive, and Luna was ordered to immediately move inland, leaving only a small contingent of soldiers to hold the port (figure 2.21).

The viceroy also ordered Luna to build two new ships, which he did

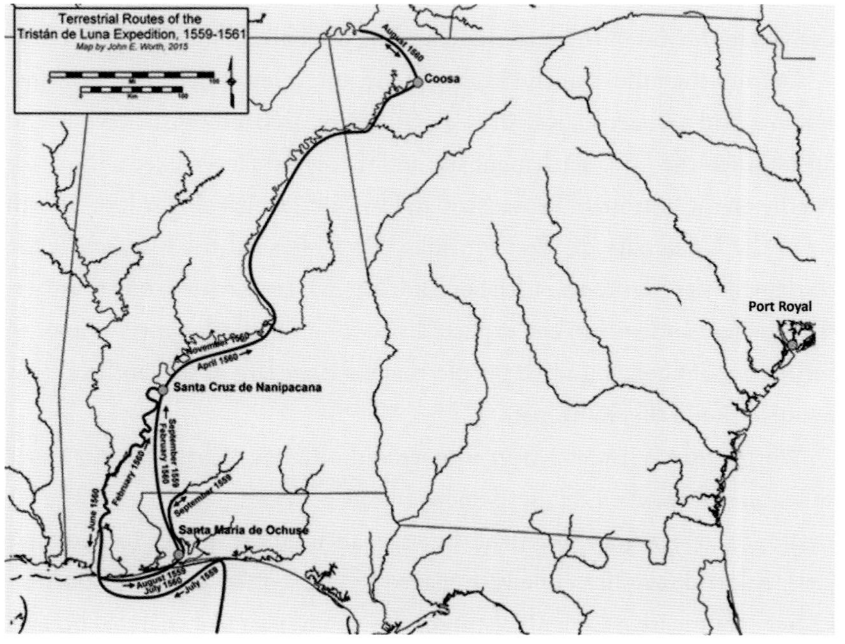

FIGURE 2.21. Map of Luna's routes.

from material salvaged from the wreckage. He then sent a military unit in the new ships up the Mobile and Alabama Rivers to locate Native villages and food. They found a large town called Nanipacana, which was probably on the Lower Alabama River. After building a new road to Ochuse, most colonists went there to settle. From Nanipacana, another group was dispatched farther upriver to find the Coosa, which they did. Seven months later, when they returned to Nanipacana, they found the colonists had already given up and left for Ochuse. Fortunately, a relief fleet from New Spain soon arrived, and Luna was ordered to proceed immediately to Port Royal, leaving a small military unit at Ochuse. Luna quickly dispatched ships to head for Port Royal, with a planned stop in Havana for supplies, but bad weather prevented docking there, and the vessels detoured to New Spain. Luna then tried to move inland, but the officers refused, and the group became fractious. Documents reveal that by August 1560, less than a year after the colonists' arrival, only about five hundred people remained, as many of the hurricane survivors had returned to New Spain with the four relief fleets.

By September 1560, Luna's poor leadership and repeated illnesses led to increased opposition, and he had not yet carried out his orders to go to Coosa. As a result, the viceroy sent a replacement, Angel de Villafañe, who ordered Luna back to Spain. Most of the remaining men left for Port Royal, but after they arrived, Villafañe decided it was not a suitable location for a settlement and returned to Havana. Villafañe went back to Ochuse in August 1561 and evacuated the rest of the men there, ending the Luna colonization attempt.

Despite the failure of the Luna expedition, it left a rich legacy of documents and archaeological sites. Fortunately, archaeologists have found and studied the Luna settlement site and three of their wrecked ships lying nearby on the bottom of Pensacola Bay. Historical archaeologist John Worth from the University of West Florida (UWF) has led the research at the settlement site (figure 2.22). The occupied area is large (thirty-one to thirty-seven acres) and within the expected size for a sixteenth-century Spanish settlement of fifteen hundred people, making it the largest sixteenth-century Spanish site in the Southeast.

Worth and his students have recovered thousands of artifacts and scores of features from the Luna settlement (figure 2.23 and figure 2.24). The ceramic artifacts include fragments of large jars used for storage (called olive jars), colorful majolica tableware, glazed serving bowls, and Aztec pottery. Other ceramic items include a spindle whorl and part of a charcoal brazier.

Metal artifacts include wrought-iron nails and spikes, distinctive carat-head horseshoe nails, crossbow tips, lead shot, and pieces of armor. Lead shot for harquebuses and crossbow tips are evidence of the Spanish shoulder weapons. Other types of items are clothing fasteners and decorations, a scale weight, a key, and a finger ring. These artifacts provide a view into the daily life of a large group of colonists and the military that protected them. The remnants of the posts from several buildings indicate construction methods. Archaeology has also revealed that the settlers ate local fish, shellfish, and deer.

FIGURE 2.22. Site of the Luna settlement, 1559–1561, on Pensacola Bay.

One of the most fascinating aspects of the archaeology of Luna's colonization attempt is the discovery of three shipwrecks. They are all embedded in the bay bottom just offshore of the settlement site and have been studied since 1992, when then–state underwater archaeologist Roger C. Smith discovered the first shipwreck. It was buried in a sandbar in only twelve feet of water, and a second wreck was found about four hundred yards away in the same sandbar. In 2016, underwater archaeologists discovered a third ship-

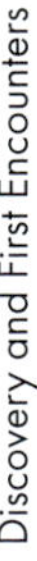

FIGURE 2.23. Excavating at the Luna settlement site: *top,* John Worth; *right:* UWF students.

wreck in only seven feet of water between the settlement and the other two shipwrecks. The first shipwreck, Emanuel Point I (EP I), was investigated by Smith, UWF maritime archaeologists John Bratten and Greg Cook, staff, and UWF students (figure 2.25).

EP I is the largest shipwreck. Much is preserved in the muddy bay bottom, including the stern, rudder, keel, main mast step in the keel, bilge pump, bow, large sections of the starboard hull, port covers, and internal supports (figure 2.26). A wrought-iron anchor lying just off the bow is more than ten feet long (figure 2.27). It is missing the anchor ring where a wooden stock would have been attached. There were also three hinges for the massive rudder and more than five hundred iron fasteners of all sizes used in the ship's construction. Archaeologists also found pieces of lead sheathing once attached to the hull to prevent shipworm damage and a pile of ballast stones. From the structural remains of the wreck, Smith determined that the ship was a 114-foot-long galleon, built in Europe, and was a veteran of many ocean voyages, as evidenced by its many cracks, leaks, and primary and minor repairs. Given the dimension, estimated tonnage, and other features, Smith determined that EP I is probably the *San Juan de Ulúa,* the vice flagship.

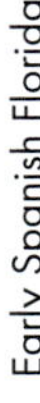

FIGURE 2.24. Spanish artifacts from the Luna settlement site, 1559–1561, on Pensacola Bay.

FIGURE 2.25. Excavating the 1559 Luna shipwreck in Pensacola Bay.

Maritime archaeologists recovered hundreds of other artifacts from the EP I wreck site, especially from the galley, reflecting life on board. These included a large copper pitcher, four copper cauldrons, cups, funnels, a saucepan, a bronze mortar and pestle, and an armor breastplate (figure 2.28). Olive jar fragments were the most frequent ceramic artifact, but there also was a complete tin-enameled majolica plate and fragments of many others, plus distinctive Aztec ceramics. In the bilge were tiny round droplets of shiny liquid mercury (quicksilver) used to process silver ore; the droplets were floating among many scraps of wood, including a complete miniature carved wood silhouette of a Spanish galleon. Perhaps the silhouette was the model used in the ship's construction, or maybe it was a good luck charm. Other items include leather shoes, wooden tool handles, chicken and cat bones, insect parts, hundreds of olive pits, stone cannonballs, lead shot, crossbow bolts, and a copper coin minted between 1471 and 1474. Despite the abundant artifacts found in and around EP I, there were no traces of its cargo because the ship's survivors salvaged it.

The second Luna shipwreck, EP II, is only about 440 yards from EP I, buried in the same sandbar. UWF maritime archaeologists and students led by Bratten and Cook found and documented the stern, midship, bilge pumps, well, buttresses, keelson, and bow. Artifacts associated with the wreck are similar to those of EP I: fragments of olive jars and majolica tableware, lead hull sheathing, iron fasteners, gudgeon straps, and a large ballast pile. This ship is only sixty-five feet long, half the length of EP I, and the bows of both ships are facing the shore.

FIGURE 2.26. 3D rendering of Luna's sunken 1559 vice flagship in Pensacola Bay.

FIGURE 2.27. Anchor from Luna's shipwreck in Pensacola Bay.

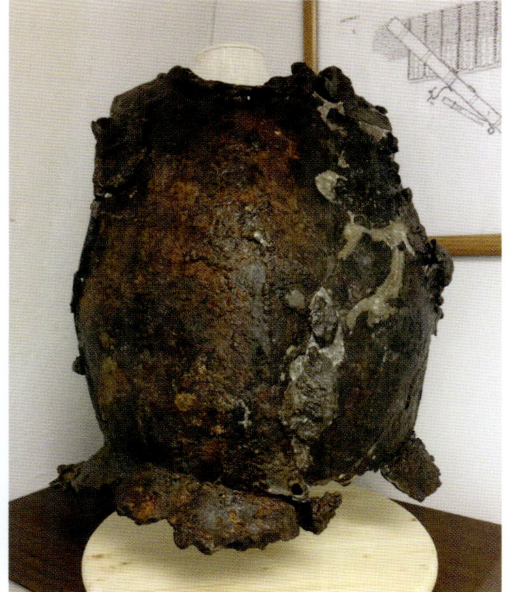

FIGURE 2.28. Spanish soldier's breastplate from the Luna shipwreck in Pensacola Bay, conserved and reconstructed.

The materials on the shipwrecks tell the story of shipboard life and what was expected to be needed for colonization. For example, passengers and crew in the sixteenth century ate sea rations of wine, salted pork and fish, beans and peas, and sometimes beef or cheese. Archaeologists found evidence of most of these staples on the shipwreck. They also found supplementary food, such as olives, plums or prunes, cherries, hazelnuts, and various other fruits and nuts. Pests such as cockroaches and rats were also on board. The many broken olive jars used to store a variety of wet and dry goods indicate that the group's food supplies were ruined. Pieces of clothing, leather shoes, and personal items were also preserved. The complete breastplate, stone cannonballs, crossbow tips, lead shot, and other military hardware reflect the presence of soldiers and their supplies.

To sum up, the Luna expedition was the Spanish government's largest, most expensive, most well-supplied, and best-funded effort to colonize La Florida. The plan was to build three settlements connected by roads and one, long road to New Spain. Native people were to be well treated and evangelized, not enslaved. It was a good plan, and the colonists were well supplied. But the massive hurricane strike only five weeks after landing doomed the effort. Luna sent several exploratory units into the interior and finally found the Coosa chiefdom, but there was never enough food, and starvation was always looming. Native groups were hostile wherever the Spanish went. Fewer than half of the colonists survived, and the failure ruined Luna's career. The rich documentary and archaeological records left behind reveal details of the short-lived settlement at Santa María de Ochuse on Pensacola Bay. The abandoned settlement and the wrecks of three ships have revealed a wide range of artifacts reflective of the people's lives on board ship and on land, as well as details of the preparation for such a significant colonization effort. However, for the fifteen hundred people of the Luna expedition, their venture failed and cost half of them their lives, starting with the bad luck of a hurricane strike soon after landing, ruining their supplies and changing everything.

Summary of Discovery and First Encounters

In 1492, Spain was a feudal medieval agrarian society on the backwaters of Europe that stumbled into a vast new world with riches beyond measure, inhabited by people with a less developed technology, no metal weapons, and no domesticated work animals. As a result, the Spanish thought they could militarily defeat the Native people, subjugate them, and take their lands and possessions, as had been done in Europe for centuries. This was the mindset of the Spanish in the so-called New World, and for seventy years, the Spanish had almost all the Americas to themselves.

Historians agree that there must have been many unrecorded trips to the Florida peninsula in search of Natives to enslave before the first documented arrival by Ponce de León in 1513. De León was attacked wherever he landed on the South Florida coast, implying that other Spaniards with ill intentions toward the Native groups must have preceded him. So, from the very beginning of our Florida, the Spanish were the enemy of the Florida Natives and were to be resisted, driven off, or avoided at all costs. De León returned to southwest Florida to establish a colony in 1521 on Estero Bay, where previously the Calusas had attacked him and driven him away. The Calusas immediately and relentlessly attacked the colonists, driving them off again, and this time fatally wounding de León.

In 1528, Narváez landed on Tampa Bay and experienced the same hostility. Told that there was gold and food in North Florida, the entrada marched to Apalachee near Tallahassee. They seized a village, but waves of Apalachee archers drove them off, so the Spanish retreated to the coast and fled. When the de Soto army landed at Tampa Bay eleven years later, in 1539, Native groups also immediately attacked them. De Soto quickly moved north, camping near villages, capturing chiefs and their family members as hostages for protection and information, enslaving others to serve the army as porters, and stealing food. All along the way, Native groups waged guerrilla warfare on de Soto's army, attacking them in hit-and-run raids. The Spanish seized the abandoned principal village, Anhaica, in Tallahassee, spending five months there and building a stockade for protection from the constant attacks by Apalachee archers. The de Soto army headed north following rumors of treasure, moving from one chiefdom to another as far as South Carolina, then west across the Appalachians following river valleys. The Coosa duped the army into a vicious battle at Mabila on the Alabama River, devastating both sides. The army became mutinous, so de Soto pushed them north, away from the coast and the resupply fleet at Pensacola Bay. For two more years, they wandered north and west, crossing the Mississippi River in 1543, where de Soto died. Natives continually harassed the remnants of the army, and they never found enough food. The soldiers eventually gave up, retreating down the Mississippi and escaping to New Spain.

After the failure of the first three explorations and attempts to colonize

Spanish Florida along with the fierce resistance to the invasion from the Native people, it was clear that the Natives could not be defeated with traditional European warfare methods. There was also no gold or silver or large agricultural populations to be exploited. As a result, the Spanish government changed its policy toward Indians to a peaceful approach: sending a group of settlers protected by a military unit to start a colonial settlement. Tristán de Luna led this effort to settle Spanish Florida with the goal of establishing two new port settlements at Pensacola and Port Royal and a town in the interior with the Coosa. Unfortunately, only weeks after the group of fifteen hundred people with an army to protect them landed, a massive hurricane struck Pensacola, wrecking six of their ships and ruining their food supply. Forced to seek food from Natives once more, the expedition searched for Indian villages to help support them, but there was never enough food. Within two years, in 1561, the fourth attempt to settle Spanish Florida was declared another failure.

Mining the many documents and sites left behind from the first four expeditions, archaeologists and ethnohistorians have projected the paths of each expedition and found and studied several of their encampments, settlements, and ships. All these studies have shed light on what happened on these excursions and how the Spanish lived in a hostile and challenging land. Despite these challenges and failures, the Spanish did not give up. They needed Florida to protect their lucrative silver mines in New Spain and the ships transporting their treasure to Spain. Meanwhile, Florida's Native Americans had lost many battles with the Spanish, but they were winning the war. They had driven the Spanish armies out of their homelands.

Suggested Readings

Patricia Galloway. *The Hernando de Soto Expedition.* Lincoln: University of Nebraska Press, 1997.

Michael Gannon. *The History of Florida.* Gainesville: University Press of Florida, 2018.

Charles Hudson. *Knights of Spain, Warriors of the Sun: Hernando de Soto and the South's Ancient Chiefdoms.* Athens: University of Georgia Press, 1997.

Jerald T. Milanich and Susan Milbrath, eds. *First Encounters: Spanish Explorations in the Caribbean and the United States, 1492–1570.* Gainesville: University Press of Florida, 1991.

Roger C. Smith. *Florida's Lost Galleon: The "Emanuel Point" Shipwreck.* Gainesville: University Press of Florida, 2018.

Álvar Núñez Cabeza de Vaca. *Chronicle of the Narváez Expedition.* New York: Penguin Classics, 2002.
Álvar Núñez Cabeza de Vaca. *Castaways: The Narrative of Alvar Nuñez Cabeza de Vaca.* Berkeley: University of California Press, 1993.

Places to Visit

Archaeology Institute Museum, Pensacola. University of West Florida campus, Pensacola, Florida.
Florida Museum of Natural History. 3215 Hull Road, Gainesville, Florida.
Museum of Florida History. 500 S. Bronough Street, Tallahassee, Florida.
Soto Winter Encampment Site, 1539–1540. Governor Martin House, 1001 Desoto Park Drive Tallahassee, Florida.

Website to Visit

Hernando de Soto 1539–1540 Winter Encampment at Anhaica Apalachee. https://dos.myflorida.com/historical/archaeology/projects/hernando-de-soto-1539-1540-winter-encampment-at-anhaica-apalachee/

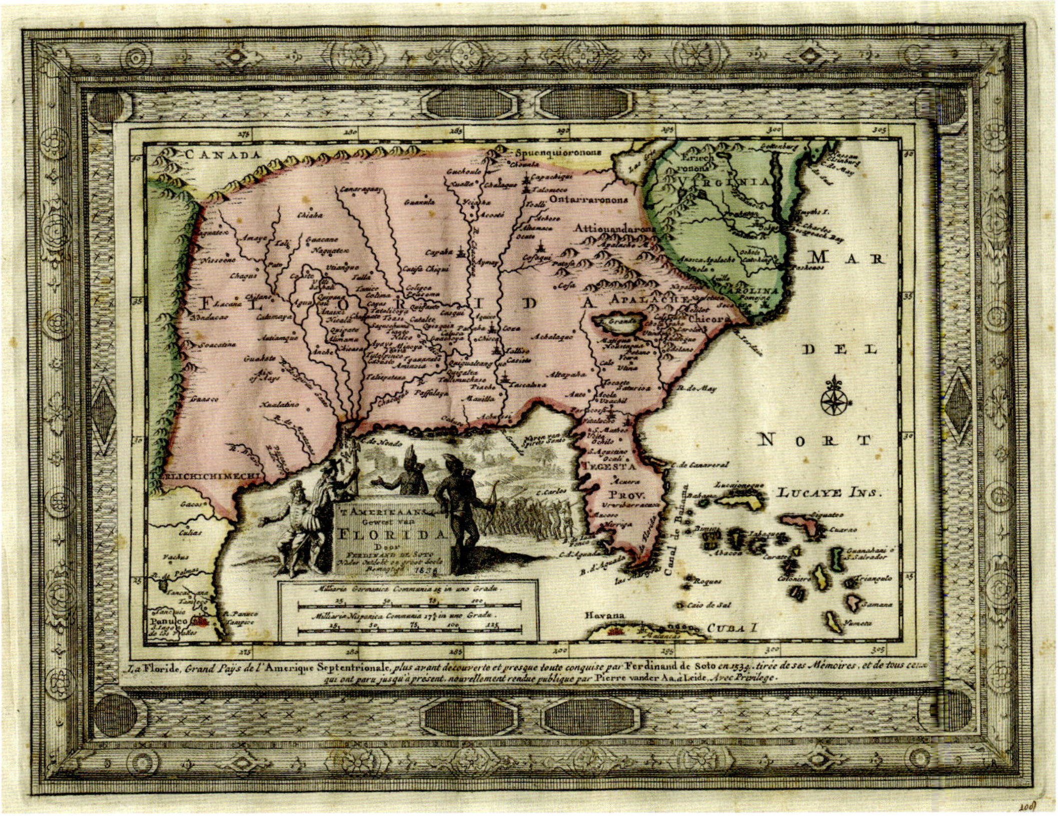

FIGURE 3.1. Map of La Florida as defined in 1543.

FIGURE 3.2. Map of Menéndez's settlements, 1565–1569.

THREE

COMPETITION AND COLONIZATION

Hernando de Soto's expedition from 1539 to 1543 defined the extent of Spain's La Florida province, encompassing most of Southeastern North America (figure 3.1). After the failure of four costly colonization attempts, the Spanish King Philip was disenchanted with trying to settle La Florida. After the failure of the Luna colonies in 1561, the king put a hold on any further plans to settle Florida. However, the French saw the opportunity to seize La Florida and soon secretly built two forts on the Atlantic Coast in preparation for future settlements. This discovery so alarmed the Spanish that they sent Pedro Menéndez to remove the French threat and colonize Florida. He was successful, building fifteen forts and missions from Tampa Bay on the Gulf to Port Royal on the Atlantic Coast and deep into the Appalachian Mountains of eastern Tennessee. For the first time, the Spanish settled and fortified La Florida. Historians and archaeologists have found and studied several Menéndez towns, missions, and forts, revealing their bleak and short existences. Ignoring orders not to harm the Native people, the Spanish abused them wherever they went. Incensed at this treatment, attempts to take their homelands, and challenges to their beliefs, local Indigenous groups attacked the Spanish, killing and driving them out everywhere except St. Augustine, which became the first permanent Spanish settlement in the United States. This chapter will recount the evidence that historians and archaeologists have discovered that explains the clashes between European rivals and the responses of local Native Americans to the imperial claims on their homelands and cultures (figure 3.2).

The French Arrive

In the 1550s, several books were published in Europe describing Southeastern North America and its people, based on the narratives from the de León, Narváez, de Soto, and Luna expeditions. The books revealed Spain's inability to settle Florida. They revived the legend of Chicora from the de Soto

FIGURE 3.3.
Jean Ribault.

expedition, a supposed kingdom with an abundance of silver, pearls, and excellent agricultural soil. Importantly, the books also revealed the exact degree of latitude of the supposed entryway to Chicora: Port Royal Sound, near today's Beaufort, South Carolina. The French were the first to take advantage of a vacant Spanish Florida, spurred on by the promise of great wealth to the successful colonizer of Chicora. France had a growing desire for a colonial empire like that of the Spanish, and French pirates were successfully seizing Spanish ships and sacking their ports in the Caribbean, including Havana, with alarming frequency. Competition for an unoccupied La Florida and a vulnerable Havana was a big new problem for the Spanish—they no longer had the Americas to themselves. The Spanish treasure galleons gathered annually in Havana and sailed from there in a fleet along the Atlantic Coast of La Florida, riding the Gulf Stream before turning east to Spain. Spanish ships containing incredible wealth in gold, silver, and gems were increasingly lost to piracy along with the usual maritime hazards such as reefs, shoals, and storms, especially hurricanes.

In 1562, immediately following the abandonment of the Luna colonization attempt, the French launched a secret expedition led by Jean Ribault, a French Huguenot (Protestant) naval officer and navigator, to explore La Florida's Atlantic Coast and find a site for a future settlement (figure 3.3). Sailing far north of the normal routes, the French made a clandestine landfall just north of present-day St. Augustine, Florida, on April 30, 1562 (figure 3.4). From there, they proceeded to the mouth of the St. Johns River near Jacksonville, Florida, and established French claim to the area by placing there a marble column engraved with the coat of arms of the king of France (figure 3.5). After a brief survey of their surroundings and a friendly meeting with the local Timucua Indians, the Ribault expedition traveled north to Port Royal Sound, South Carolina, and planted another column to stake their claim to northern Spanish Florida. Even though Ribault was only supposed to survey and identify potential sites for a colony, he was so impressed with the high quality of the land and the good harbor there that he built a small fort named Charlesfort and left twenty-six men to protect the claim. Ribault promised a speedy return with colonists and supplies, but when

FIGURE 3.4. Ribault's fleet landing near Jacksonville, 1562.

FIGURE 3.5. Ribault and Timucuans at the French column marker near Jacksonville, 1562.

FIGURE 3.6.

Excavated moat showing the outline of the fort wall and bastion around French Charlesfort (1562) and Spanish Fort San Felipe (1574).

FIGURE 3.7.
Engraving believed to show Charlesfort under construction, 1562.

he got home, France was in a civil war between the Catholic Crown and the Protestant Huguenots. He went to England to request assistance but was imprisoned there as a spy. Meanwhile, the men left behind by Ribault waited ten months for his return, enduring many hardships, including losing all their supplies and food to a fire. The despairing crew built an open ship, sailed for Europe, and made it to the English Channel, where they were rescued.

After years of searching for the French-built Charlesfort, archaeologists determined, to everyone's surprise, that it was hiding in plain sight. They found it under the remains of a later Spanish fort, San Felipe, built in 1574 to protect a new town on Parris Island called Santa Elena. Archaeologists Stanley South and Chester DePratter discovered that the Spanish had cleaned out and used the old Charlesfort moat (figure 3.6). Because the French occupation lasted only a few months, while the Spanish occupied the fort for at least ten years, there were more Spanish materials than French in the moat. While no remains of the French fort have been found, experts think that a sketch of it was made during construction (figure 3.7).

Rumors of the French intrusion into La Florida concerned the Spanish king, and in May 1564, he sent Hernando Manrique de Rojas from Havana to the mouth of the St. Johns River and to Port Royal to determine the truth. Rojas did not find the stone column set at the mouth of the St. Johns River but did find the one at Charlesfort; he removed it and burned the

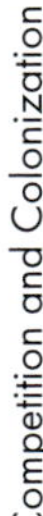

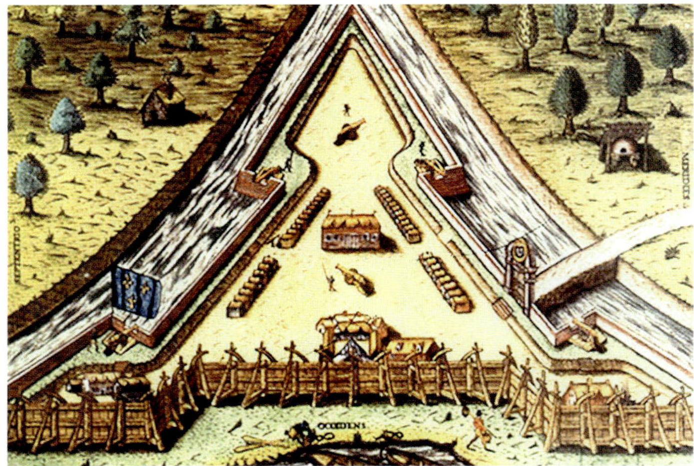

FIGURE 3.8.
Fort Caroline.

abandoned French Charlesfort to the ground. Meanwhile, a French fleet had quietly returned to the mouth of the St. Johns River, led by Ribault's second in command, René Goulaine de Laudonnière. He found the stone column Ribault had placed there two years before, which had become important to the local Timucuan people. Laudonnière built a new fort there, Fort Caroline, as a base from which to attack Spanish ships, as a refuge for Protestant Huguenots, and to give legitimacy to a French claim to Southeastern North America. Assuming the local Timucua Indians would supply the garrison with food, Laudonnière sent his ships back to France; however, problems soon began. The Timucuans became hostile, and there were several military mutinies. Some mutineers stole boats and attacked passing Spanish vessels. They also attacked nearby Native Timucuan settlements for food. By late August 1565, supplies ran low, and the colonists decided to abandon Fort Caroline. But just as they were leaving, a relief fleet led by Jean Ribault arrived full of supplies and one thousand soldiers for the colony.

Historians have discovered many informative documents about Fort Caroline, including drawings by the first European artist to visit the New World, a French illustrator and cartographer named Jacques Le Moyne, who accompanied Laudonnière in 1564. Le Moyne traveled through today's northeast Florida, sketching the fort (figure 3.8), Timucuan villages and people, and interactions between the Timucua and the French, such as the scene around the stone column shown in figure 3.5. His drawings portray details of the Native people and their ways of life, but experts have questioned their accuracy.

THE STRANGE TALE OF JACQUES LE MOYNE'S DRAWINGS

In the days before photography, artists recorded many important events and places for their sponsors. In 1564, artist Jacques Le Moyne was assigned to René Goulaine de Laudonnière's French expedition to colonize Spanish Florida in 1564. Spending more than a year at Fort Caroline, he recorded in detail the local Timucua people, the landscape, the construction of forts, and the coast in a wide area around today's Jacksonville, Florida. His forty-three watercolors are the earliest known drawings of Native Floridians and their way of life. Unfortunately, Pedro Menéndez made a surprise attack on Fort Caroline in 1565. Le Moyne escaped but probably lost all but one of his original drawings. Historians believe that he later redrew them from memory. Theodor de Bry, a German engraver and publisher, purchased these sketches shortly after Le Moyne's death. Bry made engravings of many and, with Le Moyne's descriptive captions, published them in a book in 1587. Experts debate the authenticity of Le Moyne's drawings because the Indians look like Mediterranean Europeans and the illustrations include what we now know are tribal customs and artifacts that existed far from Florida. However, the Le Moyne drawings published by De Bry provide one of the first views sixteenth-century Europeans had of the people and landscapes in America.

Even though the Spanish scout Manrique de Rojas did not find a French settlement at the mouth of the St. Johns River, Spain's King Philip II kept hearing reports about a French fort and that the English were also exploring the southern Atlantic Coast for a new colony. Concerned that Spanish Florida could be taken by his rivals, in March 1565, King Philip worked out a contract with the widely admired Spanish Admiral Pedro Menéndez de Avilés to lead the fifth Spanish attempt to colonize Florida (figure 3.9). Menéndez was to fund the expedition, and any profits were to be split with the king. At about the same time, the king learned of Laudonnière's arrival and details about Fort Caroline's construction. Meanwhile, Menéndez was

FIGURE 3.9.
Pedro Menéndez de Avilés.

putting together his colonization expedition in Spain, while Ribault was assembling his fleet in France to resupply and reinforce Fort Caroline. Both men and their governments learned of the other's activities and plans, which caused the transition of both ventures into military campaigns against the rival European power. Troop numbers increased for both fleets, and Menéndez's priority shifted; he was to remove the French from Spanish Florida before establishing a series of forts, missions, and settlements. Likewise, Ribault's top priority became defending Fort Caroline rather than just resupplying and reinforcing it. A race to claim La Florida was ignited.

Both fleets sailed for La Florida at the same time. Ribault's fleet arrived at Fort Caroline in late August 1565, and within a few days, the Menéndez fleet arrived (figure 3.10). After a small naval skirmish offshore of Fort Caroline with no clear victor, Menéndez withdrew to a harbor about thirty miles south. At this site, which would become St. Augustine, Menéndez built some crude defenses, expecting a retaliatory assault by Ribault. The French forces did arrive at the harbor to retaliate, but almost immediately, a hurricane struck, scattering and sinking most of Ribault's ships and troops, ending their attack. Menéndez calculated that very few troops had been left at Fort Caroline and that they would not expect an attack during a hurricane. So, he marched his troops thirty miles overland, through the storm, and took the fort without resistance. After killing or capturing all the French soldiers, women, and children at Fort Caroline, Menéndez returned to St. Augustine. From there, he immediately began hunting down and killing shipwrecked French troops and sailors south of St. Augustine, executing several hundred Frenchmen, including Ribault, at Matanzas Inlet. Only about twenty-four Frenchmen, including Laudonnière and the artist Le Moyne, escaped the Spanish attack and the hurricane in a small boat that eventually reached England.

Archaeologists have found an archaeological site near the beach in the Cape Canaveral National Seashore that appears to have been occupied by some of the shipwrecked French survivors. They found sixteenth-century French coins, iron tools, nails, and metal objects that had been reworked using European metallurgy techniques, suggesting that the surviving ship-

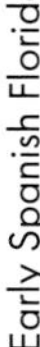

wrecked Frenchmen may have had an encampment there for a few months before being found and killed by Menéndez.

To everyone's surprise, in 2016, maritime archaeologists discovered the wreckage of *La Trinité,* the flagship of Ribault's doomed fleet that sank in the 1565 hurricane, on the bottom of the Atlantic off Cape Canaveral. Amazingly, the cargo on the sunken ship includes at least one of the marble columns bearing the symbol of France's coat of arms and the fleur-de-lis, identical to the monuments Ribault set at the mouth of the St. Johns River and Charlesfort three years earlier to claim La Florida for France. Other artifacts in the shipwreck are twenty-two cannons embossed with the fleur-de-lis, several anchors, and a stone grinding wheel. An agreement was reached in 2018 between France and the State of Florida to work together to preserve the 450-year-old shipwreck, exhibit some of the ship's cargo, and explain the role Jean Ribault played in Florida's history.

After they drove the French out, Menéndez completed the remainder of his mission to fortify and colonize La Florida. Within two years, Menéndez had built fifteen forts, founded the capital town of Santa Elena, and established a presidio (fortified military settlement) at St. Augustine.

Menéndez's First Encampment at St. Augustine

After the skirmish with Ribault's fleet off Fort Caroline, Menéndez's fleet entered an inlet of the Matanzas River on September 8, 1565, landing at the

FIGURE 3.10.
Ribault's fleet arriving at Fort Caroline.

FIGURE 3.11.
Menéndez's army arriving at Chief Seloy's town, 1565.

village of Chief Seloy, the leader of the Timucuan town. Menéndez selected the location quickly because the town offered safety from Ribault's expected retaliation. Seloy gave Menéndez a large house in his town and permission for his group to build a large warehouse there for their supplies. Thus began the first permanent and the oldest European settlement in the United States. There were about 800 Spaniards with Menéndez, consisting of 500 soldiers, 200 seamen, and 100 "others" such as civilians, clergy, and the wives and children of 26 soldiers. Included among the 500 soldiers were 138 who held licenses in various trades and 117 who were farmers, ready to settle and farm the land (figure 3.11).

After the Spanish captured Fort Caroline, they renamed it San Mateo and made it an outpost protected by three hundred soldiers. They soon built a second outpost, Santa Lucía de Ais, near the mouth of the Indian River on Jupiter Island, 230 miles to the south; they stationed another three hundred men there. By November 1565, only about two hundred people were left at St. Augustine, and by January, only about one hundred remained due to loss of life from illness and attacks by Native people. These conditions led to an unsuccessful mutiny in the spring of 1566. In April 1566, the Spanish warehouse in Seloy's village burned, and the Spanish decided to move across the river to Anastasia Island for safety.

Historians and archaeologists long suspected that the site of Timucuan Chief Seloy's village and the first encampment of the Menéndez colonists was in today's Fountain of Youth Park in St. Augustine. This site has been a popular tourist attraction promoting Ponce de León and the story of the Fountain of Youth (figure 3.12). Native Americans and Europeans have lived there for more than four thousand years, and archaeologists, primarily from the University of Florida and the Florida Museum of Natural History (FLMNH) in Gainesville, have studied it for more than seventy years. Both archaeologist Kathleen Deagan of the FLMNH and historians have gathered information from the Early Spanish occupation there and conducted excavations confirming it as the site of the first Menéndez encampment (figure 3.13).

The seven-month encampment of the Menéndez colonists at the Timucuan village of Seloy was on the edge of the Native village on a small peninsula surrounded by marshes and a creek on three sides. The peninsula was connected to the mainland village by a narrow neck where the Spanish built a 262-foot-long wall. The encampment had an open central plaza that was

CHARNEL HOUSES

Many Native Americans in the Southeast used special buildings to house the bodies of deceased persons prior to communal burial. The individuals placed in charnel houses were buried together when a special leader died. A specific person was usually assigned to protect the charnel house and sometimes to clean the bones. A special funeral ceremony was usually held for the chief and the remains of the people who were chosen to be buried at the same time. Many such burials were located on top of a mound and covered with a layer of earth while others were located beneath the surface of the ground.

Native American charnel house in North Carolina.

FIGURE 3.12.
Entrance of Fountain of Youth Archaeological Park.

FIGURE 3.13.
Kathleen Deagan working at the site of the 1565 Menéndez encampment.

the focus of activities, and Spanish artifacts were concentrated there. The colonists built at least six rectangular shelters of wood and thatch (probably palm fronds) on logs laid directly on the ground and with corner posts. Near the plaza, they built a large, rectangular wooden structure believed to have been a fortified warehouse; it was about sixty-six feet by fifty feet, resting on large timber beams with a raised wooden floor (figure 3.14). The smaller rectangular structures were divided into rooms with dirt floors, and trash pits were located just outside the buildings. Near the camp's periphery, there were several small, circular thatch houses, believed to be soldiers' huts. There is also a large circular structure about forty feet in diameter; there is provocative, but not definitive, evidence this was Chief Seloy's council house, which he gave to the Spanish for their use. Inside there are indications of internal "cabins" for guests and rows of benches for events. It appears that the Spanish modified this circular house by adding rectangular partitions and perhaps a wood floor. At that time, Native groups throughout Florida and the Southeast traditionally used circular council houses for community gatherings, special events, and guest lodging (figure 3.15). Based on archaeological and historical evidence, artists have depicted the first encampment

FIGURE 3.14. Timber stains mark the Menéndez encampment warehouse floor, constructed in 1565.

FIGURE 3.15.
Cutaway drawing of the Chote council house showing benches, central fire, entrance, and internal structure.

of the Menéndez colonists as a small, crowded space with Spanish-style buildings of wood and thatch and circular huts surrounding a central open plaza (figure 3.16).

Scholars have conducted significant historical and archaeological research on life at Menéndez's first encampment. Historians such as Eugene Lyon have combed through the initial and additional supply lists, and archaeologists have recovered thousands of artifacts from refuse pits, wells, and the surface the first group of colonists walked on. For the seven months they lived there, the nearly two hundred residents preferred to live in traditional Spanish houses and use the supplies they had brought. However, artifacts found by archaeologists indicate they also used locally made Indian pottery and ate local food. For example, half of the ceramic pieces found in the two Spanish wells are from Indian-made containers, undoubtedly obtained from the villagers. From the start, food was in short supply; much of the food brought for the colony was lost on a ship that left to avoid the French and never returned. In addition, food stored at San Mateo (Fort Caroline) burned in a warehouse fire a month after the Spanish arrival. To make matters worse, even though Menéndez made several large purchases of food at Havana, there was never enough, and hunger caused

FIGURE 3.16.
Re-creation of 1565 Menéndez encampment in Seloy's village.

unrest and mutinies. Although most food does not leave a trace archaeologically, animal bones and shellfish were recovered, revealing that the colonists caught and ate various local fish, shellfish, and deer. Remnants of their clothing (buttons, straight pins, beads, a buckle), jewelry (glass beads), household items (candlestick holders, a glass bottle), and furniture (brass upholstery tacks) provide us a glimpse of their daily life. Evidence of a child is seen in a clenched-fist amulet protectively tied around a baby's neck. Over time, however, relations with the local Timucuans became increasingly hostile, probably due to increasing Spanish demands for food, among other things, and the colony was moved across the river to Anastasia Island for safety.

The confirmation and description of Menéndez's first encampment is an outstanding achievement for historical archaeology in Florida and the nation. It had been speculated about for decades, but with careful research, historians and archaeologists have identified the actual site. It was the first Spanish foothold in North America, and St. Augustine became the oldest continuously occupied city in the United States. Keep in mind that St. Augustinians were raising their *grandchildren* when the English arrived at Jamestown in 1607, forty-two years after Menéndez set up camp in Chief Seloy's village.

From the perspective of the local Timucua Natives, the seven months the Spanish lived in their village began with friendship and support, but by the time the Spanish left, had become hostile. The usual reason for such a downturn in relations is increasing demands of the Spanish for food, support, and often, women. Also, wherever the Spanish went, local Natives soon realized the Spaniards, especially the soldiers, considered them inferior. The Spanish claimed the Natives' homelands for Spain, declared that they were subjects of the Spanish king, and pressured them to change their way of life by becoming Catholic and serving the Spanish king and his representatives. By 1565, Spanish policy forbade enslaving the Natives or forcing them to labor and support the invaders, but the Spanish continued to treat Native people very poorly. Timucuans resented this treatment and made it known the Spanish were no longer welcome. The Timucuans vastly outnumbered the Spanish and forced them to retreat to an island they thought they could secure.

Menéndez's Florida Forts and Missions

Soon after the first encampment was started, Menéndez began to carry out the rest of his orders to fortify the coast of Florida (figure 3.17). In the fall

FIGURE 3.17. Map of forts, missions, and towns Menéndez established between 1565 and 1570.

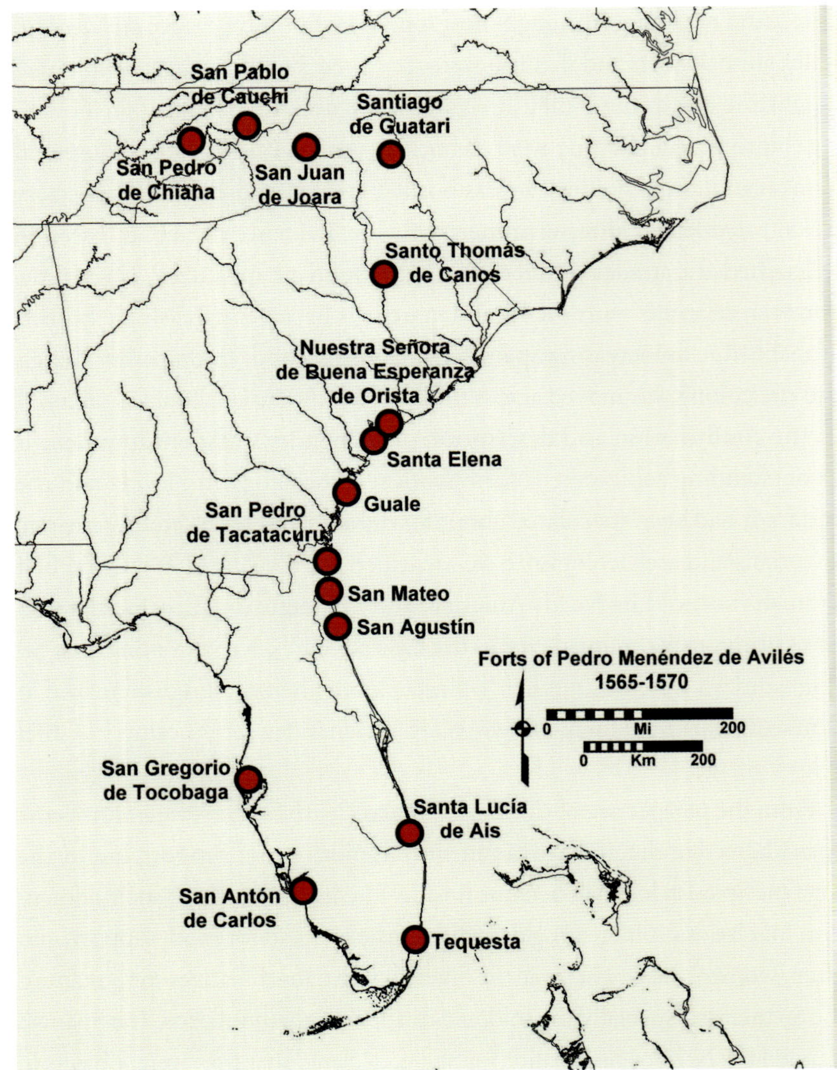

of 1565, on his way to Cuba to arrange for supplies, Menéndez stopped near today's St. Lucie Inlet on the southeast Florida coast to capture and kill the last of Ribault's men. He built a fort there among the Ais Indians and named it Santa Lucía; he left thirty soldiers there and moved on to Havana. After arranging for supplies in Cuba in early 1566, Menéndez sailed along the southwest Florida peninsula to Caloosahatchee Bay. There, like his predecessor Juan Ponce de León had done more than fifty years before, he encountered the remarkable capital town of the Calusa chiefdom with its tall mounds made of shells and the large council house of their paramount chief, Carlos (figure 3.18). Later, in the fall of 1566, Menéndez returned to this location and built a fort and a Jesuit mission, San Antón de Carlos, on

top of a tall flat-topped mound in the heart of the Calusa capital on Mound Key, near today's Cape Coral.

FIGURE 3.18. The Calusa chief's large council house, which could hold three thousand people.

Menéndez was always on the lookout for a waterway that would provide a shortcut across the Florida peninsula, and the Calusa told him that one existed farther up the coast where the Tocobaga lived, on today's Tampa Bay. Leaving a small garrison at San Antón, Menéndez went to Tampa Bay. Not surprisingly, the local Tocobaga were hostile to this third Spanish invasion, having already met Narváez in 1528 and de Soto in 1539. Despite the resistance, Menéndez built a fort there and established a mission called San Gregorio de Tocobaga. Because of reports of hostile Native groups to the east, however, he did not search for the water route across the peninsula. Leaving a military unit at the Tocobaga fort and missionaries at the mission, Menéndez sailed south around the peninsula to the land of the Tequestas near present-day Miami, establishing another mission and fort there. Traveling north, past St. Augustine, Menéndez established a mission on Cumberland Island, San Pedro de Tacatacuru. Local Natives strongly resisted all these military and religious intrusions into their homelands and, within a year, destroyed all but St. Augustine (then known as San Agustín) and killed the Spaniards. San Antón lasted another year but met the same fate. At each fort, local Indigenous people killed or drove the Spanish out of their territory because of their constant demands for food, their abuse of Native women, and the Catholic priests' insistence they change their traditional beliefs and ways of life.

FIGURE 3.19.
Fort San Antón excavations.

FIGURE 3.20.
Spanish artifacts found at Fort San Antón.

Two of Menéndez's forts/missions have been found: San Antón and San Gregorio. Historical archaeologists Victor and Amanda Thompson and William Marquardt found and investigated Fort San Antón de Carlos, built at the island capital of the Calusa. It is located on Mound Key in Estero Bay, near today's Fort Myers. Spanish documents describe the fort walls as being made of brushwood and lumber, enclosing thirty-six buildings. On top of a thirty-foot-high flat-topped mound built of shells, the archaeologists found part of the fort wall and possibly a bastion or gate, along with the foundations of two structures (figure 3.19). The walls of the structures were made of posts set in a trench, which was then filled with a crude cement mixture called tabby, made by mixing lime from burned shells with sand, water, and ash. The use of tabby at Fort San Antón is the earliest documented case in the United States. Not surprisingly, tabby was a traditional building material in Spain. The excavations recovered Spanish artifacts, including iron spikes, an iron hoe, pieces of large ceramic storage jars, and colorful majolica tableware (figure 3.20). Despite this evidence of a strong presence at San Antón, the Calusa killed the Spanish soldiers and priests in 1569. The Calusa chiefdom continued unmolested by the Spanish for almost two centuries.

Fort and Mission San Gregorio were built in the capital village of the Tocobaga on Old Tampa Bay. Today, the remains are in a neighborhood city park in Safety Harbor near Clearwater. There is a large, long, flat-topped mound with a ramp to the top. On the mound summit can be found traces of a building and an open central plaza. The remains of a large village stretch more than three miles along the bay shore. An early archaeologist, S. T. Walker, visited the site in 1879, and Clarence B. Moore mapped the site in 1900. Several archaeologists have since studied the site. Although it has been damaged by looting, Spanish materials have been recovered, including an iron axe, pipe bowls, and ceramic olive jar fragments.

After Menéndez founded eight forts and missions on the Florida peninsula and Atlantic Coast, he implemented the last of the king's orders: to establish a new capital at Port Royal and build a road from there to New Spain. The town, named Santa Elena, was built on Parris Island near present-day Beaufort, South Carolina. The road to the silver mines in Zacatecas, Mexico, was thought to be only about 750 miles away; it was, in fact, more than 1,700 miles away. As he sailed along the Atlantic Coast north of St. Augustine, Menéndez stopped at several sea islands looking for Frenchmen and meeting with the Native inhabitants, declaring possession of their lands and people for the Spanish king. Within a few months, he stationed five Spanish soldiers and several missionaries on the sea islands.

Menéndez arrived at Port Royal in April 1566 and started constructing a fort and the capital town of Santa Elena. Soon, the king sent 250 military reinforcements led by Captain Juan Pardo. The soldiers helped build the fort, but the fledgling colony could not feed such a large military company for long. So Menéndez sent Pardo and half his army into the interior to start the new road to Zacatecas and claim the people and lands he encountered for Spain. He was to build a series of forts in Native villages along the proposed highway and station a small garrison at each. Pardo also was expected to evangelize and pacify local Native groups along the way. He led two expeditions into the interior, in 1566 and in 1567, returning to Santa Elena in the interim. The army traveled through the mountainous terrain on foot, carrying what they needed on their backs, expecting to be fed and housed by local villagers. Fortunately, Pardo had a scribe and notary, Juan de la Bandera, who made detailed notes and observations on his expeditions. Bandera's records are invaluable eyewitness accounts of the landscape, towns, villages, and Native people they encountered. These documents are a gold mine of information for historians and archaeologists.

Like de Soto, Pardo traveled from one Native town and chiefdom to another, following river valleys up to the fall line and Piedmont across the Appalachians into eastern Tennessee. Unlike de Soto, Pardo implemented the new Spanish policy of treating Indigenous people peacefully. In return, they received food and Native cooperation in constructing forts and houses for the soldiers in Indian towns. When the chiefs first met Pardo, they treated him and his army as potential military allies who could help them defeat their enemies. Pardo's goal was to reach the Coosa chiefdom and then go on to Zacatecas. However, when the army reached eastern Tennessee, Native groups warned Pardo that the Coosa groups downstream had assembled a large army and planned to ambush the Spanish in revenge for de Soto's harsh treatment and their horrific loss at the battle at Mabila twenty-five years earlier. Pardo avoided this imminent attack by turning back to Santa Elena, where he established five forts and a mission in Native towns. He left a small unit of soldiers at each fort, and often a priest, to live there while he moved on. Unfortunately, the soldiers he left behind mistreated the local villagers, and within two years, the Natives had burned all the forts and killed all the Spaniards.

The Pardo, de Soto, and Luna expeditions traveled similar routes in some

FIGURE 3.21. Fort San Juan de Joara, 1566–1568.

areas. By using the eyewitness accounts of all three entradas, ethnohistorian Charles Hudson and his colleagues identified the general locations of the five towns where Pardo built a fort and stationed a garrison. The narratives of the three expeditions recorded the names and locations of the towns and chiefdoms the Spanish encountered; distances between them; and geographical landmarks such as rivers, swamps, mountains, and mountain passes. The narratives also recorded details of the towns, such as their population sizes, numbers of mounds, fortifications, and geographical settings. As ethnohistorians identified probable locations and descriptions of specific towns from the narratives, archaeologists searched for nearby archaeological sites that matched the eyewitness descriptions and contained mid-sixteenth-century Spanish artifacts. Using this method, scholars have discovered the remains of two Pardo-founded forts, Santo Tomás de Canos (Cofitachequi) and San Juan de Joara, and the search for the others continues.

Pardo's most important fort in the interior of northeast Spanish Florida was Fort San Juan, built in the large Cherokee/Catawba village of Joara. Pardo arrived in November 1566, and with the chief's permission, his army

FIGURE 3.22. Aerial view of the moat around a bastion of Fort San Juan (light-colored area), 1566–1568.

and village residents spent three weeks constructing a stockade fort and houses for the soldiers on the edge of the Native town (figure 3.21). Historical archaeologist David Moore found the archaeological remains of Joara at the Berry Site near Morganton, North Carolina. Long-term excavations by archaeologists Robin Beck, Christopher Rodning, and David Moore found the filled-in moat surrounding the fort and the cluster of houses where Spanish soldiers lived for eighteen months (figure 3.22).

Some sites occupied after European contact can be identified through historical documents and archaeological materials, and they can then be given their historical names. This was the case with the Berry Site, which was determined to be the Indian town of Joara and the Spanish outpost of Fort San Juan, and the Martin Site, which was demonstrated to be the Apalachee town of Anhaica. In the mid-twentieth century in the United States, the government began recording archaeological sites according to the state and county where they were found and a sequential number. Each site now has an official three-part number. For example, site 8ES22 is in the state of Florida (eighth state alphabetically), is in Escambia County (ES), and is the twenty-second site recorded in that county. Today, archaeological sites can have one or more informal names but only one formal, official number.

The Spanish soldiers at Joara lived adjacent to the fort, in a compound of

four houses and a kitchen. Their homes were built the same way as Native residences. They were square, with shallow basin floors, wattle-and-daub walls, and thatch roofs. They were all burned in 1568, apparently after most usable items had been removed. Thus far, archaeologists have discovered and studied the remains of five structures in the compound. Due to the excellent preservation of the charred timbers and thatch, researchers know that they were built with typical Native American materials and that Spanish sharp-edged metal tools were used to gather and shape the materials.

On the burned house floors were charred food remains, such as animal bones, especially deer, and maize, nuts, beans, and squash (figure 3.23). Excavations in the compound found an abundance of Native American materials, especially pottery, along with a small number of distinctive sixteenth-century Spanish artifacts, such as wrought-iron nails, chain mail and armor, iron buckles, copper alloy clothing aglets, copper alloy bells, earthenware and majolica pottery sherds, and glass beads (figure 3.24). There also are some copper alloy items, including rolled beads and pieces of brass or copper scrap that the people of Joara crafted from scrap metal acquired from Pardo and his men.

Information from the burned houses reflects how relations with the villagers changed at Fort San Juan during the eighteen months the soldiers lived there. For example, the first house was constructed by the Natives with some help from Spanish metal tools, but the last structure, the kitchen, was more crudely constructed, primarily with metal tools, and was weaker than the earlier buildings. Archaeologists interpret the changes in house construction as reflecting good initial relations with the villagers who built the first structures for the soldiers. However, the Spanish built the kitchen building late in their occupation, and it was a poorly constructed, weaker structure than those built by the Natives. This difference is seen as reflecting a deterioration of

HOW ARCHAEOLOGICAL SITES ARE NAMED

The original names of almost all Native American archaeological sites have been lost, especially those that were occupied before European contact. When archaeological sites on land or underwater are first found, they are usually named for one of the following:

a prominent nearby landmark (for example, Emanuel Point Shipwreck I or Fig Springs)

the name of the landowner at the time it was discovered (for example, Tatham Mound)

a famous person who once lived there (for example, Martin Site)

a nearby community (for example, Weeki Wachee Site)

FIGURE 3.23. Burned Spanish soldier's house at Fort San Juan, 1566–1568.

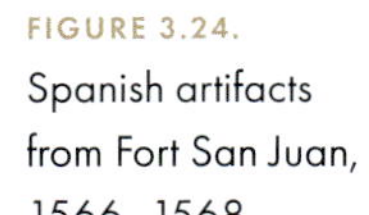

FIGURE 3.24. Spanish artifacts from Fort San Juan, 1566–1568.

relations between the soldiers and Natives. Another sign of the erosion of ties with the Joarans was a change in the meat provided to the Spanish. At first, most of the meat supplied to the soldiers was the favored bear meat, which arrived in their compound already butchered and ready to cook. Some deer were also butchered in their compound. By the end, bear meat made up less than half of their diet, and deer meat was the majority. The shift from a preferred meat to an everyday one reflects a reversal in the relations between Native and Spanish men. Testimonies of a Native man and a woman who married a resident of Joara when the Spanish were there stated that the soldiers' continued demands for food and their improprieties with Native women angered the Native men. Seeing the growing hostility, the soldiers could have denied entry of Native men into their area but could not have copied their expertise in constructing the kitchen. On the other hand, a strong presence of Native women is seen throughout the soldiers' occupation in the abundant locally made ceramic cooking pots and the charred remains of local fruits and traditional corn- and nut-based meals prepared by women for the soldiers.

The initial segregation of the Spanish compound from the village at Joara and the construction of a defensive fort very likely set a tone of distrust between the villagers and soldiers. Despite this, relationships between the two groups seem to have begun on a friendly note and have become increasingly hostile over time. Joara was a large town with a prominent flat-topped mound and a powerful chief, and the residents greatly outnumbered the thirty Spanish soldiers. After eighteen months of growing problems from the soldiers, the residents had had enough, so they killed the soldiers and burned their fort and houses to the ground. According to solid archaeological and documentary evidence, the town of Joara persisted long after the Natives dispatched the Spanish. A similar pattern of increasing hostility between Spanish soldiers and Natives must have occurred at all the other forts and the mission Pardo built, which met the same fate as Fort San Juan. Native resistance to mistreatment was successful in stopping the Spanish invasion into the interior.

Santa Elena

Despite the destruction of all the interior forts by resistant Natives, the fledgling capital of Santa Elena on Port Royal harbor continued. In 1568, Menéndez brought a group of 225 colonists, primarily small farming families, to Santa Elena from the Castile area of Spain with a guarantee of two years of support. The settlers cleared and planted agricultural fields, built homes on granted lots in the town, and started a local government. By the end of summer 1569, there were thirty-six households; by October, 327 people were living there.

Historian Eugene Lyon describes this Spanish frontier society as similar to their homeland communities in Castile. It was socially stratified from commoners to the elite, who lived in luxuriously furnished homes. Local civil and criminal courts dispensed justice, and the surviving lawsuits reveal much about the sixteenth-century society. The Spanish farmers learned to cultivate corn from local Native people and successfully grew grapes, fruit, and olives. Colonists sent lumber to Spain, along with pine resin and pitch for shipbuilding, and they sent deerskins acquired through trade with Native groups. Soon, a series of poor harvests caused a famine, and many settlers left. In order to survive, Menéndez sent groups of soldiers to live in Native villages. In 1570, the Spanish king established a subsidy called the *situado* to support the royal garrisons at Santa Elena and St. Augustine. With this new financial stability for the military, Menéndez moved his family to Santa Elena.

Meanwhile, the Jesuit missionaries who had been sent into the surrounding area to pacify the local Orista people and convert them to Christianity and obedience to the Spanish were far from successful. In fact, they caused increasing problems. Native groups resisted the changes to their customs that the priests required, such as planting a surplus of corn for Spanish use, living year-round in large settlements, and forgoing their religious beliefs. In 1571, Native groups killed Jesuit missionaries on lower Chesapeake Bay, and, in retaliation, Menéndez sent a punitive military expedition that hanged several Indigenous leaders. The Jesuits consequently terminated all their Florida missions. The plan to use priests to pacify Native groups through conversion and subsequent obedience had failed. The remains of the Jesuit mission on Chesapeake Bay have not been found, but historians speculate it probably was in Virginia, near Yorktown and Williamsburg or Fredericksburg.

Native hostility toward the Spanish increased around Santa Elena to the point where it was too dangerous for farmers to work in their fields. By 1576, the local Orista were attacking the Spaniards at will, and there were increasing food shortages. After a Spanish military patrol was massacred in 1576, the Spanish community gathered in their fort for safety, while the local Natives attacked and sacked the town. This violence caused the colonists to abandon Santa Elena and flee to St. Augustine. Outraged Natives then burned the town and the fort to the ground.

Almost immediately after Santa Elena was abandoned and destroyed, in 1577, the French sent a ship, the *Prince,* to scout the area for a possible occupation of the site. However, the ship ran aground while trying to enter Port Royal Sound, and the shipwrecked crew constructed a small fort nearby for protection. The local Orista soon attacked the French fort, killing two hundred and capturing about eighty. The next year, in 1578, the Spanish found the deserted fort with the remains of several Frenchmen inside. They dismantled the fort and searched for the remaining French crew, finding and killing about thirty Frenchmen.

The French threat to take Port Royal spurred the Spanish to return to Santa Elena the following year. This time, the Spanish deliberately waged war with local Orista groups. Military units burned Native villages, destroyed their food supplies, and killed all the residents, including Frenchmen hiding in the villages. In 1579, the Spanish built a new fort, San Marcos, at Santa Elena, and by 1580, they had built sixty new houses in the rejuvenated town. However, Native animosity only increased. Once again, the colonists were confined to the town and fort, unable to work their fields or orchards. In 1585, the British encroached into Spanish Florida, founding the Roanoke Island colony on the coast of North Carolina. The following year, Sir Francis Drake's British fleet attacked and sacked major Spanish ports in the Caribbean and attacked St. Augustine, burning the town to the ground. Drake was on his way to attack Santa Elena next but missed the Port Royal Sound entrance. Drake abandoned his plan to strike Santa Elena and continued up the coast to rescue the English colonists at Roanoke Island.

The impact of Drake's Caribbean sweep and burning of St. Augustine, plus the inability to suppress Indian hostilities around Santa Elena, made the Spanish realize that they could not defend two widely separated settlements, so they combined the two settlements at St. Augustine. In August 1587, Santa Elena was abandoned for good, the fort was torn down, and the town was burned. The abandonment of Santa Elena signaled the first reduction of the northern boundary of Spanish La Florida from Port Royal, South Carolina, to Savannah, Georgia, and St. Augustine became the second capital of La Florida.

For the second time, the Orista people had succeeded in driving the Spanish from their lands. Defiant in defending their homeland, the Orista won the war waged against them despite many vicious attacks, reprisals, killings, and destruction of their villages, food, and fields by the Spanish military.

The Orista made the establishment of a Spanish colonial town at Santa Elena impossible.

For more than three hundred years, Santa Elena was known only through historical documents, and its location was unknown. But in 1923, a major in the US Marine Corps stationed at Parris Island, George H. Osterhout, conducted excavations on the southern tip of the island and found many colonial artifacts, the outline of a partially filled-in moat, a stockade wall, and the remains of buildings. He interpreted these remains as part of French Charlesfort (1562–1563), but historians and archaeologists debated this claim for more than half a century. In 1979, historical archaeologist Stanley South from the University of South Carolina and historian Eugene Lyon investigated Osterhout's finds, which were then underneath an extensive golf course. They determined that Osterhout had *not* found French Charlesfort, but the second of three Spanish forts built at Santa Elena, Fort San Marcos.

Archaeologists Stanley South and Chester DePratter and historian Eugene Lyon conducted several years of research at Santa Elena in the 1980s and 1990s. Analysis of the historical documents by Lyon gave the archaeologists important information about what to expect in the ground and details of the events the colonists experienced there. The archaeologists found and studied two Spanish forts, San Felipe (1574–1576) and San Marcos (1577–1587), located about five hundred feet apart on the riverfront. Between the two Spanish forts lay the remains of the town of Santa Elena, which encompassed about twenty acres. In the town South and DePratter's team found a Spanish pottery kiln, the oldest of its kind in North America (figure 3.25). In their excavations, they also discovered that the remains of the 1562 French Charlesfort lay underneath the Spanish Fort San Felipe.

Forts San Felipe and San Marcos were similar in design. While only about half of each fort had survived riverbank erosion, much was learned about them. The moats for both forts were trapezoidal; corner bastions surrounded large rectangular two-story blockhouses where the soldiers lived, with an artillery deck on the flat rooftop (figure 3.26). The Spanish built both forts under threat of attacks by the Orista. Fort San Felipe was built in stages. The blockhouses were built first, and archaeologists found and excavated one. Traces remained of an initial temporary barrier nine feet high made of bundles of small logs placed in a ditch to protect the soldiers building the first floor of the blockhouse. Two years later, the moat, bastions, and stockade wall were added. The walls of the last fort, Fort San Marcos, were constructed in secret by a group of soldiers who stole back to Santa Elena

FIGURE 3.25. Excavating the residential compound of Santa Elena, 1566–1587, on the US Marine Corps Recruit Depot on Parris Island, South Carolina.

from St. Augustine before the Orista realized they were there. Quickly, they put up a wall of prefabricated sections of a post-and-board wall (like giant privacy fence sections) previously made in St. Augustine.

Documents state that the town was organized in the traditional Spanish manner around a central plaza lined with public buildings and residences radiating out in a grid pattern. The residential compound of a wealthy family was extensively excavated, along with a nearby hut that was probably used by soldiers (figure 3.27). This residential compound had three long, narrow, and rectangular houses around a central courtyard. There was a well in the

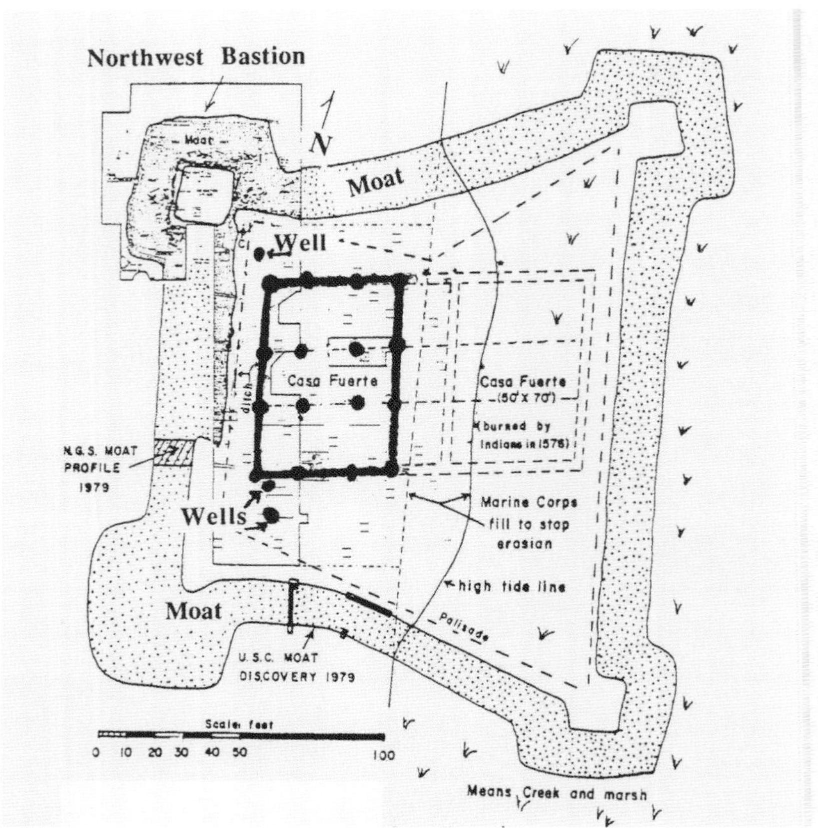

FIGURE 3.26. Drawing of Spanish Fort San Felipe, which was built over the ruins of French Charlesfort in 1566.

corner of the compound and more than a dozen pits filled to the brim with refuse from the occupants. The houses were traditional Spanish buildings with wattle-and-daub walls and large perimeter posts. This type of construction had been common in Spain for generations and was easy to build. Roofs were gabled and covered with thatch, probably palmetto fronds. The Spanish dug pits initially to mix the daub to cover the house walls, and they later filled them with trash (figure 3.28). The material in these pits included the remains of a variety of everyday materials such as food, pottery, nails, crossbows, personal and religious ornaments, thimbles, pins, and scores of other things that tell the story of the daily lives of the people who lived in Santa Elena.

In sum, Santa Elena was the first capital of La Florida and was intended to be the eastern hub of a new fortified road to the silver mines of New Spain. But soon after the colonists and army arrived, claiming the area and people

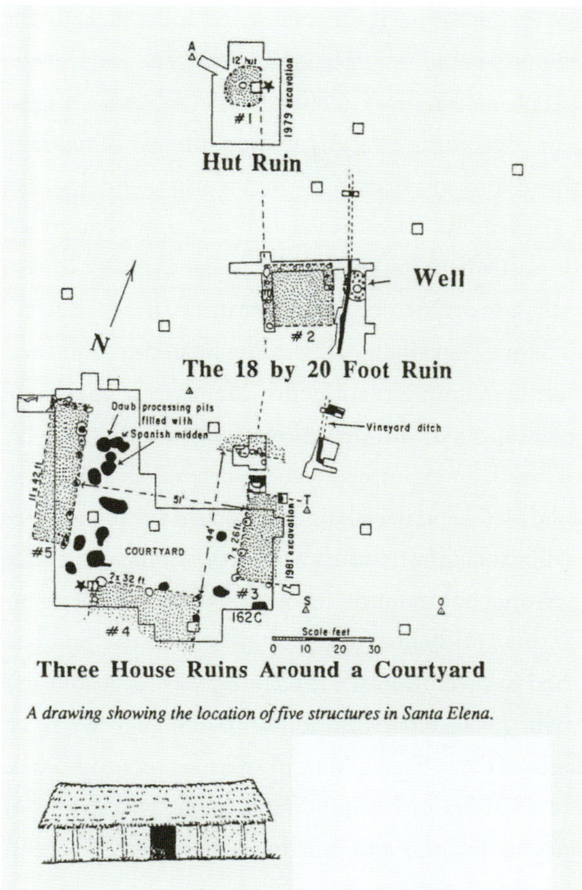

FIGURE 3.27. Drawing of archaeological remains of a household lot in Santa Elena, 1566–1587.

FIGURE 3.28. Broken Spanish ceramic tablewares in a household refuse pit at Santa Elena, 1566–1587.

SANTA ELENA HISTORY

Forts

French Charlesfort 1562–1563

Spanish San Salvador 1566

Spanish San Felipe 1574–1576

Spanish San Marcos 1577–1587

Settlements

First occupation 1566–1576

Second occupation 1577–1587

Abandonment 1587

for Spain, the local Orista resisted and attacked. The military could not defend the colonists, and in 1576, after fourteen years of effort, they fled to St. Augustine. Becoming aware of French interest in retaking the abandoned Santa Elena location, the Spanish returned, but with the same result; they abandoned the settlement for good ten years later, in 1587. Historians and archaeologists have learned that the society at Santa Elena included wealthy Spaniards and their families, among them Pedro Menéndez. They were well supplied, and the colonists lived a Spanish way of life. They exported local resources such as lumber, pine pitch, and deerskins and enjoyed the finer things of life, including jewelry, wines, nice homes, and large personal compounds. They grew fruit and olive orchards and field crops. But each time the Spanish tried to sustain a town there, they were attacked and driven out by the Orista, who protected their homelands despite many Spanish attacks on their villages and the destruction of their crops and homes. The presence of the remains of Spanish Santa Elena on the golf course of the US Marine Corps installation was and remains a very special place in the history of Florida and our country.

Summary of Competition and Colonization

After four failures to establish a settlement in Spanish Florida, by 1561 Spain's claim to the colonial province of La Florida was tenuous at best. It was very vulnerable to other European nations seeking to establish a colonial empire. The French were the first to test the Spanish hold on Southeastern North America when they secretly built Charlesfort at Port Royal in 1561 and Fort Caroline at the mouth of the St. Johns River in 1562. Archaeologists have found the elusive Charlesfort underneath a later Spanish fort, but Fort Caroline is still lost. This early French intrusion was a wake-up call to the Spanish to make a serious commitment to colonize Spanish Florida. Between 1565 and 1568, Menéndez built fifteen forts, garrisons, and missions around the Florida peninsula, up the Atlantic Coast to Port Royal, and deep into the interior across the Appalachian Mountains. Historical archaeologists have found and studied five of these early colonial settlements: the first Menéndez encampment at St. Augustine, the first capital of Florida at Santa Elena, two Menéndez forts on the Florida peninsula (San Antón and Tocobaga), and Fort San Juan, in western North Carolina. Details unearthed from the ground and in historical documents about these and other early settlements have provided crucial insights into how the colonists lived and died on the far edge of their colonial empire. They were guarding La Florida and the vulnerable shipping route along which the astronomical wealth in gold and silver was riding the Gulf Stream along the Atlantic Coast before turning for Spain. From the Natives' perspective, time after time, they drove the Spaniards out of their homelands and destroyed all their forts, towns, and missions except one, St. Augustine. Throughout this period, the Natives continued their successful resistance to Spanish claims on their lands and culture. By 1587, the Spanish grip on La Florida was still there but not strong. Keep in mind that all of this happened half a century before the founding of Jamestown.

Suggested Readings

Eugene Lyon. *The Enterprise of Florida: Pedro Menéndez de Avilés and the Spanish Conquest of 1565–1568.* Gainesville: University Press of Florida, 1983.

John T. McGrath. *The French in Early Florida.* Gainesville: University Press of Florida, 2000.

Stanley South. *Archaeology at Santa Elena: Doorway to the Past.* Columbia: South Carolina Institute of Archaeology and Anthropology, University of South Carolina, 1996. Available online at https://scholarcommons.sc.edu/popular_series/2.

Michael van Groesen and Larry E. Tise. *Theodore de Bry: America.* Cologne, Germany: Taschen, 2019. Available on amazon.com.

Places to Visit

Fort Caroline in the Timucuan Ecological and Historic Preserve National Park outside Jacksonville, Florida. Visit the reconstruction of Fort Caroline, exhibits, and reenactments along with the Ribault memorial.

Fountain of Youth Archaeological Park, 11 Magnolia Avenue, St. Augustine, Florida. Site of Menéndez's first encampment and 1587 Spanish mission of Nombre de Dios.

Mound Key Archaeological State Park in Estero, Florida. The island is accessible to the public only by boat. Once you get to the island, you can hike the trails with interpretive signs, and you can see the two big shell mounds, the canal that crosses the island, and the "water courts," or fishponds, where the Calusa stored vast amounts of live fish. Bring your own boat and enjoy a very interesting day.

Websites to Visit

Fort Caroline National Memorial: https://www.nps.gov/places/foca.htm

Luna Settlement: https://uwf.edu/cassh/community-outreach/anthropology-and-archaeology/research/faculty-and-staff-projects/luna-settlement/

Menéndez Fort and Camp, Original Site of St. Augustine, 1565–1566: https://www.floridamuseum.ufl.edu/histarch/research/st-augustine/menendez/

Santa Elena, The 1500s Capital of Spanish Florida in South Carolina: https://www.nps.gov/articles/santa-elena-the-1500s-capital-of-spanish-florida.htm

Symposium: The Tristan de Luna Shipwrecks and Settlement (1559–1561) in Pensacola, Florida: https://core.tdar.org/collection/65659/symposium-the-tristan-de-luna-shipwrecks-and-settlement-1559-1561-in-pensacola-florida

FOUR

TRANSFORMATION

The Spanish first attempted to colonize the Indigenous people of the Southeast by conquering them militarily. But, as you learned in chapter 3, between 1528 and 1543, the armies of Narváez and de Soto faced fierce resistance from the Native groups they encountered. They did not find what they were seeking: gold or silver deposits or large agricultural societies, and the few expedition survivors barely escaped with their lives. In the mid-sixteenth century, the Spanish tried a more traditional approach to colonization: they sent large groups of Spanish settlers to start three agricultural communities, each protected by a fort and garrison. They planned to build roads connecting the new communities to each other and to New Spain, protected by strategically placed military installations. Luna and Menéndez attempted two such colonization efforts, but after almost three decades of efforts, only the subsidized presidio at St. Augustine remained.

Realizing they could neither defeat the Southeastern Indian groups nor establish successful colonial settlements among them, yet still needing to settle La Florida, the Spanish tried a third strategy: missionization. The plan was to work within the Native political system by establishing voluntary alliances with chiefs of agricultural villages and towns. The Spanish would provide large annual gifts of prestigious European goods and military protection, and, in return, the chiefs were to build missions in their villages and provide food and labor for the mission, St. Augustine, and the military. Historians and archaeologists have long studied the story of Spanish missionization, and this chapter will share what they have learned about this unique approach to colonization and the tens of thousands of Native people who underwent missionization.

As the mission system developed, the British and French rapidly started new colonies in Spanish Florida (in Louisiana, the Carolinas, and Georgia) and met with little resistance from Spain. British and French traders developed a lucrative network with Native groups in the interior, and established plantations along the Atlantic Coast and in the Mississippi Valley. The new plantations as well as those well established in the Caribbean islands depended on enslaved labor, creating a constant demand for slaves. This chapter will explain how the combination of high demand for enslaved labor, successful British trade with Indian groups, and the traditional Native practice of taking war captives developed into a devastating Indian slave trade in the South. Militant and armed Native societies who were allied with the British conducted raids on unarmed Native groups for captives to be traded to the British for firearms and ammunition. The Natives would sell their captives to British slave dealers, who then sold them to planters, primarily in the Caribbean. This was the Indian slave trade. Spanish missions, with their large numbers of undefended, unarmed Native farmers, became prime targets of the Indian slavers. Raids for captives eventually destroyed the Spanish mission system and disrupted traditional Native American groups throughout the Southeast. This chapter will reveal this little-known and terrifying episode of Florida's past.

Between 1650 and 1750, the combination of the Spanish mission system, population loss from epidemics of European diseases, and the Indian slave trade transformed Spanish Florida. Spanish and Indigenous people were overwhelmed, and the boundaries of Spanish Florida shrank almost to those of our state today. Spanish Florida and lands along the Atlantic Coast became vacant of Native people, while the militant captive-trading societies coalesced in the interior and became powerful. This transformation of Spanish Florida and its Native people was shocking.

Spanish Missions

Following the failure of the Jesuits in Spain's earliest, mid-sixteenth-century missions, Menéndez selected a new religious order, the Franciscans, to pacify Native Americans through their form of missionization. The process began with invitations from colonial administrators to local chiefs of agricultural towns and villages to visit officials in St. Augustine. There, the Spanish treated them as high-status guests, giving them many valuable European gifts with much ceremony and usually baptizing them as Catholics. Spanish colonial officials then asked the chiefs to enter into an alliance contract with them. The alliance would ensure that chiefs would be given special gifts annually and would receive military protection. In return, each chief had to agree to build a church and friary for a missionary in their primary town to teach their people the Catholic faith (figure 4.1). The chiefs also had to agree to expand their corn production to supply the village mission and St

Augustine, provide annual laborers to the Spanish for construction and maintenance projects in the region, and form a militia of warriors to aid the Spanish military when needed. Both parties would benefit from the proposed alliance. The chiefs personally benefited by improving their social and political status, plus they had the added security of the Spanish military and a resident friar to intercede for them with the colonial administrators and military. The Spanish benefited from the increased food and labor supply and strong alliances with Native mission villages and towns.

FIGURE 4.1. Rendering of a seventeenth-century Franciscan priest, Father Francisco López de Mendoza Grajales.

Initially, both the friars and Native people benefited from their new relationship. Between 1587 and 1700, a handful of Franciscan priests converted thousands of Indigenous people and established at least seventy-six missions among the Guale, Mocama, Timucua, and Apalachee (figure 4.2). Since the friars hoped to convert and assimilate Native Americans into Spanish peasant colonists, they focused primarily on those aspects of Native culture that directly conflicted with Catholicism, such as polygamy, polytheism, so-called idolatrous behavior, and their popular and violent ball game resembling lacrosse. The missionaries introduced new domestic plants, such as peaches, watermelons, and wheat, and new domestic animals, including cattle, horses, and pigs. They also introduced iron tools and other items manufactured in Europe. There was a great deal of variation in how Native groups accepted European goods, materials, plants, animals, and religion, but the Franciscans soon began to transform Native economies, social structures, and family life. Researchers agree that while tens of thousands of Native people were baptized and participated in the Catholic Church and its rituals, they also retained the integrity of their own religion, finding ways to combine the old and new religions and practice both simultaneously. They were not as Hispanicized as were many Indigenous groups in Mexico and Latin America.

From the Native American perspective, villagers were continuing practices they had been doing for hundreds of years, such as paying tributes of

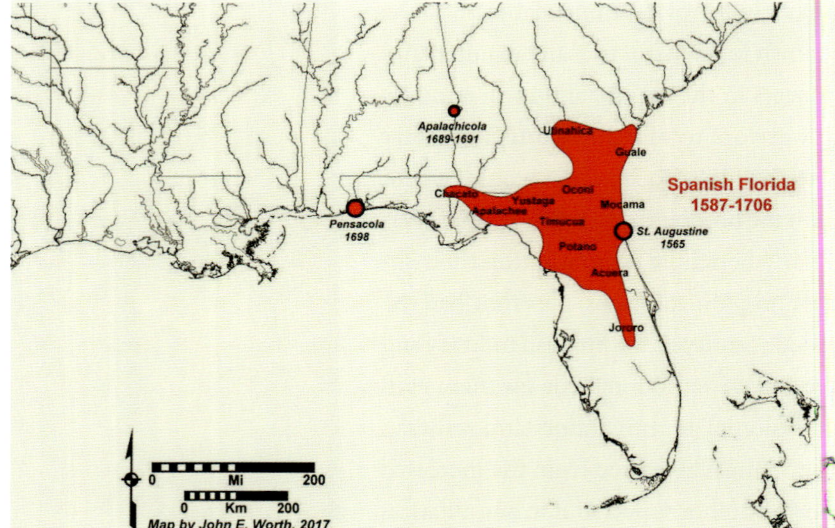

FIGURE 4.2. Map of missionized Native groups.

food and labor to their chiefs and priests. Chiefs were also accustomed to making political alliances with more powerful chiefs, in which they regularly received high-status gifts for tributes of food and labor. Chiefs also had traditionally received military support from their political allies and were expected to provide military assistance when necessary. The main differences in their new political alliances were that the new ally was Spanish rather than another powerful chief, and the new priest was a missionizing Catholic friar with an agenda of transforming them into Spanish peasants.

From the Spanish perspective, the voluntary alliances with the chiefs were their first peaceful contractual relationships with Native Americans. The costs of the alliances were very low for the Spanish, consisting only of relatively cheap trade goods—hats, jackets, blankets, glass jewelry, quartz crystals, and ceramics—that were highly valued by the chiefs. The costs of the few soldiers and friars for the missions were also low and paid for by the Crown. For these few expenses, the Spanish received a significant amount of food and very cheap labor, both of which they desperately needed.

While the Franciscans and Spanish administrators promised the chiefs of newly missionized groups a bright future, everyday people soon realized that they had to pay a high price for the chief's gifts and political affiliation with the Spanish. Most of the groups that accepted the missionaries had previously been independent; they now found their status reduced from being a sovereign people to being Spanish subjects on the bottom rung of a new colonial social order. The chiefs had agreed to supply labor groups to the Spanish, who used them as poorly paid workers to build their facilities and forts, operate ferries, maintain roadways, and work for the military and Spanish colonists, especially in St. Augustine. The work was hard, paid extremely low wages, and required the men to be away from home for extended periods. The demand for Native food and labor from the missions only increased over time as the Spanish Crown's support for St. Augustine dwindled.

Under these pressures, all newly missionized groups revolted. They murdered priests and soldiers and desecrated and burned churches and friaries. The Spanish were quick and vicious in their response to these revolts, sending military units and Native militias after the rebels and killing or humiliating the leaders. For example, after the 1647 revolt of the Apalachee, the Spanish immediately sent soldiers from St. Augustine along with a militia of five hundred Timucua warriors. A huge battle ensued, and both sides suffered heavy losses. The rebels surrendered, and the leaders were hung or sent to St. Augustine as enslaved laborers. This pattern of revolt, harsh punishment, and subjugation of the survivors was repeated throughout the mission system. The oppressive punishment deterred additional large revolts, new chiefs emerged who were more submissive and peaceful, and the villagers returned. Friars and military officials also continually interfered in local Native politics by promoting pro-Spanish chiefs, causing internal divisions and power struggles between the elite lineages throughout the chiefdoms—a classic divide-and-conquer tactic.

In addition, European diseases, to which Native Americans had no natural immunity, devastated mission communities. As exposure to the Spanish increased, the health of Native workers decreased, and waves of epidemics swept through mission towns. Native populations suffered repeated episodes of deadly diseases such as smallpox, measles, and influenza. The population of missionized groups thus rapidly declined, due not only to disease but also to the stress of forced labor at home and away. Biological anthropologists have determined that missionized Native people suffered from malnutrition and had severe and physically damaging injuries and other health risks from being in displaced work camps, especially in St. Augustine. To deal with the steady population decline of missionized Native groups, and for convenience, the Spanish consolidated missions and moved them to locations along interior roads or the shipping lanes in the Atlantic Sea Islands.

In the face of these many adversities, disillusioned, missionized Native individuals, families, and even entire communities began to flee Spanish

Florida. Some went to the new British colonies where Christian religion was not pressed on them, starting new villages and new lives. There, many of the refugees entered the British Indian trade, exchanging animal skins, captives, and other commodities for high-quality European goods and firearms, which were either forbidden to everyday people or unavailable from the Spanish. Other groups went to French Louisiana, where practicing the Catholic faith was voluntary. They founded new villages and traded their agricultural products and animal pelts to the French colonists for trade goods and firearms.

How We Find Mission Communities in Spanish Florida

Spanish missions have drawn the interest of historians, archaeologists, and the public since the nineteenth century. Attention was initially focused on the Southwest, where missions arrived late and, in the arid climate, many still have standing structures; some missions even have active churches today or have become historical parks and tourist attractions. Spanish Florida's mission buildings are up to four centuries older than those in the Southwest, and the structures were made of organic materials that either burned, collapsed, or decomposed in the wet, humid environment. In other words, nothing is left aboveground of the scores of mission sites in Spanish Florida, with their hundreds of buildings. But an abundance of information lies just beneath the surface and buried in historical documents. Although many Florida missions are identified in Spanish documents, and distances between them are sometimes recorded, their exact locations are rarely pinpointed. As a result, almost all the locations of missions in Spanish Florida were lost.

Historians, however, have found documentary evidence of more than seventy different missions in Spanish Florida, and some suggest that there were more than one hundred. Despite a scarcity of historical maps of the mission locations, historians and archaeologists have found and identified many of them (figure 4.3). One by one, researchers have been able to tie locations to the only two existing historical mission maps or create new maps of confirmed locations of missions. For historians, the big question is, Where are the missions? For archaeologists, the big question often is Which mission have we found? Bit by bit, though, they are piecing together a map of the missions. As I write this, seventy-six different missions have been historically documented, and thirty-three of those have been archaeologically investigated.

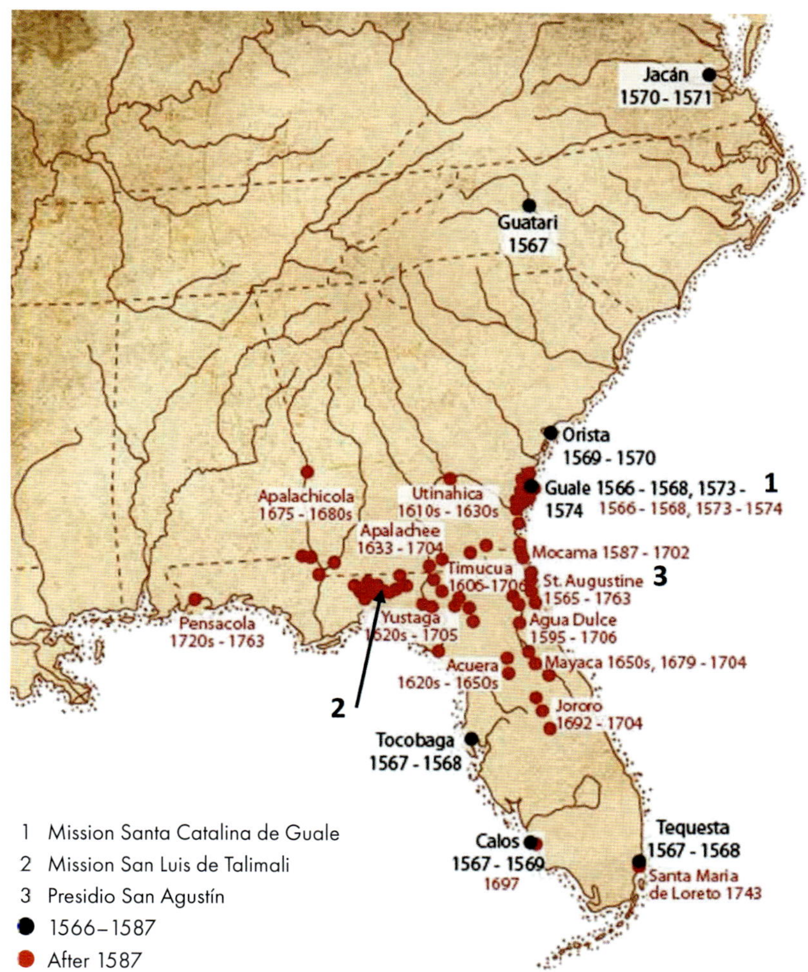

FIGURE 4.3. Map of Spanish missions, 1566–1763.

This research lets us imagine what a mission in Spanish Florida looked like. Picture a Native town or village with houses and public buildings (council house, chief's house) built in their traditional style. Usually, the only Spanish-style buildings in the mission were the church, friary, and kitchen. The people living there were Native Americans with only one or maybe two Spanish friars and a few soldiers. As the best targets for missionizing, the Spanish selected settled Native groups who had been farming corn, beans, and squash for centuries, along with hunting in winter and gathering nuts and fruits. Most of the people usually lived year-round in the mission towns and villages and walked to work in their nearby fields. However, there were also small hamlets scattered in the countryside next to fertile soil, and the people who lived there went to the nearby mission town for religious services, rituals, festivals, and games. People farmed much like they always had, except that they grew much more corn, to support the mission and to send to St. Augustine, and they now used metal hoes. Hunting, however, was reduced with the introduction of domestic animals, especially cattle and hogs.

Historical archaeologists have produced a trove of information about life in Indian mission villages. Two relatively large mission towns, Mission Santa Catalina de Guale and San Luis de Talimali de Apalachee, have been intensively studied, providing extensive information, which is summarized below. Both were chiefdom capital towns. Santa Catalina was an early coastal mission near the northern limit of the system, and Mission San Luis was near the western edge of the mission system in present-day Tallahassee.

Mission Santa Catalina de Guale

David Hurst Thomas of the American Museum of Natural History led a fifteen-year study of Santa Catalina de Guale. It is located on St. Catherines Island near Savannah, Georgia, about 180 miles north of the mission headquarters in St. Augustine. Before Spanish contact, the Guale (pronounced "Walie") lived on the mainland along rivers and tidal creeks and had a diversified subsistence base that included hunting, fishing, gathering seasonal wild plants, and gardening. Organized into chiefdoms, the Guale had two principal towns and a hereditary chief. The leaders and their families lived in the towns in large, round community buildings situated around a spacious, open plaza where their traditional ball games were held. Individual families moved in and out of the principal towns to harvest seasonally available wild foods, hunt, and tend their fields and gardens.

The Guale were among the first Indigenous people met by the Spaniard Lucas Vázquez de Ayllón in 1526, in his failed attempt to establish a colony at the mouth of the Sapelo River near Darien, Georgia. By 1584, a handful of Franciscan friars were in the area, and three years later, they established a mission in the Guale town on St. Catherines Island. There was violence in the Guale chiefdom in 1597, due either to internal political unrest between chiefs or oppression by the friars and their insistence on cultural and social changes or perhaps both. In the fighting, the Guale killed the friars and burned the mission to the ground. After a brutal and vicious Spanish retaliation, the Franciscans reestablished the mission town in 1603, along with eight other coastal missions between the Ogeechee and St. Marys Rivers.

Beginning in 1662, however, the British began to challenge the Spanish

FIGURE 4.4. Rendering of Mission Santa Catalina de Guale, 1680.

hold over these mission communities. Expanding out of Virginia, the British and their Native allies, especially the militant Westos, attacked the northernmost Spanish missions on the Atlantic Coast, capturing people for the new slave trade. A small Spanish military garrison was sent from St. Augustine to protect Mission Santa Catalina, and the church was fortified. However, after nearly two decades of relative peace, British-led raiders from Charleston attacked the mission twice in 1680, burning the town and mission to the ground. Frightened by the attacks, the Guale refused to rebuild the mission. The Spanish then moved the mission south for safety, first to Sapelo Island and later to Amelia Island, where it was destroyed in 1702 by the British. The survivors fled to St. Augustine.

Thus abandoned, the Santa Catalina mission on St. Catherines Island fell into ruins after 1680, became overgrown with dense woods, and disappeared from the landscape. While the mission was not forgotten, its location was lost. In 1981, three centuries after it was abandoned, archaeologist David Hurst Thomas and his team found the mission, after three years of searching and much sleuthing. To their astonishment, the archaeological remains of the Santa Catalina de Guale mission were exceptionally well preserved, mainly because the site had never been plowed. Also, the burning of the mission preserved portions of several buildings by charring the wood and hardening the clay floors and clay-covered walls. The archaeological team found the remains of the two churches, friary, and kitchen on the village's central plaza. The mission town has been brought to life by artist Richard Thornton (figure 4.4).

FIGURE 4.5. Rendering of the church at Mission Santa Catalina.

History and archaeology revealed that Native Guale builders constructed the church in the Spanish tradition, framing it with large posts set in the ground. On three sides, they covered the wall posts with a lower section of pine boards and an upper section of woven small branches (wattle). Then they covered the wattle with a thick layer of a clay mixture called daub (clay mixed with water and vegetation such as Spanish moss). However, the fourth wall, the front facade, was completely covered with wattle-and-daub. They made the roof with gables and thatched it with local palmetto fronds (figure 4.5). The church excavation revealed a raised altar and even a cache of charred wheat grains, probably intended for making the host—the flatbread used in Communion. Archaeologists also found fragments of clay figures that once decorated the church interior. The Guale made a square churchyard outside the front door and covered the ground with small white shells. As was the customary practice in Franciscan mission churches, a cemetery was under the church floor, with 431 interments, primarily of missionized Natives. While the Spanish burial tradition was to wrap the body in a shroud and place it in a grave, the graves under Santa Catalina church were different as the Native people followed their own tradition of placing personal items with their loved ones. The grave items include complete Spanish ceramic vessels; dozens of projectile points; a shell disk necklace or brooch with a rattlesnake engraving; a glass bottle used in Communion; two dozen religious medallions of bronze, gold, and silver; finger rings; copper disks; and more than 67,000 glass trade beads.

Across the plaza from the church, archaeologists found two superimposed friaries and a kitchen (figure 4.6). Documents relate that these buildings were built in the Spanish tradition with clay floors and rectangular wood-framed walls; the last friary had three rooms: a central room, a dining room, and a storage room. The wall facing the church had an arcade or colonnaded porch along it. In the central room floor, archaeologists found a curious rectangular platform with a basin that could have been a footbath for the friars. Interestingly, behind the friary, they found nearly four dozen fragments of large brass church bells. Because church bells are sacred and consecrated, Thomas thinks the bells were broken in the 1597 uprising. The kitchen was nearby in a separate structure, also built in the Spanish style and with one open side, probably for ventilation.

In addition to these buildings, archaeologists also found two wells in the mission complex. Both wells had shafts made of stacked barrels with the tops and bottoms removed (figure 4.7). Waterlogged artifacts were found at the base of one well, including a broken iron hatchet with part of the wooden handle still attached, two wooden balls about two inches in diameter, five

FIGURE 4.6. Excavation of the mission kitchen at Mission Santa Catalina de Guale.

FIGURE 4.7. Mission Santa Catalina, 1602–1680: excavating the deep early well showing the remains of the lowest barrel in the water.

broken Indian ceramic vessels, and two Spanish ceramic olive jars. There were many seeds and pits from grapes, peaches, and squash in the mud at the bottom of the well, indicating the friars relied primarily on the Guale for their food. They ate a predominantly Native, rather than a European, diet, but it included some European fruit and vegetables.

Historical archaeology at Santa Catalina's mission complex has revealed much about the lives of the friars and the Native Americans and how they blended Native and Spanish Catholic traditions and ways of life. From the artifacts found in the two wells and buried with the missionized Native Americans, we know that the mission was well supplied with European materials sent by boat up the coast from St. Augustine. From the array and high number of personal items placed in Native graves, it is evident that, while this practice was against church doctrine, the friars apparently considered that allowing it was a necessary step in the conversion process. However, the friars had stopped the Native practices of building burial mounds and using charnel houses. From the Guale perspective, the grave goods revealed that despite missionization, they still retained key beliefs from their own traditions. From an economic perspective, the high quantity and quality of European goods obtained by the Guale reflects their ability to produce surplus corn crops to trade for European goods. For decades, this mission provided the bulk of the Guale corn tribute, and scholars call Santa Catalina the "breadbasket" of St. Augustine during its existence. Food found in the mission complex tells us that the Spanish friars significantly shifted away from a European diet toward that of the local Guales. From the food remains in the Guale village, we know that they continued their tradition of hunting deer, trapping small mammals, and fishing. However, the increase in deer remains after the Spanish arrived indicates that hunting intensified, probably due to the importance of deerskins as a prime trade commodity for the Spanish.

Overall, however, history and archaeology show that the Guale suffered huge population losses from epidemics of European diseases that swept through their community and reduced their numbers. The destruction of the mission during a British slave raid in 1680 brought an end to this mission that had for almost eighty years supplied St. Augustine with its daily bread. While the Native town residents converted to Catholicism, they did not give up their traditional beliefs. They found a way to blend the two systems and maintain their long-established ways of life.

Mission San Luis de Talimali

Like Mission Santa Catalina, Mission San Luis de Talimali was near the edge of the mission system, about two hundred miles west of St. Augustine in today's Tallahassee. The mission was in the capital town of the Apalachee, whose province stretched between the Aucilla and Ochlockonee Rivers. The Apalachee were a densely populated society of sedentary Native agriculturalists, making them ideal for missionization. San Luis, founded in 1656, began as a traditional mission town. By about 1680, however, most Apalachees had left, and the town became primarily a Spanish settlement, which was unique among the Florida missions. The town was surrounded by small farming hamlets and farmsteads. In 1679 the Spanish also established a new fortified port nearby on the Gulf of Mexico, San Marcos de Apalachee, in today's St. Marks.

The Spanish established the first mission to the Apalachee in 1633, and soon they built at least eight more. The original capital of the Apalachee was at their capital town, Anhaica, where de Soto wintered in 1539–1540. Problems soon arose because of the friars' restriction of several Native social and religious practices, such as polygyny and their popular ball game. The Apalachee revolted against the restrictions in 1647, torturing and killing the friars, the deputy governor, and his family and burning seven of the eight mission churches. The Spanish responded immediately and violently, sending soldiers from St. Augustine and a militia of five hundred Timucua warriors, killing the ringleaders and sentencing twenty-six others to hard labor in St. Augustine. In addition, the Spanish imposed an annual labor requirement, from which the Apalachee previously had been exempt, in exchange for amnesty for the other Apalachees involved in the revolt.

A few years later, in 1656, the neighboring Timucua revolted, causing the Spanish governor to insist on moving the principal Apalachee mission town of Anhaica to a more defensible position. He stationed a resident garrison at San Luis to oversee the missions and the critical food tribute that was keeping the people of St. Augustine alive. The chief of the Apalachee agreed to move his community to a new location on the colonial road to St. Augustine, the Camino Real, and to build a church and friary, a residence for the deputy governor, and a large blockhouse for the soldiers.

Because the populations of the missionized Guale, Mocama, and Timucua were collapsing by the mid-seventeenth century, the Apalachee

El Camino Real in North Florida.

INDIAN TRAILS TO HIGHWAYS

The Southeast is a hard place to travel around in, due to its dense vegetation, big swamps, hundreds of rivers and creeks with wide, wet floodplains, narrow ridges, deep sand, and lakes. But the region was crisscrossed with a system of walkable Indian and colonial paths and trails. These passageways ran between villages, missions, and towns, and led to hunting areas, springs, and important resources such as salt, flint, and fruit and nut trees. When Europeans arrived, they immediately used existing Indian trails and paths to travel. So don't think the early Spanish explorers were constantly hacking through head-high stickers or walking through scummy swamps. Many Indian trails were widened into oxcart roads like the Camino Real, which became State Road 1, then US Highway 90, and later Interstate 10.

Brick portion of US Highway 1 near Milton, Florida.

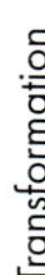

became the new breadbasket for St. Augustine and an indispensable labor source. With the protection provided by the large garrison at San Luis and the availability of rich soil for farming and cattle ranching, many people of Spanish descent, known as Floridanos, moved from St. Augustine to San Luis. They started cattle ranches and farms raising corn and wheat, all of which required Apalachee laborers. The population of San Luis grew to 1,400 in 1675, but by 1681, it had dropped again to 968, mainly due to the absence of Apalachee men laboring on the Floridano ranches and farms. The extra work, plus a series of repressive resident deputy governors, caused increasing numbers of Apalachees to leave San Luis for non-missionized areas. By about 1680, most Apalachees had left Mission San Luis, and the number of Hispanic Floridanos had increased. They tore down Apalachee houses and replaced them with Spanish ones. The Spanish stationed more and more soldiers there and built a larger blockhouse that was enclosed with a double stockade wall.

Then, at the turn of the eighteenth century, the British and their Creek allies began to attack Apalachee and Timucuan missions to the east. They burned mission villages and killed or captured most of the Native residents. Many of the surviving Apalachee moved north, joining the British. By July 1704, the English had marched very close to San Luis. Knowing their military could not defend San Luis, and unwilling to allow the fort to be captured, the Spanish decided to burn the mission and fort and abandon it. Most of the Spanish residents fled to St. Augustine, but some went to the new Spanish presidio of Santa María, on Pensacola Bay, along with about four hundred mission Indians. Because the Spanish in Pensacola could not support the large number of Indian refugees, most went on to Mobile Bay where they allied with the French colonists there. This was a pattern followed throughout the Southeast, whereby former mission Natives adapted to the disruptions of colonization by forming new alliances with other European and Native groups.

Historians and archaeologists have studied Mission San Luis since the mid-twentieth century, reconstructing a great deal of information about this community. Unlike most missions, the location of Mission San Luis was never lost after its burning and abandonment. Succeeding property owners were aware of its presence, and some of the remains of the fort were still visible in the mid-twentieth century. Archaeologist Bonnie McEwan and historian John Hann conducted a long-term intensive investigation at Mission San Luis de Talimali for more than two decades. Their work, along

FIGURE 4.8. Bird's-eye rendering of Mission San Luis de Talimali showing the mission complex, central plaza, Spanish village, and fort in the late seventeenth century.

with that of others, is the basis for the summary below and the reconstruction of the heart of the town and mission.

The layout of the mission consisted of a military complex and residential community positioned on opposite sides of the Camino Real roadway (figure 4.8). The community was arranged like a traditional Apalachee town, centered around a large circular plaza that was the hub of community activities, especially traditional Native ball games and markets. Major public buildings sat around the edge of the plaza, including a large round council house and chief's residence across from the mission church, friary, and kitchen. At first, Spanish residences were generally on the northeast side of the plaza, and Apalachee residences were around the plaza and beyond. Later, the Apalachee residences were torn down, and new Spanish residences were expanded around the plaza.

The Apalachee council house was one of the largest Native structures in the post-contact Southeast, built in the shape of a truncated cone and covered with palm thatch (figure 4.9). The council house was the seat of the Apalachee government and a center to receive delegations from visiting Native groups and Spanish officials, but it also functioned as an inn, restaurant, jail, and community auditorium (figure 4.10). Thousands of artifacts were recovered from the council house floor; almost all were of Native manufacture, such as chipped stone projectile points and Native pottery. The few Spanish artifacts were typical of gifts usually given to Apalachee leaders, including ceramics, glass beads, small brass bells, and weapons.

The chief's house was next to the council house and served as a residence

FIGURE 4.9. Reconstructed Apalachee council house and outline of chief's house at Mission San Luis, 1656–1702.

FIGURE 4.10. Rendering of the interior of an Apalachee council house in use, showing benches and floor plan, circular post structure, and central fire.

and meeting place for small groups. It was similar to the council house in shape and construction but was about half its size. Materials recovered in and around this special house included Native pottery and stone artifacts, as well as an assortment of Spanish items such as parts of a flintlock musket and a number of unusual, faceted quartz crystal beads and pendants. These artifacts are good examples of the special gifts the Spanish gave to chiefs to reinforce their status and allegiance.

FIGURE 4.11. Reconstructed mission church and friary on the central plaza at Mission San Luis, 1656–1702.

The mission complex at San Luis consisted of three buildings: a large church, a residence for the friars (friary), and a detached kitchen (figure 4.11). The church was two stories tall with walls made of vertical boards. The interior had a choir loft, and the board walls in the altar area were plastered and whitewashed. Historical inventories of the church furnishings indicate that the friars placed elaborate statues, altar hangings, banners, pictures, paintings, and engravings in the church interior. Following European custom, there was a cemetery under the floor of the church where between seven hundred and nine hundred people were buried (figure 4.12). The deceased were interred in the traditional Catholic manner of the seventeenth century: The congregants wrapped them in a shroud and placed them in a shallow pit on their back in an extended position, with their head looking east, feet facing the altar, and hands folded across the chest. As at Mission Santa Catalina, the Apalachee at San Luis continued their traditional practice of placing personal items in the graves of their loved ones, including a variety of everyday, ceremonial, and religious items.

The friary was near the church, facing the plaza with a detached kitchen behind and connected to it by a covered walkway. The kitchen had one large and two small rooms with clay floors and whitewashed walls of wattle-and-daub. In the large open room, archaeologists found the remains of a traditional Spanish clay stove, confirming that this building was a kitchen.

The Spanish at San Luis lived in rectangular-shaped homes with two rooms, clay floors, wattle-and-daub or vertical plank walls, and thatched

FIGURE 4.12. Funeral procession inside the mission church at Mission San Luis, 1656–1702.

gabled roofs (figure 4.13). The largest house, probably belonging to the deputy governor, had an enclosed patio facing the plaza. The materials found in household trash pits provide the most information about Spanish life at Mission San Luis. During house construction, the Spanish dug holes to get clay, which they used to make daub for the walls and to cover the floors. They then used the open pits to dispose of their household garbage. The material in the pits is plentiful and diverse; there are a surprising number of imported luxury items, suggesting that the residents had ready access to such goods. Most of the luxury items are things that would have been used and worn by women and children, such as glass beads, pendants, amulets, finger rings, and sequins, along with silver spoons, tableware, and food (figure 4.14 and figure 4.15). Pieces of broken pottery were the most abundant artifacts in the trash pits, and archaeologists were able to reconstruct many of the fractured vessels.

Of the tens of thousands of pieces of pottery found in and around Spanish residences at San Luis, only 9 to 10 percent are Spanish-made. An additional 8 to 10 percent are Indian-made replicas of Spanish ceramics, what archaeologists call colonoware (figure 4.16). The remaining 80 percent of the ceramics are traditional Apalachee containers. The colonoware pieces are

unusual and include handmade long-handled skillets, pitchers, plates, cups, large chamber pots, and candlesticks. Interestingly, the Apalachee potters did not make the replicas using the potter's wheel that was available but continued to use their traditional hand-coiling method.

Food remains from the Spanish village suggest that the residents ate meat, primarily from domestic animals such as cattle and hogs, along with corn grown by Native farmers. They had good supplies of wine, olive oil, olives, wheat, sheep, cattle, and pigs, since the temperate climate was ideal for European plants and livestock. They also grew peaches, barley, peas, chickpeas,

FIGURE 4.13. Depiction of Spanish houses and families in the Spanish village at Mission San Luis, 1656–1702.

FIGURE 4.14. Glass beads and pendants found at Mission San Luis.

FIGURE 4.15. Spanish ceramics and a musket barrel support found at Mission San Luis.

FIGURE 4.16.
Indian-made ceramic imitations of Spanish pitchers and a skillet found at Mission San Luis.

and watermelon. The food remains reveal that the Spanish families at San Luis enjoyed a traditional Mediterranean diet despite being out on the edge of the Florida frontier.

The Apalachee built their homes in the traditional way they had used for centuries before the Spanish arrived. Like their public buildings, their homes at San Luis were circular in shape with conical roofs. The structures had a framework of poles lashed together, covered with layers of palmetto thatch. The doorways were low, and there were no windows. Materials in and around the Apalachee residences included a high concentration of Native pottery and very few Spanish items. Traditionally, the Apalachee used their homes primarily for storage and sleeping, conducting their daytime activities outdoors.

Historical documents indicate that the first military structure at San Luis was a blockhouse. The Spanish constructed at least three blockhouses in the same place, the last of which was completed in 1697. They enclosed the blockhouse in 1702 with a double stockade wall and a dry moat (figure 4.17). The military garrison lived in the blockhouse, and it was large enough to hold the entire community in times of trouble. The blockhouse has been reconstructed based on detailed archaeological and historical information about the last blockhouse. It was a two-story structure covered with thick vertical boards and a rooftop artillery fighting deck. The Spanish covered the interior walls with a thick layer of daub, and when the blockhouse burned in 1704 along with all the mission buildings, the walls were fired hard (figure 4.18). Thus, archaeologists recovered enormous quantities of hardened daub from the burned blockhouse (sixteen tons of it!).

Thus, a picture of the settlement emerges from the archaeology and the documents. Mission San Luis de Talimali was established in 1656 as a new Native mission and Spanish provincial capital on the Camino Real. The mil-

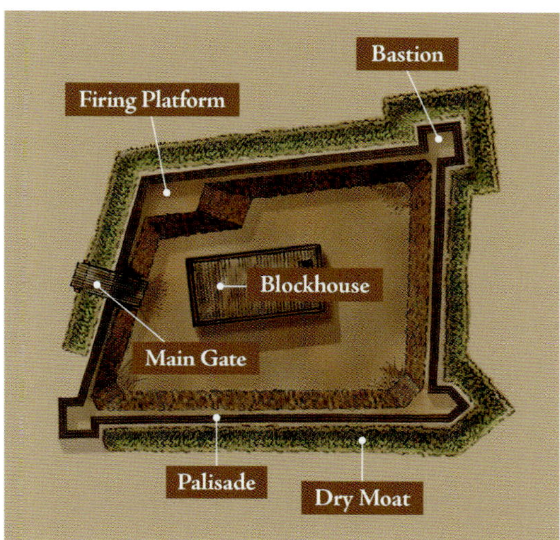

FIGURE 4.17. Blockhouse and stockade at Mission San Luis.

FIGURE 4.18. Intentional burning of the blockhouse and fort as Mission San Luis was abandoned, 1704.

itary complex included a series of three large blockhouses, the last of which was enclosed with a stockade wall and dry moat. The center of the civilian community was a large circular plaza bordered by Apalachee and Spanish public buildings. The settlement grew, but midway through its fifty-year existence, the Apalachee began moving out, and more Spaniards moved in. San Luis became more like a Spanish town but was still the seat of Apalachee leadership. Archaeologists and historians have extensively studied the major public structures on the plaza: the Apalachee council house and chief's house, mission church, friary, and kitchen. The architectural details of construction, expansion, and interiors combined with the artifacts left behind paint a picture of the political and religious life of the residents. Materials found in and around the Spanish residences reveal that, despite being on the edge of the frontier of Spanish Florida, colonists enjoyed a typical Spanish way of life that, if anything, was better than life in St. Augustine or other missions. There was plenty of Spanish food, wealth from cattle ranches and farms, and a seaport that provided access to luxury goods.

In sum, the Franciscan mission system was the preferred Spanish method of colonization for more than a century between 1587 and 1706. The missionaries tried to turn Native populations into Spanish peasant colonists, using the Native traditional political structure of hereditary chiefs who controlled the villagers. Spanish patronage of the chiefs raised their status, and, in turn, the chiefs agreed to supply food and laborers to St. Augustine and the missions. Thousands of Native laborers transported millions of pounds of food to St. Augustine on their backs and then worked there. The mission system depended on large, productive agricultural populations, and the mission communities were not unlike plantations. But European diseases, overwork, and, finally, withering attacks and enslavement caused the collapse of all the missionized Native groups. The friars did not transform Native Americans into Hispanicized colonists, despite the tens of thousands who were baptized and the scores of churches that were built. At the end of the seventeenth century, Spanish Florida was rapidly shrinking in size and almost empty of people.

The Indian Slave Trade

Between about 1650 and 1750, Native Americans in the Southeast were transformed by a new British trading system: the Indian trade. It was a commercial trade whereby the British exchanged European manufactured goods for dressed animal skins and Indian captives. Native people in the Southeast had long practiced a form of enslavement in which the victors of battles took captives to be their slaves. When the British learned of this practice, they began to purchase the Indian captives and resell them as enslaved labor on their Caribbean plantations.

The transformation of Indian captives into something to be bought and sold was a powerful new disrupting force in Native life in the Southeast. It destroyed the Spanish mission system, depopulated Florida and most of the Atlantic coastal area, and transformed traditional Native American culture. It was a terrifying time for Native Americans, with armed and vicious slavers hunting them like animals. The description below of this horrifying and extremely important time in Early Spanish Florida is based on the meticulous research of historian Alan Gallay, ethnohistorian Robbie Ethridge, historical archaeologist John Worth, and others, and it is a sad story.

Human enslavement has been practiced for millennia by many people worldwide, including Europeans and Native Americans, long before Columbus arrived in the Caribbean in 1492. For example, enslaved labor was used extensively in building the Roman Colosseum and the Greek Parthenon. In the Americas, enslavement of Indigenous people was commonly practiced by colonizing Europeans, starting with Columbus, who captured and enslaved local Native people soon after he landed. Some captured Indians were sent to Spain, and others served Columbus and the colonizers on the islands. This practice led to the quick exhaustion of local Native populations and led to importing enslaved Indians and Africans from other areas.

In Spanish Florida, it was forbidden in the mid-sixteenth century to enslave Native people, and in general, the policy was followed. While Indians were the labor force in the mission system, the chiefs, not the Spanish, required their followers to produce more corn and to labor for the Spanish, for which they were paid, if poorly. Native members of a mission town were free to leave if they considered the conditions unsafe or overdemanding, and many did so.

Most European colonizers enslaved Native Americans at some point, but not on the scale of the English in the Southeast. Many of the original British settlers of Carolina who arrived in 1663 were second-generation adult male children of successful, wealthy planters who had slave labor plantations on the Caribbean island of Barbados. The British on the Carolina coast soon began exchanging guns, ammunition, gunpowder, and other manufactured goods for Native food, furs, and captives. Some planters in the interior started to trade on a larger scale, and soon, professional traders emerged who went into the interior regularly to trade with Native groups.

Animal pelts and captives were the main trade items. Captives were more valuable than pelts to the British traders, and only for captives would they trade guns, shot, and ammunition. For the Indians, guns and ammunition were the most prized trade items. The captives-for-weapons trade started a vicious cycle in which newly armed Native groups would raid their unarmed rivals for captives to trade for more guns and ammunition. The now vulnerable, unarmed rivals then needed guns and ammunition to protect themselves, and they had to become slave raiders to get them. As slave raiding expanded, it caused shock waves that spread for hundreds of miles. Raiders traveled farther and farther for unarmed victims, and many horrified groups picked up and moved their entire societies to escape slave raiders. Some Native groups joined with others to better fend off the raiders. Any Natives who were left were forced to become part of the slave trade, and many groups became extinct after losses to disease and slave raiding.

Traders took Indian captives to Charleston to be sold at the large slave market there. Caribbean planters purchased most of the captives, especially those from Barbados, where there was a growing, and seemingly unending, demand for enslaved laborers. The official colonial government of Carolina was supposed to be the only entity that could conduct and regulate the Indian trade, but the colonists ignored the law. From the start, the trade in enslaved Indians was illegal, but it generated so much cash and labor for the new colonists that it was irresistible.

The Indian slave trade operated on the British credit system. It started with Carolina merchants borrowing money in England to buy trade goods and shipping them to Charleston. Merchants then sold the trade goods on credit to the traders, who went into Indian villages and towns in the interior. There, traders contracted with individual Natives or Native groups to obtain captives and provided them with firearms and ammunition on credit to do it. The Indian slave hunters returned with their captives, paid off their debts, and got more guns and ammunition on credit. The traders sold the captives to slave traders in Charleston, paid off their debts to the merchants, and got more trade goods—including guns and ammunition—on credit, as did the merchants. This business cycle repeated itself, year in and year out, for a century.

The British Indian slave trade was the first opportunity for unarmed Natives in the Southeast to obtain firearms, since the Spanish did not allow

Native groups access to guns. There was a huge advantage to the Native groups who were armed first. Since the only way to get British firearms and ammunition was by selling captives to traders, some groups decided to shift from their traditional diversified way of life to focus on waging war just for captives. Essentially, it was easier to get captives to trade for weapons and other manufactured goods than it was to hunt animals and process their hides. The lucrative slave trade spawned new violent and aggressive militaristic Native societies that made special alliances with the British, who used them as armies of aggression against the Spanish in Britain's expansion of its colonial empire. Native groups initially attacked their traditional enemies for captives, but the British traders and military kept encouraging them to take more and more war captives to sell on the slave market. The owners of extraordinarily profitable slave-based plantations in the Caribbean and eastern North America drove the demand for enslaved labor, a demand that historians describe as having been endless.

An example of a Native group that became a violent, militaristic slaving society is the Westos. They were an immigrant group that had fled from Virginia to Carolina and became armed militant slavers in the Virginia Indian slave trade. They allied with the Carolina British colonial government and traders and began attacking the Guale and Mocama Spanish mission towns along the coast, taking the unarmed and unprotected mission Indians captive. The mission town of Santa Catalina de Guale, the capital of the Guale, was attacked by the Westos in 1661. By the spring of 1680, all the Spanish missions on the mainland of Spanish Florida's northern frontier had been either destroyed or relocated to the barrier islands for protection, leaving the mainland vacant and open to occupation by the Westos. Those Guale and Mocama individuals who were not captured fled south and joined the Timucua and Apalachee Spanish mission towns in today's North Florida. Unfortunately for the Westos, the British now wanted their new land for rice plantations. The traders turned to a new immigrant militant Native group, the Shawnee, who agreed to attack the Westos for captives, but with no promise of receiving the Westos' land. The Shawnee succeeded in just a few years and appear to have dispersed afterward. In only twenty-three years after the first attacks on the Spanish missions, the Indian slave trade had depopulated the coastline of present-day Georgia and Carolina, and British rice plantations had expanded into the Carolina Low Country.

By 1680, Charleston had become the main slave market for exporting enslaved Indians. While some of the captives were sold to local planta-

FIGURE 4.19.
A Southeastern Indian being sold into slavery.

tions, they were apt to escape, since they knew how to survive in the region. Due to this escape problem and to strong labor demands in the Caribbean, most Southeast Indian captives were exported (figure 4.19). The value of Indian captives varied widely, but they were always less expensive than Africans, and in the Caribbean islands, Indian slaves had virtually no chance of escape. Carolina planters preferred male African slaves with plantation experience, and they often would exchange their inexperienced Indian captives for veteran African slaves at a ratio of about two-to-one or three-to-two enslaved Indians for Africans. In this way, Caribbean planters got rid of their experienced but problematic African slaves, and the Carolina planters exchanged their escape-prone Native captives for experienced adult male Africans.

By the mid-sixteenth century, the African slave trade was well developed, providing thousands of enslaved people to plantations in the Caribbean and the mid-Atlantic seaboard. Due to their large size, however, the African slave ships could only stop at major ports. Indian slave traders, with lesser numbers of slaves to sell, went to smaller ports to sell to the planters on small islands that were bypassed by the large slave ships, and they did a brisk and profitable business. In addition, in the Northeast United States, even though there were no plantations, there was a strong demand for servants and trade apprentices. Indian slave traders took their small boats with enslaved Native women and children, who were preferred for servants, up the Northeast rivers to small towns and readily sold them there.

In 1685, another immigrant Native militant slaving group, the Yamasee, moved into the coastal area south of Savannah, allied with immigrant Scots and later the English, and started slave-raiding missions deeper into the heart of Spanish Florida. At the same time, the British also established an alliance with the Lower Creeks in the interior of today's western Georgia, many of whom had relocated to the Ocmulgee River Valley by 1685. The Yamasee and Creeks became particularly violent, militarized slaving societies, and for the next three decades, British traders and military-led armies of Yamasee and

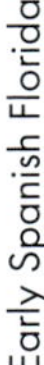

Creek warriors attacked and enslaved tens of thousands of Spanish Florida mission Indians.

The Yamasee began in 1685 by attacking the large, unarmed agricultural populations at Timucuan missions. The Spanish tried to retaliate but were ineffective. For the next few years, the Yamasee drove deeper and deeper into the missions, using both small raids and full-scale attacks. For example, in 1691, the Yamasee and Creeks attacked Mission San Juan de Guacara on the Suwannee River, killing or capturing many Timucuans and burning down the town. Soon, nearby missions were moved into the better-protected Apalachee province. The loss of these Timucuan missions created a gap in the chain of missions between St. Augustine and Tallahassee that the Yamasee immediately exploited.

Slave raids on the Spanish missions increased, and in 1702, one hundred Creek warriors destroyed Mission Santa Fé in North-Central Florida, taking many prisoners and scalps with them. The Spanish soon assembled an eight-hundred-man army of mission Indian warriors and marched north to British Georgia to retaliate, but on the way, they met a force of four hundred Creeks on the lower Flint River. In the ensuing battle, the mission Indians were completely routed, losing perhaps three hundred warriors in combat and two hundred more to desertions. Later that year, South Carolina governor and slave trader Colonel James Moore, with an army of five hundred Yamasee and Creek warriors, launched a land-based assault on St. Augustine. But Moore failed to take the Castillo, and a Spanish fleet from Havana blocked Moore's plan for a naval attack. Moore returned in early 1704 with a force of one thousand Creek warriors and fifty Englishmen, determined to eliminate the Spanish missions. He destroyed fourteen more mission villages, enslaved at least one thousand Indians, and drove two thousand more into exile. Terrified and unhappy with the lack of Spanish protection, hundreds more mission Indians left and joined the British, including at least four entire mission towns that moved and settled in southeast British Georgia. Historians also state that the populations of seven mission villages voluntarily joined Moore's army on the march. When news of Moore's attacks reached San Luis de Talimali in 1704, Spanish authorities realized they could not defend the mission and ordered its evacuation and burning. Moore and his Indian army continued to find and attack other missions in Spanish Florida, finally withdrawing in 1706, leaving behind scores of ruined missions and an essentially depopulated North Florida. The remaining demoralized Apalachee refugees fled to St. Augustine or Pensacola. By the summer of 1706, the mission population of an estimated 6,500 Indians in 1681 was reduced to 400 refugees huddled around the presidios at St. Augustine and Pensacola.

Until 1704, the chain of Spanish missions between St. Augustine and Tallahassee had been a barrier to slave-raiding attacks, preventing substantial penetration into South Florida. But with the missions eliminated, South Florida Native groups between 1704 and 1711 became the target of British-led Yamasee and Cherokee slave raiders who attacked anyone they could find, including the Calusa, Keys, Ais, and Miami (figure 4.20). These groups had no alliances with the Spanish, and they were unarmed. Thousands fled south but became trapped at the end of the peninsula and in the Keys, waiting and hoping to be rescued by Spanish ships and taken to Cuba. But the Yamasee and Creek slavers attacked them there mercilessly, and hundreds were taken into slavery each day. The slave raids of the early eighteenth century spelled the end for the last of the Native South Floridians.

There are few and often conflicting records of how many Florida Natives were captured, sold, or killed, or how many fled. Historians estimate that at least fifteen thousand and up to thirty thousand Florida Natives were sold into slavery, making up almost three-quarters of all the Natives enslaved in the South. However, researchers caution that these numbers are certainly underestimates because the Indian slave business was illegal, and records of captives or transactions were purposefully not kept. The years between 1650 and 1715 were shocking and disastrous for the Spanish and their mission

FIGURE 4.20. Creek slave raid against Florida Natives.

Indians. Spanish Florida had shrunk to essentially the size the state is today, and it was virtually depopulated.

The depopulation of Florida and the flight of many interior groups away from the British colonies caused serious problems for the Yamasee and Creek slave hunters, who were still heavily in debt to the British traders, because the latter would only accept captives as payment for the guns and ammunition advanced to them on credit. When it was evident to the traders that there were not enough potential captives to clear the Indian slavers' debt, the British informed the Yamasee and Creeks that they would take them and their families as captives to sell to settle their debts. This pressure by the traders and the English authorities resulted in a widespread rebellion in 1715 called the Yamasee War. The Yamasee and many Native allies killed hundreds of colonists, destroyed many settlements, and killed traders throughout the Southeast. The Yamasee War was one of the most disruptive and transformational conflicts of colonial America.

After the rebellion, ironically, many Yamasee and Creek groups fled to Spanish Florida, seeking refuge from the British, moving into areas newly vacated due to their own attacks in the former mission area and elsewhere in Central and West Florida. Some of their descendants still live in this area today. The killing and enslavement of the Florida Natives and the abandonment of Carolina by interior groups ended the Indian slave trade. It left the British without any Native allies and greatly reduced the power of the British in the Southeast. Former militant slaving societies such as the Creeks, Chickasaws, and Choctaws interacted and traded with all the European colonizers, playing them against each other and allying with none. These new Native societies were clearly the victors after a turbulent century of slave hunting, and they became the independent Native nations in the South today.

The end of the Indian slave trade stopped the violent attacks on Indigenous people, but it also led directly to a rapid expansion of the African slave trade in the British colonies. For example, in 1708, there were only about four thousand enslaved Africans in South Carolina, about the same number as the white population. In 1740, there were about thirty-nine thousand Black slaves in that colony alone, an increase of more than 1,000 percent that outnumbered whites by about four to one. A similar pattern occurred in all the British colonies and islands with plantation agriculture.

The rapid increase in enslaved Africans in the southern British colonies directly affected Spanish Florida, since it became a destination for self-emancipated or runaway African slaves. Always combating underpopulation, the Spanish welcomed fugitive slaves, the first of whom arrived in St. Augustine in 1687. Soon, the Spanish officially declared that runaway African slaves were welcome in their Florida colony. In 1733, the government stated it would not reimburse the English for the fugitives that arrived, and it would require four years of service in the militia for the fugitives to become free. This codified a practice that had been in place since 1687, when the first fugitive slaves were put to work building the Castillo. In 1738, the fugitives were granted plots of land about two miles north of St. Augustine, where they built a fort and settlement named Fort Mose.

In sum, the traditional practice of the Indigenous people in the Southeast of taking captives after victory in battle was hijacked by the British when they provided firearms to Native groups to meet the commercial demand for enslaved laborers on plantations. The strategic funneling of weapons and ammunition to warlike groups that specialized in commercial slave capturing transformed the traditional culture of the Indigenous people in the South into a new social order, one of coalesced militant societies that held the European colonists at bay. Tens of thousands of missionized Natives were murdered, enslaved, or forced to flee their homelands by British-led and British-sponsored commercial slave raids. At least fifty thousand Natives of Spanish Florida fell victim to this commercialized chattel slavery system, far more than in any other European colony. Once they ran out of Native Americans to enslave, planters quickly turned to the preexisting trade in enslaved Africans for the forced labor on which their plantations were based.

Summary of Transformation

Both Native and Spanish people living in the Southeast underwent cultural and personal transformations between about 1580 and 1715. The Spanish changed from using an aggressive approach of Spanish settlers and military intruding into the homelands of resistant Indigenous people to using a peaceful approach of voluntary political alliances with existing chiefs who allowed missions into their villages and became vassals in the Spanish social hierarchy. In the end, the Spanish effort to use Franciscan Catholic missionization as a colonization strategy for their Florida province, by turning missionized Native people into colonists and subjects of the Spanish Crown, simply was not sustainable. In 1704, when Mission San Luis was burned and abandoned, there were only two small, subsidized settlements in Spanish

Florida, Presidio St. Augustine and a new presidio on Pensacola Bay named Santa María. Both places were under siege by the British and French.

The Spanish had lost the entire interior and Atlantic Coast to the British, and the Native populations they had missionized were decimated. The strategy of using luxury gifts and promises of protection to coerce chiefs into agreements in which they and their people became subjects of the Crown backfired. Mission Indians suffered under the obligations of their chiefs to provide increasing amounts of food and labor to the Spanish. All four missionized groups, the Guale, Mocama, Timucua, and Apalachee, revolted against the Spanish. Spanish retaliation for the revolts was quick and so vicious that it intimidated the remaining Native leaders into submission as their populations collapsed around them.

When British colonists on the Atlantic Coast intruded into Spanish Florida, they transformed the South into a war zone of armed slave-hunting societies waging war for captives on British-selected targets and anyone else they could find. The slave raids dealt the final blow to the Spanish colonial mission system in La Florida and their claim to all of Southeastern North America. In addition, the slave raids destroyed the independent traditional Native groups in Central and South Florida and the Keys, effectively depopulating the Florida peninsula. The Indians were largely gone, and the Spanish were defeated and cornered in two small frontier presidios in St. Augustine and Pensacola.

Suggested Readings

Amy Turner Bushnell. *Situado and Sabana: Spain's Support System for the Presidio and Mission Provinces of Florida.* New York: American Museum of Natural History, 1994.

Alan Galay. *The Indian Slave Trade.* New Haven, CT: Yale University Press, 2002.

John H. Hann. *Apalachee: The Land Between the Rivers.* Gainesville: University Press of Florida, 1988.

John H. Hann and Bonnie G. McEwan. *The Apalachee Indians and Mission San Luis.* Gainesville: University Press of Florida, 1998.

Jerald T. Milanich. *Laboring in the Fields of the Lord.* Washington, DC: Smithsonian Institution Press, 1999.

David Hurst Thomas. *The Archaeology of Mission Santa Catalina de Guale.* I. *Search and Discovery.* Anthropological Papers of the American Museum of Natural History, vol. 63, part 2. New York: American Museum of Natural History, 1987.

Places to Visit

Florida Museum of Natural History. University of Florida campus, 3215 Hull Road, Gainesville, Florida.

Mission Nombre de Dios. Fountain of Youth Archaeological Park, 11 Magnolia Avenue, St. Augustine, Florida.

Mission San Luis. 2100 West Tennessee Street, Tallahassee, Florida. Historic site, gallery, and gift shop.

Websites to Visit

Mission Santa Catalina de Guale: https://www.georgiaencyclopedia.org/articles/history-archaeology/mission-santa-catalina-de-guale/

YouTube Video of David Hurst Thomas lecture: https://www.youtube.com/watch?v=-SjU2aMSvuM&ab_channel=ASUHispanicResearchCenter

Mission San Luis Living History Museum: https://www.missionsanluis.org/

Mission Nombre de Dios: https://en.wikipedia.org/wiki/Mission_Nombre_de_Dios

Fountain of Youth Archaeological Park, Nombre de Dios: https://www.fountainofyouthflorida.com/exhibits/nombre-de-dios-mission/

FIVE

ST. AUGUSTINE

St. Augustine, Florida, holds the distinction of being the oldest continuously occupied city in the United States, with its roots dating back to 1565. This chapter delves into its residents' unique and often perilous experiences during the town's first two hundred years. The former residents of this small and diverse military community, perched on the fringes of the Spanish Empire, would be astounded to see the thriving city St. Augustine has become more than 450 years later, drawing millions of visitors annually to celebrate their resilience (figure 5.1)!

During the Early Spanish period (1565 to 1763), St. Augustine was a military base and town, and beginning in 1587, it was the second capital of Spanish Florida for the next 176 years. The settlement was in a strategic position on the Atlantic to protect Spanish shipping, rescue shipwrecked sailors, salvage shipwrecks, and monitor the Gulf Stream, the critical current used by all European shipping, including the treasure fleets taking bullion to Spain. St. Augustine was also politically important in securing Spain's claim to Florida. Despite poor soil in the vicinity and the lack of any valuable natural resources, the Crown supported the garrison, colonial administration, missions, and Indians with an annual subsidy called the situado. The fleet at St. Augustine was a key part of the Spanish defense system against its colonial rivals—the French, the English, the Dutch, and their pirates, whom historian Amy Turner Bushnell describes as sharks circling the Spanish Empire's ports and seaways, looking to unload their stolen goods or plant new colonies. As you know, pressures from competing European rivals for control of colonial North America resulted in the destruction of the Spanish mission system, and the British Indian slave trade led to the demise of the Native American population. However, St. Augustine was kept afloat. It was just too important to lose.

That importance can be seen in the fact that, from its beginning, the settlement consisted of a fort, an adjacent town, and nearby Native mission villages—it addressed all the purposes of the Spanish colony. The town

FIGURE 5.1. Tourists in St. Augustine.

population was diverse, consisting of Spanish military soldiers, colonial administrators and their families, a few other Europeans, Native Americans, Africans (both free and enslaved), and people of mixed races. Townspeople lived along the Matanzas riverfront in a traditional Spanish-style town, with homes on a street grid surrounding a central plaza. Indian towns and villages and a free African community were nearby but separate from the town.

In this chapter, however, you also will learn that St. Augustine was increasingly the target of attacks by the British military and pirates, who burned the town and fort to the ground at least four times. Residents suffered from poor support from the Spanish government and a growing dependency on the mission system and illicit trade for survival. But early St. Augustinians adapted to their circumstances, solving their own problems as best they could with local resources and ingenuity, blending their diverse backgrounds into a new Spanish American culture that was different from those in their homelands and other European colonies in America. You will view the community through the eyes of the Spanish, Africans, and Native Americans who lived and worked together in this Spanish Catholic military community and see how their relationships changed through time. Native and African laborers built an extensive and unique defense system for St. Augustine.

Finally, you will learn of the little-known but extensive Spanish Indian trade network into the interior. For almost a century, the Spanish were the sole source of the European goods that Native leaders used to display and increase their personal status and political alliances. The interesting and compelling story of this community and its role in the unique Spanish colonial system during its first two hundred years unfolds below.

The Spanish Community

The Spanish community living in St. Augustine spent their first two centuries dealing with one disaster after another. They had to build new forts *ten* times, rebuild their town *four* times, suffer through waves of epidemics, and endure one attack after another, first by Indians and then by British armies and their pirates. Menéndez failed in his initial attempts to establish a self-sufficient colonial settlement protected by a military garrison. After more than twenty years, Native Americans, furious about being invaded, had destroyed all the Menéndez forts and missions except at the small, subsidized military presidio of St. Augustine (figure 5.2).

After a few months of being harassed and attacked by the local Timucuans, Menéndez quickly moved the colonists out of the Timucuan village of Seloy on the mainland to Anastasia Island across the Matanzas River. They built a fort and outposts on the island and in the local area, along with a

FIGURE 5.2. Timucuans fighting the Europeans.

FIGURE 5.3.
A 1589 map showing Sir Francis Drake's 1586 attack and capture of St. Augustine.

new settlement. However, military mutinies and the sea's erosion of the fort forced a return to the mainland in 1572, after only six years. Colonists built a second new town and fort on the mainland, but just five years later in 1577, local Indians struck again and burned much of it down.

With the disruptions during the first two tumultuous decades, involving several relocations of the settlement and much rebuilding, any visual historical record of that time has disappeared. Our first snapshot of St. Augustine is a 1589 illustrated map by Baptista Boazio showing the English privateer Sir Francis Drake's successful attack on the community in 1586 (figure 5.3). The map shows a six-sided wooden fort guarding the inlet to the Atlantic. This exceptionally detailed map and other historical documents indicate that the Spanish fort was made of cedar posts, with a raised fighting deck for fourteen cannons and a few internal buildings. The town was south of the fort along the Matanzas River, and the map legend states that the garrison of 150 soldiers lived in the town, not at the fort. The map shows that while local Natives had partially destroyed the town in 1577, it had been rebuilt in the intervening nine years. The map shows a street grid of nine residential blocks, with buildings lining the streets, and an open shared space in the center. A large government house and church are shown just north of the residential blocks, and two irregular rows of structures are shown directly on the riverfront. Outside the town there were gardens and fields. In his 1586 attack, Drake burned all the buildings and the fort to the ground.

Remnants of the Drake razing of St. Augustine initially eluded researchers, but City Archaeologist Carl Halbirt finally found them in 1998, in the center of the former sixteenth-century town. Beneath an art gallery in the modern-day town, he uncovered part of a burned floor of a Spanish house; a number of nearly intact, apparently abandoned ceramic vessels sat on the floor, in a thick layer of charcoal (figure 5.4). The ceramics were of both European and Native American make, and the pieces fit together to reveal highly decorated pitchers and plates typical of the mid-sixteenth century (figure 5.5). The discovery of Indian-made pots in a Spanish home occupied only twenty years after the town's founding suggests that a Native woman likely lived or worked in the Spanish household. While it is possible that the Indian-made vessels could have been purchased by Spanish men from Native women, who were traditionally the potters in local Native groups, historical documents consistently state that very few Spanish women were sent to St. Augustine. Soldiers regularly engaged with Indian women as wives, servants, or concubines. Throughout the Spanish colonial empire, it was an accepted and common practice for Spanish men and Native women to form relationships. If the woman converted, the Catholic Church sanctioned the marriage, and the community accepted the relationship. Their mixed-race offspring were the beginning of a new ethnic group called mestizos (Spanish and Indian), later referred to as Spanish Floridanos, originating from the first blended families of Spanish fathers, Indian mothers, and their children.

FIGURE 5.4. Overhead view of burned Spanish artifacts in a house in St. Augustine burned by Drake in 1583.

As they had done before, this robust, diverse community picked themselves up and put the settlement back together. A map made in 1593, seven years after Drake's destruction, shows a rebuilt St. Augustine, with a new fort and a small and shabby town (figure 5.6). The new wooden

FIGURE 5.5. Spanish ceramic vessels reconstructed from the floor and refuse pit in a house burned by Drake in 1583.

fort was large and triangular, with corner bastions and long arched buildings lining the two landward sides, protected by a circular perimeter wall with a keyhole-like entrance. The town is shown with only five wooden buildings and a short dock. The two structures on the riverfront are labeled as a guard-house (with cannons) and the general's house; two buildings farther back probably are residences, with a church in the middle (figure 5.7). There also was a wooden plank wall along the riverfront extending all the way to the fort. If both the Boazio and Mestas maps are representative of St. Augustine, in the intervening seven years, it appears the Spanish had focused their efforts on rebuilding the fort but not the town. Unfortunately, in 1599, the town was badly damaged by fire and a hurricane. Undeterred, the residents began rebuilding yet again, and by 1600, documents state that there was a church, a Franciscan convent, a small hospital, a market, a gristmill, 120 houses, and a population of seven hundred.

An example of the resilience of the St. Augustinians is seen in an interesting sixteenth-century archaeological feature found just outside the town: a

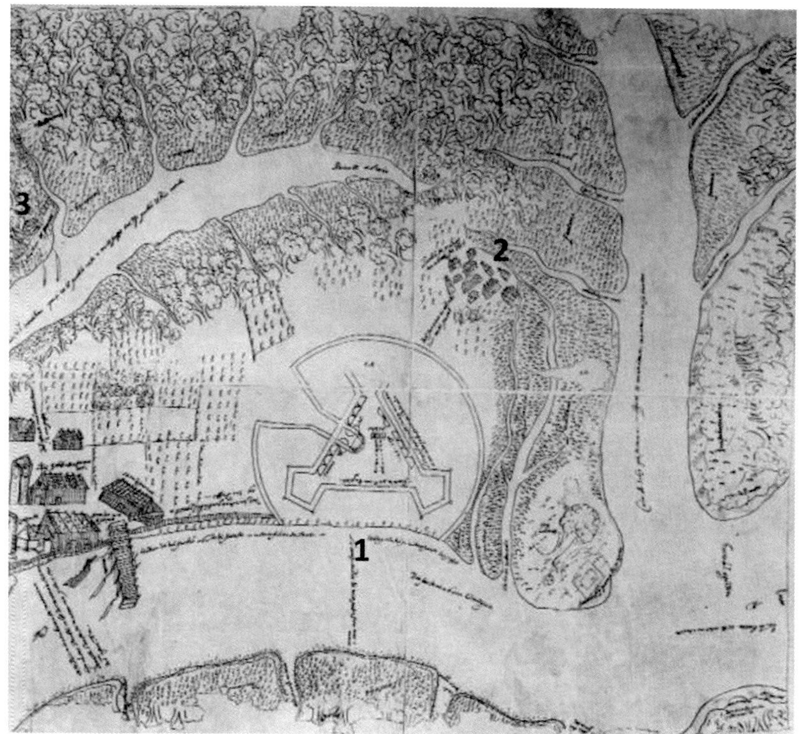

FIGURE 5.6. Map of St. Augustine in 1593 attributed to Mestas: (1) eighth wooden fort; (2) Nombre de Dios Mission; (3) San Sebastián de Yaocos Mission.

FIGURE 5.7. Close-up of riverfront town buildings on 1593 Mestas map of St. Augustine.

FIGURE 5.8. Cross section of an early sixteenth-century lime kiln near Nombre de Dios mission at Presidio San Agustín.

lime-burning kiln. It is a large, bowl-shaped pit about fifteen feet in diameter and five feet deep (figure 5.8). Inside the pit are layers of locally abundant oyster shells, dirt, and charcoal lying on a layer of white burned and powdered oyster shells (lime); the colonists used the lime to make mortar, tabby, whitewash, and plaster. Europeans developed this type of simple lime kiln in pre-Roman times, and it is still used today in rural areas. Artifacts in the kiln dated to the sixteenth century, and historical documents mention that there were lime kilns and lime production in St. Augustine by 1580. Experts think that colonists first used the lime to cover the flat-roofed structures at Santa Elena and St. Augustine. Instead of purchasing expensive imported lime or ceramic roof tiles, the Spanish in St. Augustine covered their roofs the old-fashioned way.

Historical archaeologist Kathleen Deagan conducted a multiyear study of sixteenth-century St. Augustine and determined that the town was indeed laid out in the traditional Spanish grid, as shown in the 1589 Boazio map. She archaeologically documented the remains of two churches, the town plaza, and several homesites. Focusing on *criollo* families (Spaniards born in the Americas) and their way of life, Deagan found that their houses were made of wattle-and-daub or boards and were located near the front of their house lots, along the street. The layout of the house lots included perimeter walls or fences, backyard gardens, barrel wells, and trash pits. This use of space on a house lot was common in Spain and persisted through the entire Early Spanish period in St. Augustine. Barrel wells were also placed about every forty to fifty feet along the streets for public use.

The archaeological materials from the house lots were consistently both Native American–made and Spanish-made, and there is a distinct pattern to the artifacts. Native American materials were primarily kitchen-related, especially ceramics and food-preparation items. The most frequent Native

FIGURE 5.9. Spanish ceramic tablewares and Native cooking pots.

American artifacts were pots for cooking and storage and stone manos and metates that Native Americans traditionally used for grinding corn (figure 5.9). Few, if any, Spanish cooking items were found on the house lots. On the other hand, serving tableware (plates, platters, bowls) was almost exclusively European, not Native. This pattern is thought to reflect that the kitchen was the Native woman's private domain, as she did all the food preparation and cooking. However, the dining room and table were the Spaniard husband's public domain, in which his ethnicity and social status were on display. Historical documents identify the male residents of the house lots, their occupation, and their income; archaeological research looks deeper into households and reveals how the blending of Spanish and Native cultures took place in real life, creating the new Spanish American mestizo/Floridano way of life in St. Augustine.

Thus, by the beginning of the seventeenth century, St. Augustine's population had developed many of the characteristics that lasted throughout the Early Spanish period. The core of the population was the male-dominated military garrison with soldiers rotating in and out or staying on as private citizens after leaving the military, and most activities centered on the military and the church (figure 5.10). The majority of people were of Spanish descent born in the Americas, known as criollos. A smaller number of people were born in Spain, *peninsulares,* who, regardless of their prior status

FIGURE 5.10.
Rendering of Martín de Arguelles, who served in St. Augustine and is typical of the seventeenth-century Spanish soldiers there.

at home, were at the top of the local social order. (Some individuals of noble birth also lived in St. Augustine.) People of color and mixed races, *castas,* were relegated to the lower ranks of society.

Historians depict St. Augustinians in the early seventeenth century as practical and creative in solving the problems caused by the Crown's unreliable provision of funds and supplies. Many soldiers had useful trades and skills, such as carpentry and blacksmithing, that were used in construction, and they supplemented their income with these skills. Chronically undersupplied by the government, people made the best of what they had. Colonists melted down anchors and old mortars to make much-needed iron nails and tools, and they developed a trade with local Indians, exchanging muskets (illegally) and even clothes for food. Using local natural resources and their own labor, they built what they needed and made what they could.

The biggest problem was procuring sufficient food for the growing settlement. To this end, colonists started cattle ranches and wheat farms in the interior west of St. Augustine in the 1620s, owned by Floridano families from St. Augustine who used Native American laborers. The Spanish also expanded the mission system westward to the agricultural Apalachee in the 1630s, probably more to obtain a new source of food and labor than for religious reasons. They built a new port on the northern Gulf, San Marcos de Apalachee, shortening the transportation time for agricultural and cattle products from Apalachee and Floridano farms and ranches to St. Augustine and other Spanish ports, especially Havana. With continued meager and unreliable Crown support to the colony, Apalachee food and labor became St. Augustine's lifeline.

As Spanish St. Augustinians were forming new families, rebuilding their fort and community, and expanding westward, French and English pirates steadily increased their presence along the Atlantic Coast, harassing Spanish shipping. Storms also caused many shipwrecks, and St. Augustine's naval fleet regularly rescued shipwrecked sailors and salvaged what they could

from the wreckage. The fleet at St. Augustine also captured pirate ships and put their cargoes to good use. After the British founded their Virginia colony in 1607, the Crown increased the garrison at St. Augustine to three hundred men and began to monitor the English presence closely. British and French pirates increasingly targeted St. Augustine in the mid-seventeenth century, especially after the founding of Charleston in 1670. British buccaneer Robert Searles sailed into St. Augustine in 1688 at midnight (figure 5.11). Capturing a Spanish ship, he killed sixty people, taking many well-to-do young women for ransom, and completely sacking but not burning the town (figure 5.12). The pirates destroyed government buildings and the church and captured all the Blacks and Indians they could find to sell into slavery. In 1702, James Moore, an English slave trader and governor of the Carolina colony, attacked St. Augustine and laid siege to a new stone fort, with the townsfolk and their domestic animals huddled inside. The fort

MOSQUITO CONTROL

Smudge pit for mosquito control.

Have you ever forgotten your mosquito repellent on a hot summer day or night when you were walking or camping in the woods or wetlands in Florida? Immediately, thousands of buzzing and stinging mosquitoes attacked you! What did people do before modern insect repellents? The most frequent practice of Southeastern Indians was to use small pits of slow-burning corn cobs. Called "smudge pits," the smoldering cobs produce a lot of smoke that drives away those nasty mosquitoes. In a large council house lodge of the Apalachee Indians in Tallahassee, archaeologists found an individual smudge pit full of charred corn cobs by every sleeping bench. I also found smudge pits near the officers' barracks of early eighteenth-century Spanish presidios (forts) in West Florida, and Dr. John Worth found them at an eighteenth-century Spanish mission in Escambia County. Putting other plants, such as basil, marigolds, and rosemary, in any small fire also produces smoke that will keep mosquitoes away.

FIGURE 5.11. Robert Searles (aka John Davis), English pirate.

FIGURE 5.12. Rendering of teenage criolla Estefanía de Cigarroa, who could have been taken for ransom.

held, but Moore's army burned both the Spanish and Indian towns to the ground (figure 5.13). In 1740, another governor of the British colony of Georgia, James Oglethorpe, attacked St. Augustine with an Indian army. He blockaded the port, captured four outposts, and bombarded the stone Castillo with the town's population inside for more than three weeks. However, the Spanish sent a relief fleet from Havana through the blockade, and Oglethorpe withdrew.

Other enemies also challenged the survival of the community. Hurricanes waged war on the town, devastating their wood or wattle-and-daub thatch-covered buildings several times in 1622, 1638, and 1674. Adding to the struggles of the townspeople was an invisible enemy—viruses. A yellow fever epidemic in 1649 killed Spaniards and Indians alike. A smallpox outbreak six years later killed all the African Crown slaves as well as large numbers of Spaniards. A measles epidemic struck in 1659. Health care was at best primitive, being limited to small hospitals run by clergy and only occasional physicians, who were usually foreigners captured from shipwrecks.

By the turn of the eighteenth century, there were approximately 1,000 people living in the Spanish town. The population expanded to 1,350 in 1725 and 3,000 in 1735. At the time the Spanish ceded Florida in 1763, 3,104 people lived there. People of European, primarily Spanish, descent were always the majority in St. Augustine (about 70 percent), and most were white criollos. There were more peninsulares during the 1700s than previously due to the increase in the number of soldiers recruited from Spain. Almost all the women were local criollos, descended from the original settlers and mestizos, who preferred to marry soldiers from Spain for their high social status in the community. Several hundred Spanish Canary Islanders also arrived in 1757–1761. As archaeologist Kathleen Deagan has described, the community of St. Augustine had a reputation as a European town, and its soldiers were sent directly from Spain. This contrasts with the Spanish colonial military communities elsewhere in North America, where the military and community were primarily castas and a few mulattos (mixes of African and Spanish or Indian).

Through studies by historians and archaeologists, we know much about the eighteenth-century town and its residents. The Spanish were very thorough recordkeepers, documenting individual names, real estate ownership and transactions, church records of individuals' religious milestones, and military records. The required layout of the Spanish town continued to be stable during the eighteenth century.

Using the wealth of historical documents and maps of the eighteenth-

FIGURE 5.13. Rendering of the 1702 British siege of St. Augustine.

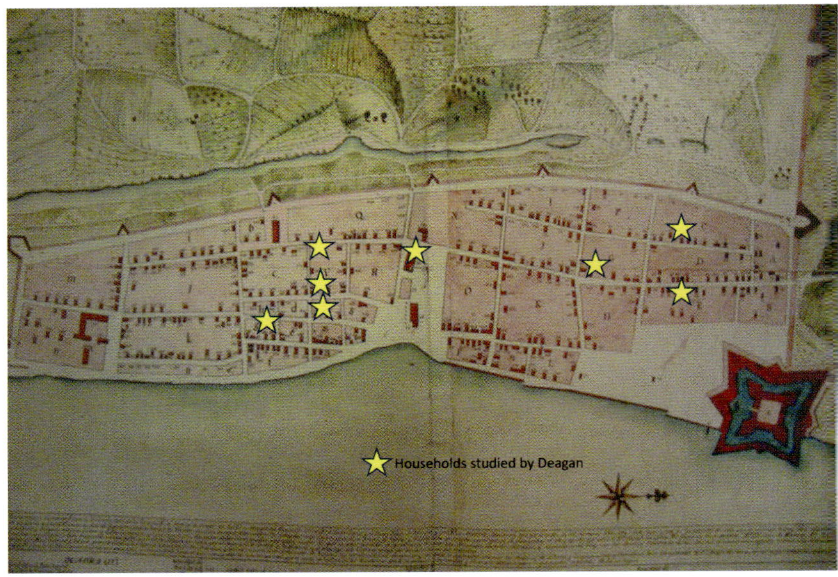

FIGURE 5.14. Puente map of St. Augustine in 1764. Households studied by archaeologist Kathleen Deagan are marked with stars; note the defensive walls around the town.

century town as a guide, Deagan studied the similarities and differences of selected house lots occupied by families with different ethnicities, occupations, incomes, and activities of the male household heads, known from documents. The locations of the eight house lots she studied are shown on the 1764 map in figure 5.14. The research revealed that the key to the differences in the materials found in the households was the social status and income of the male head of household. The higher the social status and income, the more expensive, European-made items were present in the household. As in sixteenth-century households, Indian-made materials, especially ceramic pots, were present and associated with Indian women's food preparation and cooking, while European-made materials were used in public areas. European items reflecting the owner's status included ceramic tableware, glassware, jewelry, and clothing fasteners such as buttons. Display and use of these items indicated one's social identification as "Spaniard." Lower-status households had far fewer Spanish items and many more local Native materials. The food consumed by the residents of the households also strongly reflected the social position and income status of the Spanish male head of the household. The higher the status and income, the more domesticated foods, such as corn and beef, were in the residents' diet. The lower the status and income, the more wild plants and animals, such as wild grains, birds, and fish, were in the diet.

FIGURE 5.15. Modern excavation in the colonial area of St. Augustine.

Other elements in the public realm reflected the social status and income of the male head of household, including whether the house was built in the Spanish style and its size. The organization of residential lot features also followed a Spanish plan, with the house placed by the street and wells and refuse pits in the backyard. The floor plan of most houses was a two-room rectangle without fireplaces and often with a detached kitchen. The colonists covered their house floors with a hard layer of very fine-grained white tabby three to five inches thick. When the floor became worn, it was leveled with a new layer of earth, and a new tabby floor was poured on it. There were no outhouses or privies on the house lots.

Archaeology in the town of Presidio San Agustín continues today through the City Archaeology Program, which established one of the very first city ordinances in the United States; it requires city archaeologists to investigate proposed construction sites in historically significant areas of the city. The program has discovered the remains of the early Spanish town under parking lots, lawns, and building floors in downtown St. Augustine. Excavations often reveal the oyster shell footers, coquina block foundations, and stacked tabby floors of early colonial buildings. The buried tabby floors in figure 5.15 originally were in the home of the Spanish treasurer Don Francisco Menéndez Márquez in the 1730s. The building was converted into a hospital in 1743 and remains occupied to the present day.

FIGURE 5.16. Drawing of the streetscape on colonial St. George Street, St. Augustine in the early eighteenth century.

In sum, in its first two centuries, the Spanish perspective on the way of life in St. Augustine depended on one's position in a stratified social system of an increasingly diverse Spanish Catholic community. The town resembled one in Spain with a central plaza, street grid, Spanish architecture, and residential house lots (figure 5.16). All the residents living in the town were Catholic, and the Church and its calendar ordered the community's social and religious life. Most of the population were criollo descendants of retired soldiers who had stayed on after their service and were the primary contributors to the town's population growth. The retired soldiers usually had Indian wives and started blended families who, after several generations, identified as Spanish, with a unique Spanish American blended culture known as Floridano. Spaniards born in Europe were at the top of the pecking order, and a man's status and that of his family were determined by his ethnicity, race, occupation, and income. They lived a Spanish way of life in a Spanish town. The social system was flexible, and an individual's social status could change during their lifetime. While residents of Spanish descent constituted most of the population, their society evolved into a unique Spanish American one with distinct but flexible social distinctions. Castas, people of color and mixed race, were generally relegated to the lower ranks of society. The people on the lower rungs of the social ladder could afford fewer expensive imported Spanish and European items and food and had to use more local resources and materials.

The African Community

Africans, both free and enslaved, were part of the St. Augustine community from its very beginning. The Spanish had kept slaves since the thirteenth century, but slavery did not necessarily have racial overtones. Slavery was considered a legal condition that could happen to people of any race. Slaves were people, not property, and had legal rights. Spanish slaves were permitted to earn money, buy property, buy their freedom, escape abusive owners, and earn freedom by service to the state; owners could not break up families through sales. It was common to find both enslaved and free people of African origin living together in St. Augustine, and Africans made up about 10 to 15 percent of the town's population. From the African perspective, it was far better to live with the Spanish in St. Augustine, even on the bottom rung of society, than with the British in chattel slavery, as property with no rights.

Menéndez brought fifty Africans, both free and enslaved, when he and the first colonists arrived in 1565. In 1580, a group of thirty enslaved Africans owned by the Crown arrived from Havana to work on the fort at St. Augustine. A second group of twenty Crown slaves arrived in 1597, making a total of forty-two royal slaves in St. Augustine (eight had died in the interim). They lived outside the town in houses near fields in which they grew their own food. In addition, many colonists in St. Augustine privately owned enslaved Africans. The Spanish forcibly baptized enslaved individuals and considered them Christians, at least on paper. The colonists gave them Spanish names recorded in church records and gave them Christian burials. In 1606, there were about one hundred African slaves in the town, and most (about seventy) were privately owned. Some Crown slaves were leased to soldiers or other individuals who hired them out for various services. Historian Jane Landers describes St. Augustine as a society with slaves rather than a slave society.

The British introduced chattel slavery to the region in 1670, when they expanded down the Atlantic Coast to found colonies in Carolina and Georgia. They established plantations based on the labor of enslaved individuals, and African slaves soon began to escape and flee south to St. Augustine. The first runaway slaves arrived in 1687, and they were immediately freed and put to work for the government, either in the military or constructing the new stone fort, the Castillo. This began a southern "underground railroad" to freedom for African slaves in the Deep South. Initially, if the slave owners or slave catchers found their runaway slaves in St. Augustine, the Spanish would pay the owners for them but would not send them back. Scores of desperate fugitives arrived each year, converted to Catholicism, and worked or served in the military. Former slaves took Spanish surnames after baptism, were instructed in Catholicism, and became part of Spanish civil and religious society, where they were protected as vassals of the king. Since the Spanish always needed more soldiers, the practical-minded St. Augustinians began to spread the word that escaped African slaves arriving in St. Augustine would be given sanctuary if they converted to Catholicism and worked for the government, especially building the stone Castillo or serving in the militia. They were not allowed to leave Spanish Florida.

FIGURE 5.17.
Drawing of the African militia officer Francisco Menéndez, St. Augustine.

African refugees from British plantations continued to flee to St. Augustine into the eighteenth century. When Carolina slaves revolted in 1711 and 1714, many joined the Indians in the Yamasee War against the British, almost eliminating the colony. But the British defeated the Native rebellion, and the Indians and their fugitive Black allies sought refuge with the Spanish in St. Augustine. More and more runaway African slaves followed, assisted by the Yamasee and other Natives along the southern underground railroad. In 1733, the Spanish government decreed it would no longer reimburse the English for fugitive Africans and required that Africans complete four years of paid service in the militia before their freedom was granted (figure 5.17). A Black militia was formed that became an effective offensive force, battling pirates and British attackers and raiding British plantations in Georgia. A few years later, in 1738, more than one hundred former African slaves were living in St. Augustine, and they were granted unconditional freedom by the king so that there could be no pretext for selling them back to their former owners.

In 1738, the Black militiamen and their families were given free plots of land about two miles north of St. Augustine to establish a new town, the first free Black town in what is now the United States, referred to today as Mose (pronounced mo-SAY). Their community consisted of a fort with surrounding fields that served as an advance early-warning outpost to protect the town of St. Augustine. The new homesteaders also served their own interests in fighting the British, who were determined to return them to chattel slavery. News of the Spanish sanctuary spread through the more than thirty thousand enslaved Africans on Carolina plantations, and more and more tried to flee to the Spanish. When fugitives managed to reach St. Augustine, they were received with great ceremony and declared free. Unsurprisingly, this situation infuriated and frustrated the British who, in their view, were losing valuable property at an alarming rate.

Concerned that the Spanish might attack Georgia or encourage more slave rebellions, Governor James Oglethorpe, with a colonial and Indian army, attacked St. Augustine in 1740 and took Fort Mose. But all the people escaped to the Castillo, where the town's population was secure. Oglethorpe used Fort Mose as his base of operations during his siege of St. Augustine.

In a surprise attack, Spanish soldiers and the Black militia regained Fort Mose, defeating the British forces there; however, the fort was destroyed in the process.

This led to the free Black community from Fort Mose living in St. Augustine for the next twelve years. There, they worked in various occupations, such as skilled laborers, carpenters, bakers, and blacksmiths. Several Black soldiers signed on as privateers for the Spanish, capturing British ships and providing much-needed goods for the townsfolk. Some Black women, like Native women, also sold food, such as sweet baked goods, from their homes (figure 5.18). As the need for more defenses grew, a second Fort Mose was built in 1752 (figure 5.19). The former residents had become settled into town life in St. Augustine and reluctantly moved back to the frontier with their families. The second fort was much larger, with a moat and packed-earth walls. Everyone lived inside the fort in thatch-covered rectangular huts, and there was a chapel.

FIGURE 5.18. Drawing of Juana de Herrero, Native wife of a Spanish soldier, selling chickens.

The Black community in St. Augustine and Fort Mose had many residents originally captured from different African cultures. Some also were formerly enslaved in Latin America or the Caribbean and had been sold to Carolina planters. Shared elements of their African cultures probably inspired their music, dance, clothing, and adornments. This coalescence happened in many enslaved and newly freed Black communities, such as the Gullah Geechee in the Lowcountry region of South Carolina and Georgia. Emancipated slaves formed Eatonville in Florida in the late 1800s, and it is the oldest Black-incorporated municipality in the United States. Africans and In-

FIGURE 5.19. Rendering if the second Fort Mose in 1763.

dians were allied because of their common enemy, the British, and were accepted in each other's communities. Indian-made pottery used in the everyday activities of Africans provides material evidence of Indian alliances with the Black community in St. Augustine. Documents recorded that some Black militiamen married Indian women and lived in their communities.

Historical archaeologist Kathleen Deagan conducted an investigation of Fort Mose and discovered that the second fort had packed earth walls on three sides with a moat and two corner bastions. The fourth side, which was open, followed a tidal creek. Families lived in rectangular palm-thatch houses inside the fort and worked in the agricultural fields surrounding it. In their homes, archaeologists found fragments from the daily life of free Black families, such as Native and Spanish pottery, bottle glass, and religious objects, including rosary beads and a St. Christopher medallion. They also found military paraphernalia such as guns, gunflints, lead shot, metal buckles, and hardware; household items such as pipestems, thimbles, nails, ceramics, and bottle glass; and food remnants such as charred seeds and bones.

These and other artifacts of the first free Black community in the United States provide details about their daily life and diet. From them, we know that the residents farmed but also obtained meat by hunting and fishing nearby. Animal bones from their meals indicate abundant use of locally available wild animals such as fish, shellfish, turtles, rabbits, and deer. Plant remains were scarce, but experts are confident that the residents took advantage of wild and domesticated fruits such as figs, honeysuckle berries, persimmons, and blackberries. Archaeologists also recovered food-preparation items such as cooking pots, grinding stones, spoons, and storage jars. The archaeological information reveals that the free Black military homesteader families lived a full, free—if not prosperous—life in the salt marshes north of the town of St. Augustine. They provided valuable military service, were part of the greater community, and were protected by the Crown. This was a life far better than chattel slavery, where they suffered terribly and risked their lives to escape.

Historian Jane Landers has unearthed rich historical documents that pieced together the Black families who lived at Mose. The Spanish government and the church kept meticulous records of their colonial activities and people, including births, deaths, ethnic origins, naming patterns, godparent networks, deaths, warfare, and marriages. We now know the number of freed Africans living there, many of their names, and the African nations where they were born. Church records reveal that marriages were often interracial.

Former African slaves married each other, Black residents of St. Augustine, Indians, and whites, and their children were given the mother's legal status, either slave or free.

In sum, Africans, both free and enslaved, made up about 10 to 15 percent of the town's population, and they were part of the community from the start. From their perspective, although they were on the bottom rung of the social ladder, they were recognized as people with a place in their society. They were not property and had legal rights, even as slaves, and they could advance in society. Once the British introduced plantations based on enslaved labor into Carolina, enslaved individuals began to flee south to Spanish St. Augustine, often assisted by Native Americans, on a southern underground railroad. The Spanish accepted fugitive Africans into their community, converted them to Catholicism, and put them to work as paid laborers or in the military. The Spanish spread the word that they would provide sanctuary to runaway slaves, and the numbers of fugitives increased, infuriating the British. The Spanish provided the former African slaves with land and the opportunity to build their own military outpost community two miles north of the town, Fort Mose, which became the first free Black community in the United States.

Today, the site of Fort Mose is a National Historic Landmark owned by the state of Florida and open to the public. There is a pavilion, a visitor center with interpretive exhibits, and a boardwalk trail over the marsh. At the time of this writing, the 1738 fort is being rebuilt by the Fort Mose Historical Society and Florida State Parks with funding through a grant from the Department of State and many community partners. I encourage you to visit the park and experience the site of the first free Black community in the Americas.

The Native Americans

The lives of Native Americans in St. Augustine were very different from those of the townspeople or Africans, and their relationship with the Spanish changed over the two centuries of this early period. The Spanish considered all the Indigenous people they encountered in their empire to belong to a separate race they called *indios.* At first, the local Timucua residents welcomed the sudden appearance of Menéndez's eight hundred colonists and military in 1565, believing the Spanish would give them support and assistance. Soon after landing, Menéndez's chaplain, Father Francisco López de Mendoza Grajales, built a church named Nombre de Dios for the local Timucuan people, and the first Mass in Florida was celebrated there. In 1566, the Spanish signed peace treaties with Timucuan groups west and north of the St. Johns River, but *not* with those living in the vicinity of St. Augustine, where hostilities continued and increased. The local Timucua leader, Seloy, resisted the increasing demands of the Spanish, and after only a few months of living in his village, the Spanish moved to an island across the river and fortified it. Furious at being invaded, local Timucuans considered the Spanish their enemy. Spanish efforts to pacify the local Natives through religious conversion began about 1573 when the first Franciscan friars arrived. But Native resistance continued, and in 1577, the local Timucuans attacked the newly built Spanish town on the mainland, burning most of it.

In the same year, 1577, another group of Franciscan friars arrived and succeeded in baptizing many Natives in the St. Augustine vicinity, including Doña María Meléndez, the *cacica* (chieftainess) of the local Timucuan group. She greatly favored the Spanish, as did her daughter, who inherited the leadership position in the 1590s and was very Hispanicized. The mother married a Spanish soldier, and they lived in the Nombre de Dios Indian village with their children. It was a frequent practice of Spanish governors to take children of high-ranking Native Americans into their households to be raised and educated in the Spanish tradition. They gave the children Spanish names, and the girls often married Spaniards chosen by the governor. The daughter of the cacica may have been one of these. The conversion of the local cacica and her daughter marked a turning point in the relationship between the Timucuans in the vicinity of St. Augustine and the Spanish because the two women encouraged their people to convert and embrace the Spanish presence rather than fight it. For the next eighty years, several generations of Christianized Timucuans lived peacefully and relatively independently in their town of Nombre de Dios, about a mile from the Spanish town.

When Drake attacked and burned the Spanish town and fort in 1586, he found the Indian town of Nombre de Dios temporarily deserted and did not damage it. Drake noted that it was about 1,500 yards from the Spanish town, but Boazio did not place it on the map of the 1583 Drake attack. The Indian mission town is on the 1593 Mestas map of St. Augustine, along with a second mission village named San Sebastián de Yaocos (figure 5.7).

The 1593 map shows a mission church named Nombre de Dios and ten nearby buildings (figure 5.20). The buildings appear to have some traditional

Native-style elements, such as arched doorways, some circular-shaped homes with thatch walls, and thatched cone-shaped roofs. Until the mission church was built in Nombre de Dios in 1587, Christian Timucuans attended Mass in the Spanish church in the town.

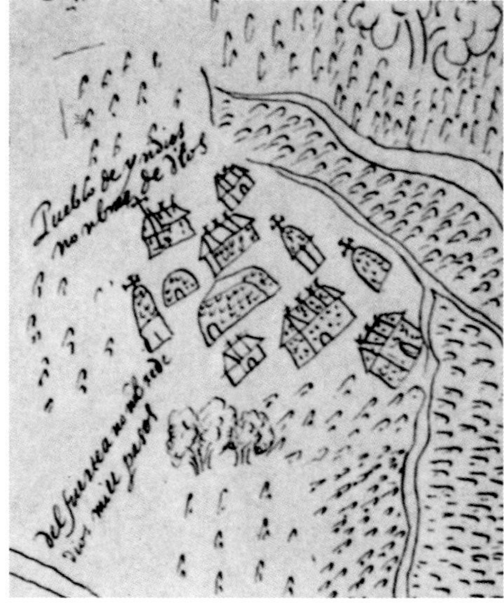

FIGURE 5.20. Close-up of Nombre de Dios mission buildings on the 1593 Mestas map.

Archaeological remains of the early Nombre de Dios Indian town have been found in today's Fountain of Youth Archaeological Park. Archaeologists from the Smithsonian Institution first discovered the cemetery beneath the church floor in 1934, and they excavated more than 112 burials. Most burials were extended on their backs in the typical Catholic fashion, but a few were in Native positions (flexed bodies or bundles of bones from charnel houses). Many personal items were placed in the graves of infants and children, such as shell and glass beads. This mixture of Christian and Native burial traditions reveals the continuation of Native beliefs and traditions within the context of Catholic missionization.

Outside of church services and festivals, the Timucuan residents of Nombre de Dios lived separate and relatively independent lives from those in the Spanish town during the late sixteenth and early seventeenth centuries. Their life blended their traditional beliefs and way of life with the Catholic faith. They worked in the fields adjacent to their town, growing food crops for themselves and the friars. Women often worked and sometimes resided in the town as servants and cooks, and some became wives of Spanish soldiers (figure 5.21). In 1606, there were eighty-four people living in the Nombre de Dios town, including the cacica, her two children, and twenty people of Spanish descent. In 1654, however, a smallpox epidemic was reported to have greatly reduced the Native population at Nombre de Dios, and it continued to decline during the rest of the seventeenth century. In 1674, there were only thirty residents in the town. The mission church was burned in 1702 by the forces of Colonel James Moore during his siege of the town, and it was ravaged again in 1728 by Colonel James Palmer, another British raider. After the Palmer raid, the governor of St. Augustine dismantled the church

FIGURE 5.21.
Rendering of Teresa Camacho, grinding corn for a meal.

and buildings at Nombre de Dios due to their exposure to attacks. By 1729, only one Timucuan was known to be alive.

As the Timucuan population declined, there was an increase in Guale and other Indian refugees from Georgia and South Carolina who were fleeing Indian slave raiders. This immigration brought a new Indian population into St. Augustine of nonlocal, diverse mission refugees. No longer were the local Indians a homogenous Timucuan group, nor did they live in their own town. Usually, the refugees from a former mission lived together in a separate village near the Spanish town. The new refugee Indian population, primarily Guale from missions in coastal Georgia, grew rapidly in the last decades of the seventeenth century. In 1690, there were 225 refugee Indians living in the area, and by 1725, there were at least ten small mission villages around St. Augustine. The number of Indian refugees grew steadily, and a 1728 census recorded 1,350 Indians living in the surrounding Indian villages.

Another source of Indian diversity in St. Augustine during the late seventeenth century was the steady increase in Indian laborers from outlying missions sent by their chiefs according to their alliance agreements with the colonial administrators. When the Castillo was under construction between 1672 and 1695, more than three hundred Indian laborers, especially Apalachee, worked on fort construction, and more were sent to grow crops for the workers.

After Nombre de Dios came under attack from British Colonel James Palmer in 1728, the overall Indian population and the number of refugee mission villages began to decline as the British continued their attacks and epidemics swept through those Indians that remained. After the Oglethorpe attack in 1740, several groups of the remaining refugees lost confidence in the ability of the Spanish at St. Augustine to protect them. They left, seeking alliances and protection with the Spanish presidio on Pensacola Bay or with the British in Georgia. By 1759, the effects of mission relocations, consolidations, diseases, and abandonment had reduced the Indian population around St. Augustine to only two mission villages with about ninety-five

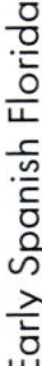

people of many ethnicities, including Yamasee, half-Timucua, half-Yamasee, Ibaja, Chickasaw, Casipuya, Chiluque, and Costa.

The inability of the Spanish to protect the mission refugees ended the last chapter of the Indian population of St. Augustine. The historical and cultural homogeneity of the original mission towns had been torn apart, and the surviving diverse refugees needed protection. In the end, the Spanish could not save them or themselves.

In sum, the Native relationship with the Spanish colonists began with hatred and resistance for the first dozen years of Spanish occupation, especially on the part of the local Timucuan group near St. Augustine. Things changed in 1577 with the missionizing Franciscan friars and the conversion of the Timucuan chieftainess, Doña María Meléndez, and her daughter, who then led their people by example to accept the Spanish religion and presence. For almost a century, missionized Timucuans lived in the town of Nombre de Dios and, though independent, interacted with the Spanish in St. Augustine. Indian women regularly married Spanish soldiers, becoming part of Spanish society and starting a new, blended way of life. From archaeological information we know that, although most Indians converted to Catholicism and were devout, they did not give up all their Native traditions and beliefs. Until their population was weakened from diseases and the British destruction of the missions, local Timucuans lived a relatively independent life outside of the Spanish town. However, once the Timucuan mission population began to decline and with the Spanish no longer being able to protect them from British raids, the remaining Timucuans died out and were replaced by immigrant nonlocal refugee Indians, especially Guale, who fled to the St. Augustine area from the besieged missions. But the Spanish could not protect the more than 1,300 new and diverse Native Americans who lived in the nearby mission villages. By 1763, there existed only two small villages with fewer than one hundred residents. In the end, the Indians had been failed by the Spanish, and they paid with their lives.

Defending St. Augustine

Defending St. Augustine and its diverse community is the huge stone fortress of Castillo de San Marcos on the riverfront. Built between 1672 and 1695, it still stands today and is the oldest masonry fort in the continental United States. Located on the Matanzas River at the inlet to the Atlantic, it stands

FIGURE 5.22. Present-day Castillo in St. Augustine.

FIGURE 5.23. Drawing of the east wall of the Castillo under construction, 1675.

guard over the old city (figure 5.22). The community's other defenses were a series of town walls and outposts protecting its perimeter. These defenses were all built during the Early Spanish period and are briefly described below.

FIGURE 5.24. Drawing of quarrying coquina blocks on Anastasia Island, 1671.

After building nine wooden forts, each lasting only a few short years due to natural decay, storms, and British attacks, Spanish Queen Regent Mariana declared that the tenth fort would be much more substantial and provided the funds for constructing a stone building. Almost all the building materials, especially coquina limestone, oyster-shell mortar, and timber, were available locally, as was a labor force of Indians drafted from outlying missions, soldiers, African Crown slaves, convicts, and English prisoners (figure 5.23).

The influx of workers, especially drafted mission Indians, swelled the population of the city. Native laborers were usually assigned to quarry limestone, and more were tasked to raise fields of corn to feed the enlarged labor force. The number of mission Indian laborers at St. Augustine grew to about three hundred during the Castillo construction. While contractually they were supposed to work there for only a year, they often were held much longer. It took twenty-three years to complete the stone fort. The coquina quarry was located on Anastasia Island across the river, and Native laborers rafted large limestone blocks to the construction site (figure 5.24). Two big new lime kilns were also built near the new fort for burning oyster shells to be made into lime mortar.

The new stone fort was of a state-of-the-art modern European design. It had a square of thick curtain walls with large diamond-shaped bastions on the corners and a triangular-shaped protection for the single entrance (figure 5.25). Although the Castillo took twenty-three years to complete, within three years (by 1675), three of the stone curtain walls were finished, and a strong wooden stockade for the fourth wall made it defensible. When completed, the walls were thirty feet high and ten to fourteen feet thick at the base, sloping to five feet thick at the top. While the initial fortress has been enhanced over the centuries, it stands today as one of the most visited

National Historic Landmarks in the United States. When you are inside it, you can feel the strength of its walls, huge bastions, and wide protective moat. A true fortress, it was never taken by force.

The first test of the Castillo came in 1702 from the army of James Moore. In preparation for a siege, the Spanish governor ordered the destruction of all buildings within a musket shot (about 750 feet) of the Castillo, and 1,500 civilians, along with their stored food and domestic animals, moved inside the fort. While the English fired their cannons at the fort, the thick, soft coquina walls of the Castillo absorbed the cannonballs like a sponge. Moore gave up, burned the town, and retreated.

COQUINA LIMESTONE

Along the east coast of the Florida peninsula from St. Augustine to West Palm Beach, there is a unique form of limestone made primarily from the cemented shells of millions of small shellfish called coquinas that live in the surf zone. Coquina limestone is soft enough to be quarried with hand tools such as picks yet hard enough to form the walls of forts and buildings. The most famous use of coquina limestone is the Castillo fortress in St. Augustine, where the thick walls absorbed cannonballs and protected the colonial population. Because of this, coquina limestone is known as "the rock that saved St. Augustine." The fortress was built in the late 1600s and still stands today as a testament to its durability. The Spanish built a smaller fort of coquina limestone in 1742, Fort Matanzas, which also still stands today in a National Monument of that name located about twenty miles south of St. Augustine. The best places to see coquina limestone outcrops on Florida's Atlantic beach are at the House of Refuge in Martin County near Stuart or Washington Oaks Gardens State Park in Flagler County.

Coquina limestone.

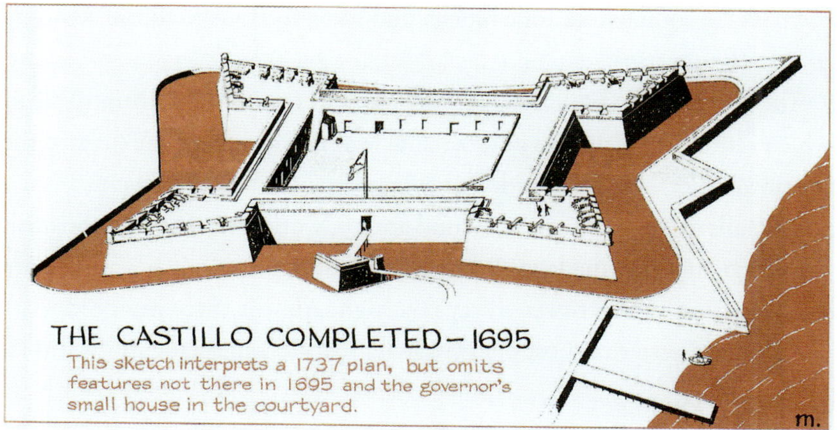

FIGURE 5.25. Drawing of the completed Castillo as it looked in 1695.

FIGURE 5.26. The Old City Gates of St. Augustine: *left,* 1881; *right,* 2016.

Thus, in 1702, the Castillo could protect the population, but it could not protect the town from destruction. The town lies on a narrow peninsula of land, surrounded by a river and creek on three sides and open to the north. The Spanish eventually built three defensive walls with moats across the northern neck of the peninsula to fend off land attacks. They built a new city gate into the first wall protecting the city, which still exists today (figure 5.26). A fourth wall surrounded the town. All the defensive walls were made of local materials: packed earth, palm logs, and sod with rows of sharp-leaved Spanish bayonet and yucca plants growing on top. There also were bastions along the walls and at the corners so that soldiers could defend the walls. The Spanish replaced part of the fourth earthen wall around the town with coquina limestone blocks, and some sections were still standing in 1871 (figure 5.27).

The Spanish also built defenses outside the city, the most formidable of which is the Fort Matanzas outpost, fourteen miles south of the town at the Matanzas Inlet, where it guarded a critical entrance from the Atlantic (figure 5.28). Built in 1742, it was the second and only other stone fort in Spanish Florida at the time made with blocks of coquina. It is a fifty-foot-square single bastion with a tower thirty feet high. Almost three hundred years old, this impressive outpost is a National Historic Landmark and National

FIGURE 5.27.
Photograph of a remaining section of the Rosario line wall in St. Augustine in 1871.

FIGURE 5.28.
Fort Matanzas outpost today.

Monument open to the public. The visit includes a short ferry ride from the visitors' center to the fort for a close-up experience of Florida's early Spanish history.

At various times St. Augustine had many other smaller, wooden, defensive outposts guarding various roads and crossings of the St. Johns and St. Marys Rivers. The Spanish placed other military batteries and redoubts (defensive works) armed with cannons along the rivers. Batteries on Amelia Island protected the mouth of the St. Johns. Some of the remaining missions were also fortified. Unfortunately, the British overran all these outlying military positions, so they provided little protection for the people or the strategic positions they guarded. But the Castillo was impregnable, and it saved the people of the town twice.

In a nutshell, the new stone Castillo was a success, withstanding two British attacks in 1702 and 1740. The substantial town walls successfully deterred enemies and protected the town, which was not burned again after Moore's attack in 1702. St. Augustine, in the early eighteenth century, with its town walls and stone fortress, was the most well-defended town in all of Spanish Florida and northern New Spain.

Spanish Indian Trade

A little-known aspect of Early Spanish Florida is its successful Indian trade in the interior of the Southeast and the effect it had on Native Americans. Facing continual harassment by the British and dwindling resources arriving from the mother country, the Spanish revived interest in Menéndez's initial vision of a Florida that included most of Southeastern North America. They sent search parties into the Carolinas to check out the stories told by de Soto's men of gold mines, diamonds, and freshwater pearls free for the taking. One party reached Cofitachequi near today's Camden, South Carolina, but the Crown did not want to extend the northern boundary of Florida that far from St. Augustine in the difficult terrain of the Appalachian Mountains. When de Soto passed through the Georgia Piedmont in 1540, he encountered many chiefdoms in the rich river valleys of the coastal plain. Ethnohistorian Robbie Ethridge has determined that ten years after de Soto's march, some groups had moved upstream and into the uplands to get away from future Spanish invasions, but others, such as the Ocute in South Carolina and the Apalachicola in the river valley of that name, began to develop trade relations with the Spanish (figure 5.29).

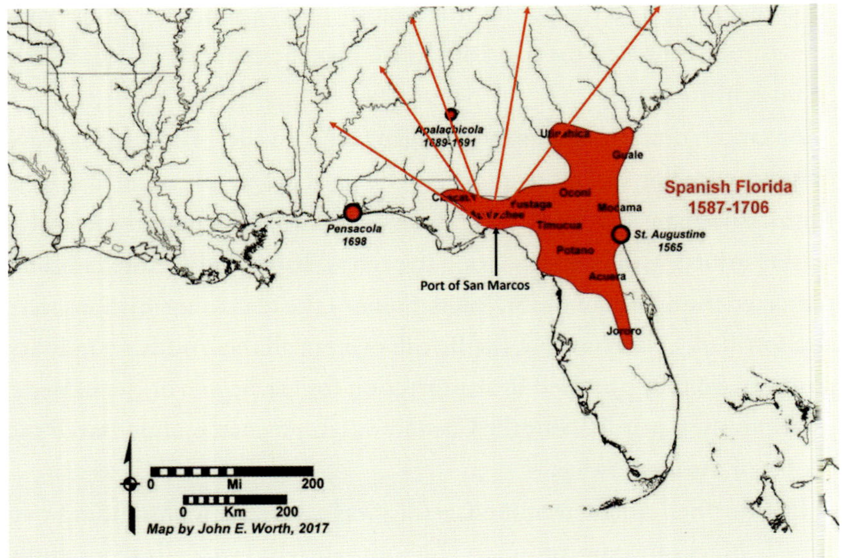

FIGURE 5.29. Map of the missionized Native groups and the range of the Spanish trade network in the interior based out of the port at San Marcos on the Gulf.

Some villages moved closer to the Spanish to take advantage of the access to high-status trade goods such as sheet brass, brass bells, glass beads, firearms, iron chisels, celts, and axes. Colonists used the port of San Marcos on the northern Gulf of Mexico to secretly ship goods, especially furs and hides from the Indian trade in the interior, to sell in Havana and other ports in Spain's South American colonies without being taxed by officials in St. Augustine. This trade was highly illegal, but friars, soldiers, and some governors apparently looked the other way and made a profit. By 1650, a strong Spanish trade network had developed with Native groups across the coastal plain, and archaeologists have found seventeenth-century Spanish trade goods reflecting that network on many Native sites in the interior river systems.

The Spanish did not missionize or establish formal colonial relations with their Native trading partners in the interior, but their trade network extended Spanish influence into the Appalachian foothills. In this sense, the Spanish retained influence in much of their original land claim of the Southeast well into the seventeenth century because until the last decades of that century they were the sole source of the European trade goods that Native Americans, especially their leaders, highly desired. However, the British and French eventually hijacked the Spanish trade and broke the Spanish monopoly with their higher-quality trade goods at better prices, as they commercialized the Indian trade into an industrial, credit-driven model.

Summary of St. Augustine

St. Augustine survived as the capital of Spanish Florida from 1587 until the treaty ending the Seven Years' War (also known as the French and Indian War) awarded Britain all of Florida in 1763. Over time, the town was organized into a typical Spanish layout with a central plaza ringed by government buildings and the main church. Residences were arranged on a rectangular street grid radiating out from the plaza. With the continual influx of Spaniards from Spain and Havana, the culture of the residents retained many Spanish cultural traditions, especially the Catholic religion and social institutions. However, the social and physical environments in colonial St. Augustine were different from those in Spain.

From the Spanish perspective, St. Augustine was an island of their homeland culture on the frontier. Although the city became ethnically diverse and there were many relationships with non-Spaniards, there was always a majority of people of Spanish descent. Everyone was Catholic and followed those religious and social traditions. Other Europeans were also present, as either visitors or prisoners, along with Africans, Indians, and mixed-race castas. The social system was flexible, with a person's place in it based on race, occupation, and income. People born in Spain and with some nobility or wealth (peninsulares) were at the top rung of society in the city and lived a Spanish way of life that was emulated down the social ladder to whatever extent residents could afford it. The social standing of households is visible archaeologically in the proportions of expensive European versus inexpensive Native materials and foods. Spaniards born in the Americas (criollos) had good occupations and incomes and could afford many Spanish goods that they conspicuously placed in public parts of their households. They often had Indian wives who preferred their own cooking containers and food-preparation items, but these items were relegated to the kitchen and out of public view. Their mixed-race offspring (mestizos) began a new hybrid ethnicity in St. Augustine that blended the two cultures.

People of color and of mixed race (castas) were low on the social ladder, and their households had few Spanish materials. Africans, both free and enslaved, always made up between 10 and 15 percent of the community.

Although on the bottom rung of society, African slaves were recognized as people with rights and opportunities, not chattel property. The Spanish welcomed and freed runaway slaves from other colonies, and many were given land and formed their own community at Fort Mose. Their households contained a mix of a few Spanish and many Native materials, reflecting their alliances with and assistance from Indians.

The Native American perspective on the Spanish evolved over time from one of resistance to acceptance to disappointment. Indians lived apart from the Spanish community, excepting the women who married Spanish men and lived in the town. Most Indians in the area were missionized and lived in their own villages outside the city. Local Timucuans occupied the first Indian town of Nombre de Dios just outside St. Augustine, but with their demise from disease and the eventual destruction of their town, groups of diverse refugees arrived from outlying missions that were under attack and repopulated the St. Augustine area. However, the Spanish could provide no safety, and most Natives eventually either died in the violence or fled to other areas.

Military pressure from the British instigated the construction of a series of defenses, especially the stone fortress Castillo de San Marcos. It succeeded in protecting the population within its walls, thwarting two major British attacks, but the town continued to be sacked and burned. To counter this problem, in the eighteenth century the Spanish built a series of four defensive walls and several outposts for protection, of which the largest was Fort Matanzas. Fort Mose with its militia of freed fugitive African slaves guarded the northern approach to St. Augustine. The St. Augustine community had grown to more than three thousand people in 1763, when by treaty, Britain gained control of Florida and forcibly evacuated all the Spanish and their allies.

Suggested Readings

Kathleen Deagan, Darcie MacMahon, and Jane Landers. *Fort Mose: Colonial America's Black Fortress of Freedom.* 2nd ed. Gainesville: University Press of Florida, 2025.

Albert Mancy. *Sixteenth-Century St. Augustine: The People and Their Homes.* Gainesville: University Press of Florida, 1997.

Places to Visit

Castillo de San Marcos National Monument, St. Augustine. https://www.nps.gov/casa/index.htm

Fort Matanzas National Monument, St. Augustine. https://www.nps.gov/foma/index.htm

Fort Mose Historic State Park, St. Augustine. https://www.floridastateparks.org/parks-and-trails/fort-mose-historic-state-park

Fountain of Youth Archaeological Park, 11 Magnolia Avenue, St. Augustine. https://en.wikipedia.org/wiki/Fountain_of_Youth_Archaeological_Park; https://www.fountainofyouthflorida.com

Websites to Visit

City of St. Augustine Archaeology Program: https://www.facebook.com/CityStAugArchaeology/

Development and Expansion of St. Augustine: https://storymaps.arcgis.com/stories/3b8466ed40bb42ce8420d015a122880a

Digital documentation of the Castillo de San Marcos: https://www.nps.gov/casa/learn/management/3d-digital-documentation-project.htm

Fort Mose Historical Society: https://fortmose.org/

Virtual tour of Castillo San Marcos: https://www.nps.gov/casa/index.htm

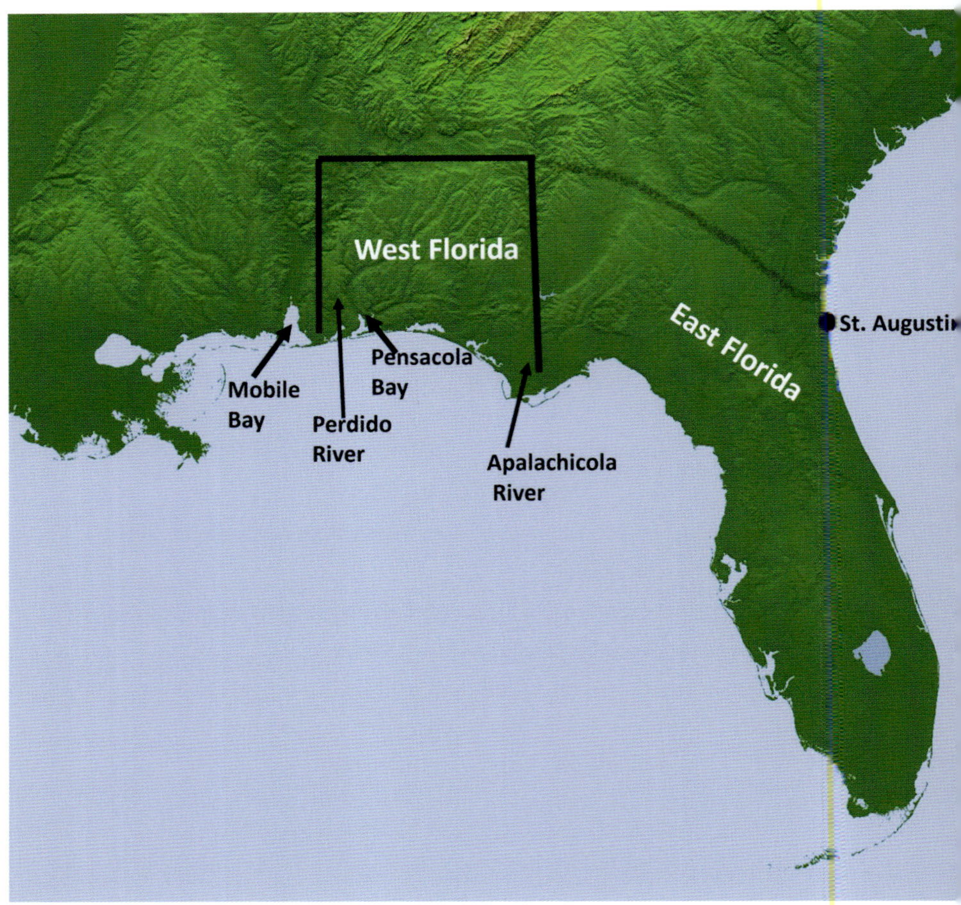

FIGURE 6.1. Map of West and East Florida.

SIX

SPANISH WEST FLORIDA, 1698–1763

Spanish West Florida encompassed the area from the Apalachicola to the Perdido Rivers and north to about central Alabama (figure 6.1). The first Spanish attempt to establish a settlement on Pensacola Bay was in 1559 by the Tristán de Luna expedition, organized and launched from Veracruz. A killer hurricane struck Pensacola Bay soon after they landed, dooming their efforts, and the entrada was abandoned in 1561. The Spanish returned 137 years later, in 1698, in response to increasing pressure from their colonial rivals for Pensacola Bay. This bay was important because of its location on the northern Gulf Coast, which provided easy access to Mexico and its silver mines, plus its deepwater entrance and bay, which could accommodate the largest colonial ships. It is the only natural deepwater harbor between Tampa Bay and New Orleans.

Thus, the Spanish needed Pensacola Bay and West Florida to be securely under their control. From their Florida colonial capital at St. Augustine, the Spanish could provide support and protection for missions and settlements only as far away as the Tallahassee Hills in North Florida, a distance of about two hundred miles. There were only a few small, short-lived missions and military outposts west of Tallahassee on the Chattahoochee River, a main feeder of the Apalachicola. By the late seventeenth century, Spain's colonial rivals, Britain and France, were planning to take Pensacola Bay, and the Spanish knew it had to be occupied and protected. Still, it was too expensive and too far from St. Augustine to manage—four hundred miles by land over rugged terrain or more than one thousand miles by sea. The solution was to add the new installation on Pensacola Bay to the Windward Fleet based in Veracruz. This fleet policed the sea lanes in the Gulf of Mexico and the Caribbean Sea to protect Spanish shipping and coastal settlements. Pensacola Bay is an easy sail from Veracruz, the main port of New Spain, and Windward Fleet ships could add a coastal presidio to their mission and service it on their patrols. This connection to Veracruz and New Spain (Mexico) strongly affected the demography, supplies, and administration of West Florida, which were very different from St. Augustine's close connection to Havana, Cuba, and Spain. The different connections of East and West Florida to the Spanish colonial empire resulted in distinct cultural and material variations between the two communities.

This chapter will summarize the history and archaeology unearthed in the archives and the ground from the Spanish occupation of West Florida between 1698 and 1763, regionally called the Presidio Period. It will also discuss the remains of a wrecked ship in Pensacola Bay that served the presidio in 1705. Finally, it describes the experiences of the two ethnic groups who built, worked, defended, and lived in West Florida: the military contingent sent from New Spain and the recently settled Native American refugees from other areas. Both groups were outsiders away from their homelands, entering a vacant but contested region. This is a surprising tale.

The Presidios

The West Florida presidio (a fort and garrison) extended Spanish control two hundred miles west from the mission chain at Tallahassee to Pensacola Bay on the Gulf Coast, anchoring a new western border of Spanish Florida. It survived despite understaffing, undersupply, almost continuous attacks, and destructive hurricanes. Four hundred miles west of San Augustín, the western presidio was a strategic safeguard protecting the northern Gulf Coast and western border of La Florida against invasion by French and British competitors. Located on the edge of the Spanish colonial empire, the West Florida presidio was a frontier military community far from the nearest permanent Spanish settlements of St. Augustine and Veracruz.

In eighteenth-century West Florida, there was a consistent constellation of three types of settlements: presidios, military outposts, and refugee Indian mission villages. There were a total of four presidio locations, six military outposts, four allied refugee Native mission villages, and two brief settlements of hostile Native Americans (figure 6.2). All the settlements and installations were short-lived, and many changed locations; at any given time, there was one presidio, two or three military outposts, and one or two refugee Indian mission villages. The presidio was the largest installation and the administrative headquarters. The Spanish built three presidios on Pen-

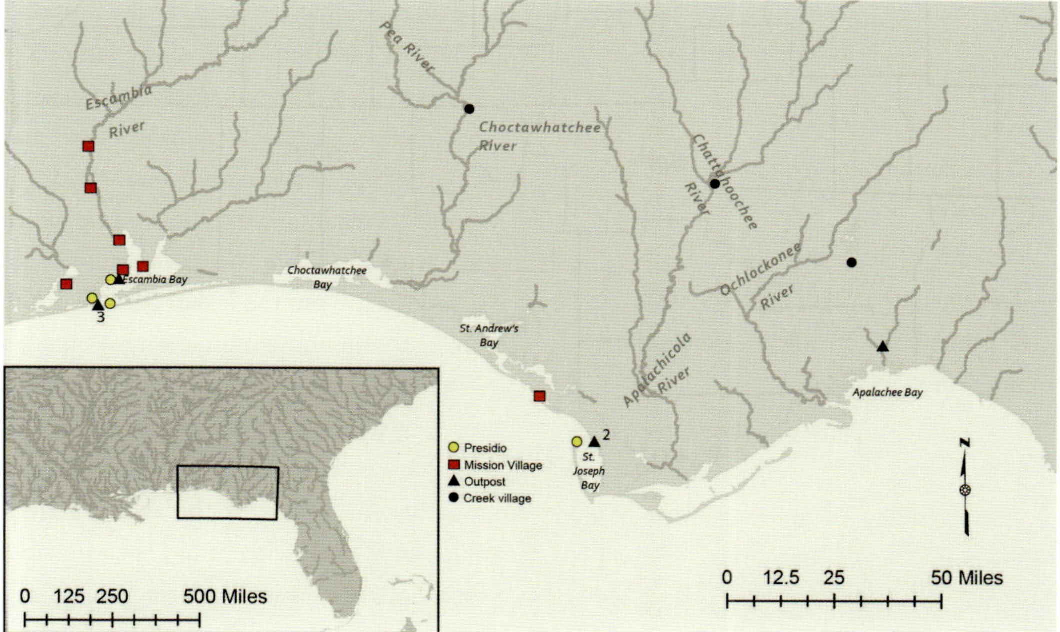

FIGURE 6.2. Early Spanish sites in West Florida.

sacola Bay and one on St. Joseph Bay, 115 miles to the east. A small rotating military unit manned the outposts, which protected strategic positions and facilities. Groups of refugee families from the missions formed villages some ten to thirty miles from the presidios. There was a formal alliance between the Spanish and the refugee Native groups. The presidio provided military protection, a church, a resident friar, and rations, while the Natives provided the fort with food and other commodities for purchase along with paid laborers, including hunters and fishers. The mission villagers also traded with interior Native groups, often functioning as intermediaries to buy British goods and horses, which they then sold to the Spanish.

Building and abandoning military installations were expensive, time-consuming, and demanding projects, creating extensive paperwork. The fact that the Spanish built a presidio four times in different places reflects the importance of holding on to Pensacola Bay. With each move, they had to build from scratch a new fort, barracks, churches, warehouses, officers' houses, powder magazines, and many other structures. Being meticulous recordkeepers and fastidious about maintaining their documents, the Spanish left a trove of military records associated with each presidio for historians to mine. The usual case was for presidios to stay in one place, as the Castillo in St. Augustine did, and over time, their discarded materials and structures build up and are mixed together. However, in West Florida,

PRESIDIOS IN SPANISH WEST FLORIDA

Santa María de Galve, 1698–1719
Pensacola Bay on a bluff overlooking bay entrance

San Joseph de Panzacola, 1719–1723
St. Joseph Bay on barrier spit near bay entrance

Isla Santa Rosa Punta de Sigüenza, 1723–1757
Pensacola Bay on barrier island near bay entrance

San Miguel de Panzacola, 1757–1763
Pensacola Bay coastline, eight miles from entrance to Gulf

the archaeological remains of the four presidios are like four layers of the same cake but located in different places. Each layer is geographically separate from the others, and the dates of each occupation are well documented. Luckily, archaeologists have found and studied all four West Florida presidio sites and have put the "cake" back together. This rare and unusual situation has enabled researchers to see changes and adjustments made by the military and Native communities that would usually be invisible or blurred together for historians and archaeologists alike. In West Florida, it has been possible for scholars to separate and track on quite a fine scale how the military and Natives lived and implemented new policies and practices on the ground between 1698 and 1763.

There is uneven information from each presidio, however, depending on the length of the occupation, degree of preservation, and amount of research that scholars have conducted. For example, about 60 percent of the archaeological remains of the fort at the first presidio, Santa María de Galve, are well preserved, and I directed a multiyear investigation there with the University of West Florida (UWF). Historians went to archives in Mexico and Spain to find and study the reams of documents, and archaeologists spent four summers finding and excavating the fort and village. As a result of this extensive research, we know a lot about the Santa María presidio community. We also know a lot about the third presidio, Isla Santa Rosa, where about 25 to 30 percent of the settlement is preserved, and scholars have conducted two major investigations. The remains of the fourth presidio, San Miguel de Panzacola, lie under downtown Pensacola. While the total extent of the preserved remains of this presidio is unknown, investigations have discovered and studied intact deposits in several places. Because this was the presidio the Spanish turned over to the British in 1763, numerous documents and maps associated with the official transfer contain many details about this community. Unfortunately, the remains of the second presidio, San Joseph de Panzacola, on St. Joseph Bay, have been destroyed by shoreline erosion over the last sixty years.

FIGURE 6.3. Presidio Santa María de Galve in 1719.

Archaeologists conducted one small, unreported excavation in the 1960s, and historians have conducted limited research. As a result, we know little about Presidio San Joseph.

We can make some generalizations about the occupation of the West Florida presidios. All were short-lived and occupied for different lengths of time. Santa Rosa (thirty-four years) and Santa María (twenty-one years) were occupied for the longest, and San Miguel (nine years) and San Joseph (four years) for the shortest periods of time. The reasons for abandoning the presidios varied. Santa María was attacked and burned to the ground by the French from Mobile. Hurricanes destroyed Santa Rosa. San Joseph was disassembled and abandoned, and San Miguel was transferred intact to the British.

Geographical factors also affected the placement and length of occupation of the presidios. The Spanish placed two presidios on the mainland and two on a barrier island or spit. The first presidio, Santa María, was on the mainland on a high coastal bluff with a view of the entrance from the Gulf, which was about a mile and a half away. Unfortunately, the entrance was past the range of Spanish cannons, but the bluff was a good observation point of the pass from Pensacola Bay to the Gulf. For eight years (1707–1715), British-led Native armies frequently attacked and besieged this presidio (figure 6.3). In 1719, a French fleet from Mobile twice entered the bay and bombarded

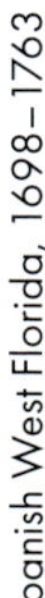

FIGURE 6.4.
Rendering of the French attack on Presidio Santa María de Galve, 1719.

the fort into surrender (figure 6.4). The Spanish then retreated to St. Joseph Bay, where they had had an earlier outpost. They positioned the second presidio, San Joseph, near the tip of a long, thin barrier spit separating the Gulf from the bay. Protected on three sides by water, this position successfully diminished the chances of a land attack. When they returned to Pensacola Bay, they placed the third presidio, Santa Rosa, in a similar location on a barrier island near the bay entrance. While British-led Creeks conducted some raids on Santa Rosa, there were no significant attacks. However, after hurricanes destroyed this presidio twice, the Spanish moved across the bay to the coast of the mainland, about eight miles from the bay entrance. This last presidio, San Miguel, was not attacked, despite its location on the mainland, but its outposts were.

THE FORTS

Forts were essential to survival in West Florida, and eleven were built: six at presidios and five at outposts. All the forts and buildings were made of wood. The largest forts were on the mainland at Presidios Santa María and San Miguel and were designed to defend against attacks from both land

and sea. The smallest fort was on Santa Rosa Island, as water protected the community on three sides and only a small fort was needed to defend the narrow land access. We know very little of the fort at San Joseph.

The two large mainland forts were variations of a popular European design consisting of a square or rectangle of upright pointed pine logs with diamond-shaped extensions called bastions on all or most corners. The Spanish built Fort San Carlos immediately after landing at Santa María (figure 6.3 and figure 6.5), but Fort San Miguel was constructed *after* the community had been built and occupied for several years (figure 6.6). Only after the threat of an imminent Indian attack did the Spanish construct a fort around San Miguel; several buildings had to be demolished or detoured

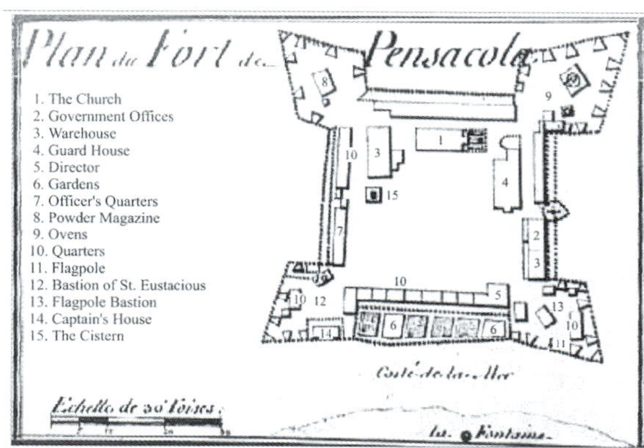

FIGURE 6.5. Map of Fort San Carlos at Presidio Santa María de Galve, 1719.

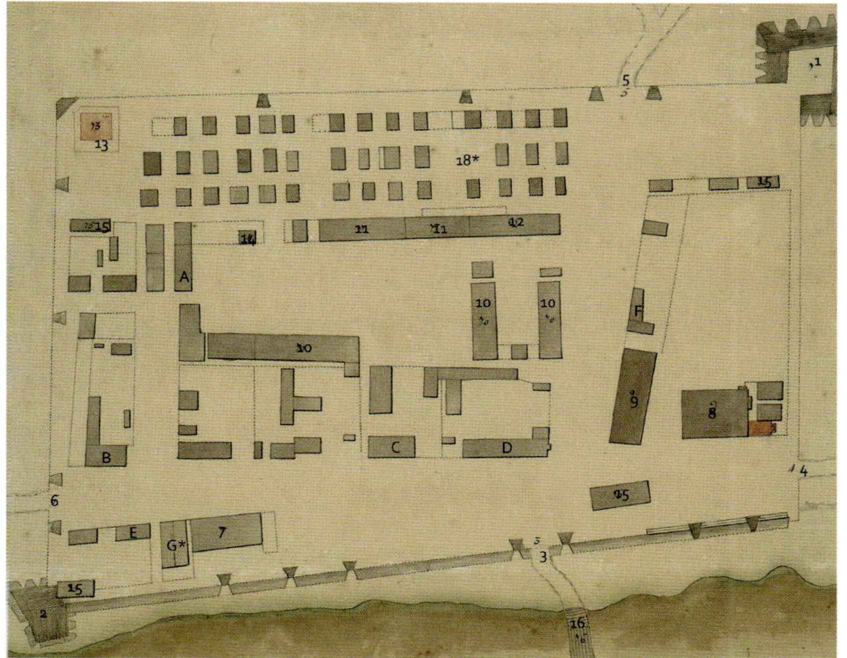

FIGURE 6.6. Presidio San Miguel: official transfer map of Fort San Miguel for the British, 1763.

FIGURE 6.7. Drawing of the fort at Presidio Santa Rosa, 1743.

around, and as a result, the fort was not symmetrical or square. The military saw little need to build a big fort at Santa Rosa because of its location on isolated Santa Rosa Island surrounded on three sides by water.

Over time, the Spanish modified all their presidio forts. Forts San Carlos, Santa Rosa, and San Miguel were built on the bay shore, where the wind and water eroded the shoreline walls, requiring the reduction or elimination of the corner bastions. San Miguel's seawall and bastions were terreplein—parallel double stockade walls with sand between them—to resist cannon fire. All the walls of Fort San Carlos were initially terreplein, but the wet sand decayed the soft pine posts so quickly that the sand and outer walls were soon removed, leaving only a single stockade wall that was damaged by erosion of the bay bluff. We don't know the details of the first fort at Santa Rosa, but a 1743 sketch of the settlement depicts the second fort with walls of vertical boards (figure 6.7). Three forts were built at Santa Rosa due to repeated destruction by hurricanes. The first and second forts were built on the shoreline, but the third appears to have been built a short distance inland.

The presidio forts shared several construction features. The walls of three forts were square or rectangular enclosures of single or double stockades with corner bastions on all or some corners. One fort had walls of vertical boards, and we do not know the details of the remaining two forts. All fort walls were made from the abundant pines in the region; even though pine wood is soft and subject to decay and insects, it is the only locally abundant tree with a tall and straight trunk. Historical documents contain continual complaints about having to repair or replace the low-quality pine posts soon after they were raised. The archaeological remains of the walls of Fort San Carlos showed evidence of many repairs to and replacement of the pine poles. However, there was no local stone or other source of wood for tall posts, so the Spanish continued to use pine for the walls of fortifications throughout the Presidio Period.

INSIDE THE FORTS

Moving within the fort walls, scholars have conducted extensive studies inside the two mainland forts, San Carlos and San Miguel. They have documented that the officers and senior administrators enjoyed the best facilities in both installations, including housing, food, and access to material items. Soldiers' facilities were second best, and convicts' and laborers' facilities were the worst. Both forts enclosed many of the same kinds of buildings, such as warehouses, guardhouses, powder magazines, hospitals, churches, and housing.

Fort San Carlos at Presidio Santa María was initially intended to be only a secure place for supplies, a guard unit, housing for the governor, and a refuge for the community when attacked. During times of peace, the population lived in an adjacent village. The fort was not particularly large, enclosing about 2.5 acres (about 100 yards square with corner bastions). Due to steady increases in the number and size of attacks by British-led Indian forces, by 1707, the village was not safe. The population of four to five hundred people had to move inside the fort, where they lived for eight years. It was crowded inside, and it was necessary to build new facilities and housing for the population. The Spaniards kept the center of the fort open for use as a public plaza and parade ground, and this area was lined with significant buildings such as warehouses, churches, and government offices. Historians have found several maps of the fort and its internal buildings, and each one is different because the wooden structures came and went over the years due to fire, decay, and demolition. The residents also built new structures and repurposed other buildings. One facility that did not change, however, was the northwest corner bastion that housed the powder magazine. Once archaeologists found this bastion, they were able to use the historical maps to find several buildings inside the fort, including three barracks, a church with a subfloor cemetery, a warehouse, and a warehouse converted into a hospital (figure 6.8).

In addition to information from historical documents and maps, archaeological excavations in the barracks for officers, for soldiers, and for laborers/convicts revealed that they differed according to rank in both the quality of the construction and the materials found in and around them. Excavations of the officers' barracks revealed the building had large square corner posts with horizontal timbers embedded in shallow trenches between them, which supported the wall studs and a raised wooden floor. The walls had

FIGURE 6.8. Burned stockade walls of northwest bastion of Fort San Carlos, 1719.

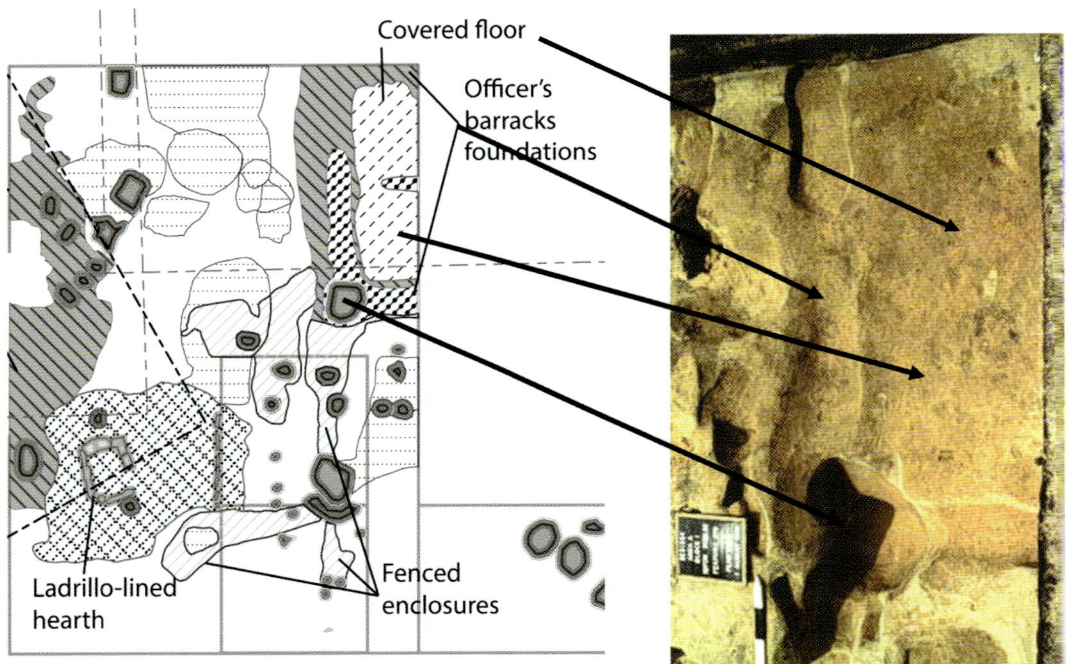

FIGURE 6.9. A photo of the remains of officers' barracks and adjacent features inside Fort San Carlos, with a sketch of the layout.

windows with glass panes, and the exterior siding was made of boards (figure 6.9). The roof was covered with boards or shingles, and the edges were sealed with lead sheeting to prevent decay. The soldiers' barracks had walls of irregularly spaced vertical posts set in shallow trenches, and several posts were replacements. The rooms were small, about eight feet wide, with a dirt floor and large pits in the floor, probably for storage. The convicts'/laborers' barracks resembled a long, shoddily constructed shed. It was made of small, irregularly sized single posts, most of which had been replaced, and a dirt floor with no evidence of individual rooms.

Behind the officers' barracks was a fenced-in area, probably for gardens, and nearby were a brick-lined hearth for outdoor cooking and a myriad of refuse pits (figure 6.10 and figure 6.11). Archaeologists recovered materials associated with each barracks, reflecting differential access to goods, food, and personal accessories based on rank. Officers had higher-quality material and more of it than the lower ranks. Officers used more Mexican tableware, decorative glassware, and window glass (figure 6.12). They also had almost all the rare items, such as gaming dice, finger rings with settings, amber pendants, silver uniform brocade, shoe buckles, and coins. There were also tacks from upholstered furniture; parts of a musket; domesticated foods such as chickens, peaches, and beef; and a variety of shellfish and fish. Compared to the meager materials found at the other barracks, the officers and their companions at Presidio Santa María clearly had the best of what was available at this frontier installation.

FIGURE 6.10. Brick-lined hearth near officers' barracks inside Fort San Carlos.

FIGURE 6.11. Sketch of officers cooking on the outdoor hearth that was located next to the officers' barracks.

Several interesting items in the convicts' barracks reflected the wide range of people housed there and what they did. For example, an iron pulley and shovel blade indicate hard labor activities and, perhaps, frequent repair of their poor structure. On the other hand, writing materials (slate and an ink bottle), a unique glass flask, a pharmaceutical bottle, and a peach pit are unexpected possessions and food for prisoners and laborers. They indicate literacy, access to personal and medical materials, and rare fresh fruit. Prisoners came from all ranks of society in New Spain; apparently, some were from the upper castas.

By contrast, Fort San Miguel was three times larger than Fort San Carlos, enclosing more than six acres. At least eighty-seven buildings were inside the fort when it was transferred to the British in 1763. Like Fort San Carlos, it had an open plaza or parade ground in the center, but otherwise, the forts are different, likely because the San Miguel community developed before the fort walls were built. The large governor's compound sat against the fort's east wall and gate, taking up about 20 percent of the interior, and a fence surrounded it. The 1763 map identified six of the nine buildings in the governor's compound: a large residence with an attached kitchen, two outbuildings, stables, a warehouse, and a guardhouse. Housing for senior officers and administrators was along the bayshore section of the fort.

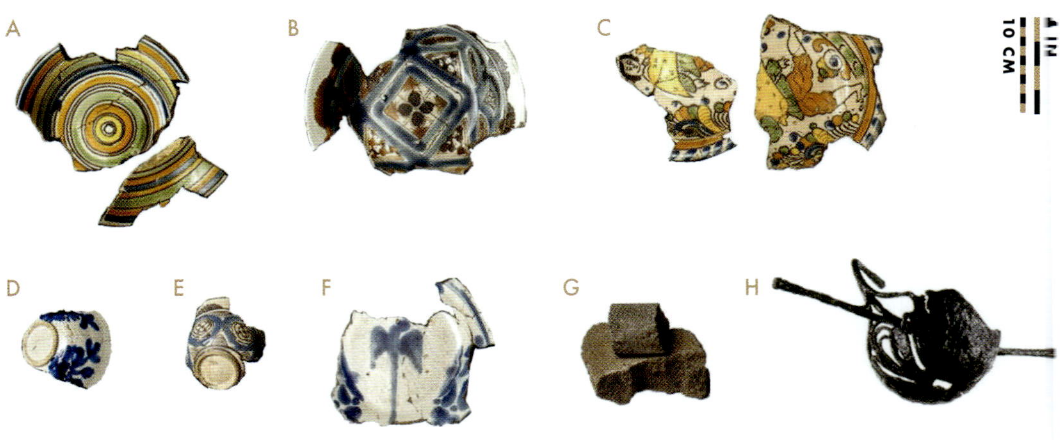

FIGURE 6.12. Artifacts from Presidio Santa María: examples of Spanish (*a–f*) ceramics; (*g*) basalt mano and metate fragments; and (*h*) iron sword hilt

where they could catch the sea breeze. These were fenced multi-structure residential compounds for the King's House (treasury), commandant, and cavalry captain, among others. Barracks for soldiers and convicts and a hospital lined the parade ground, and forty-nine small cabins for married soldiers were at the back of the fort, arranged in orderly rows. This housing arrangement reflects the hierarchy of the military community. The church and friary were near the paymaster's house in the southwest corner of the fort. As at Fort San Carlos, the powder magazine was in the northwest corner of the fort.

FIGURE 6.13. Captain Luis Joseph de Ullate's residential compound at Fort San Miguel.

One of the residential compounds in Fort San Miguel that has been found and studied is that of Captain Don Luis Joseph de Ullate, head of the cavalry unit. He lived in one of the prominent residential compounds across the street from the church near the fort's west gate. Luckily, a historical document describes his residential compound in detail. His house had two stories, plastered walls, wood floors, two apartments on the second floor with a balcony, and a loft. The outbuildings comprised a kitchen, a storehouse, and a small house (figure 6.13). In Ullate's backyard near the kitchen, archaeologists found the remains of two water wells with shafts made of wooden barrels, a root cellar, and many pits filled with refuse. The

FIGURE 6.14.
Large features in Ullate's backyard: (1, 2) barrel wells; (3) root cellar.

wells and cellar were clustered and built sequentially (figure 6.14). Most of the bottom barrel in one of the wells was preserved and had holes drilled through it for water flow. The root cellar extended down to just above the water table. It consisted of a rectangular shaft lined with wood and covered with metal sheeting.

Trash pits outside the Ullate kitchen were filled to the brim with materials discarded from the house (figure 6.15). They contained some unusual food bones, such as a complete alligator skull and the lower shell of a big sea turtle. Most of the refuse was broken ceramics and food bones, but there also were iron barrel bands, plaster, broken bricks, tiles and, fittingly, pieces of expensive large porcelain bowls (figure 6.16). The refuse revealed new information about the house interior, such as decorative ceramic tiles that probably lined a brick fireplace and evidence that there may have been a brick floor. Some of the pieces of plaster had impressions of small boards, probably laths, indicating that the captain's interior walls were made of laths covered with plaster. Almost all the Ullate tablewares were imported from New Spain. The food bones indicate the captain had his choice of domesticated animal meat, such as beef, pork, and chicken. But he also consumed local delicacies such as alligator and sea turtle, along with sharks and a variety of fish. Other

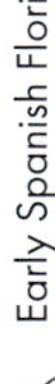

FIGURE 6.15. Full refuse pits in Ullate's backyard.

FIGURE 6.16. Refitted porcelain tableware found near Ullate's house lot.

distinctive artifacts reflecting Ullate's high status were pieces of jewelry; delicate stemmed glassware; brass, bone, and pewter buttons; clothing; and shoe buckles. Other interesting objects include a metal canteen, a pen nib, and a jar for face cream.

In sum, the mainland presidio forts of San Carlos and San Miguel were the first and last built in West Florida. The former was smaller, built at the beginning of the occupation, and was designed to have the population live in a nearby village; the latter was built around an existing community to protect it. The organization of buildings inside the two forts differed according to the residents' rank and position, with officers and senior administrators having the best housing and placement in the fort. The materials associated with the high-ranking residents inside both forts reflected their access to the best of what was available in their frontier garrisons, such as high-quality housing, special and domesticated foods, imported tableware and serving vessels, and personal accessories. Soldiers lived in barracks or small cabins, and convicts or laborers were housed in shed-like structures or in a large room of a multipurpose structure.

LIFE OUTSIDE THE FORTS

We have glimpses of life outside the three forts on Pensacola Bay, and it was a bit different at each presidio. At Santa María and San Miguel, where there were prominent forts, few people lived outside their protective walls. At Santa Rosa, there was a very small fort, and almost everyone lived outside it.

At Santa María, for the first nine years (1698–1707), almost everyone lived adjacent to the fort in a village with a church, friary, and cemetery. Documents state that the first houses for the soldiers were thatch huts, which were soon replaced with wooden houses. Some records imply that the Spanish arranged houses along a street grid. Archaeologists found the remains of one Spanish-style house in the Santa María village that was similar in construction to the officers' barracks inside the fort. It was a square or rectangular building with large corner posts and a raised floor (figure 6.17). The two refuse pits adjacent to the house revealed some surprises about the people who lived inside. The first surprise was that two-thirds of the pottery was made by the Indians, not the Spanish, which is the opposite of the proportions of the ceramics found inside the fort. This pattern is more like the proportions found in contemporary St. Augustine, where there was a Native woman in the household who did the cooking for a Hispanic man and his family. The second surprise was that a high-status officer apparently lived in the house, as reflected in pieces of expensive glass windowpanes in the refuse pits, along with the house construction style. Also in the refuse pits were parts of a metal necklace chain, a writing slate, three silver coins, and silver brocade from an officer's uniform. The combination of high-quality house construction and high-status artifacts with Indian pottery point to a household of a high-status Hispanic officer and an Indian woman, perhaps with children.

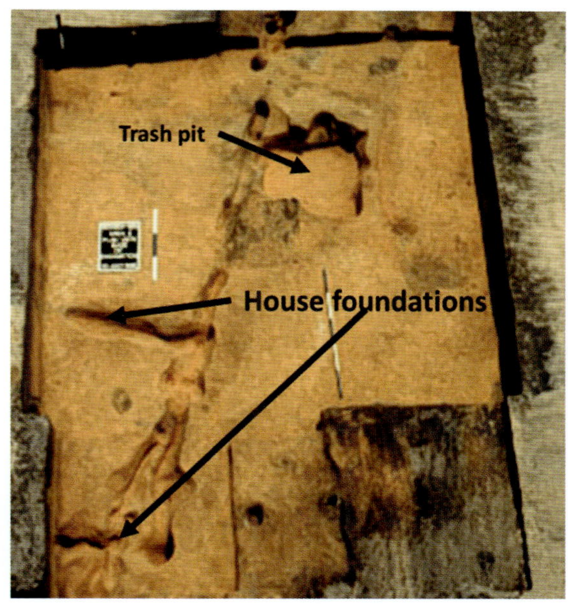

FIGURE 6.17. Spanish house foundations and refuse pit in Presidio Santa María village.

At Presidio Santa Rosa, the situation was very different because everyone lived outside the fort. The presidio was located in a strategic military position on the end of a long, thin barrier island near the entrance to Pensacola Bay. With water protecting three sides, only a small fort was necessary to guard the narrow land access. As a result, the community spread out along the shore. However, a barrier island is merely a strip of sand between the Gulf and Pensacola Bay, and living there has definite drawbacks. It is only a few feet above sea level at its highest point, and the water table is just below the surface. The vegetation is desert-like, with patches of low shrubs, a few stands of pines, open sand dunes, and marshes. There is no soil, only coarse, loose sand easily eroded by water and wind. Barrier islands are exposed to the full brunt of weather coming in from the Gulf. The Santa Rosa community was repeatedly battered by storms and hurricanes. In fact, the very day the contingent arrived with building materials from Presidio San Joseph, a hurricane struck, killing an officer and two soldiers. At least ten tropical storms or hurricanes battered the low-lying settlement with wind, torrential rains, and washovers of seawater from the Gulf, flooding the settlement and washing away homes, forts, and other buildings. Twice, the settlement was completely destroyed. After the first hurricane, in 1740, the Spanish completely rebuilt the settlement and fort, but after two back-to-back hurricanes in August and September of 1752, they declared the location uninhabitable. Significant hurricane damage to Santa Rosa Island occurred in 2004 during Hurricane Ivan, when the Gulf washed over the island, leveling the dunes and creating several new breaches across the island near the former site of the Santa Rosa presidio (figure 6.18).

The only image of Presidio Santa Rosa is a 1743 drawing made by Dominic

FIGURE 6.18. New breaks or washovers of Santa Rosa Island after Hurricane Ivan, 2004.

FIGURE 6.19. Presidio Santa Rosa, 1743.

Serres after the complete rebuilding following the destruction from the 1740 hurricane (figure 6.19). The drawing shows almost fifty one- and two-story wooden buildings along the shore and lining two streets. Researchers question the validity of the elaborate church and governor's house, and scholars have not yet found evidence to prove or disprove their existence. The walls of the small wooden fort appear to be made of boards fastened to posts and rails; the fort enclosed only four buildings.

To gain additional knowledge beyond the drawing, two historical archaeology investigations were conducted at Presidio Santa Rosa. The first was in 1964, led by Hale Smith from Florida State University (FSU), and the second was between 2000 and 2004, led by me from UWF. Historians searched the documents while archaeologists excavated large areas in the remains of the community. The Serres drawing and other documents showed all the buildings were made of wood with board siding and roofs. Serres's drawing shows no vegetation in or near the community, and the protective primary dune line along the Gulf is missing, probably flattened in the 1740 hurricane. Between one hundred and four hundred people lived in the Santa Rosa presidio at any time, and all were vulnerable to the extremes of weather common on the edge of the Gulf.

Archaeological excavations in the residential areas of Santa Rosa revealed a maze of house foundations and an unusually large and diverse artifact assemblage. Almost all the structures rested on large horizontal timbers set in shallow trenches between corner posts that supported the walls and roof (figure 6.20 and figure 6.21). A few small buildings had walls made of small vertical posts set side-by-side into the sand. Regardless of the building method, all the structures were barely anchored in the loose sand above the water table. Even under normal conditions, there was constant deterioration, but the flooding and high winds in storms and hurricanes damaged and destroyed the structures time after time. Hundreds of building foundations were found as dark stains in the light gray sand, reflecting continual construction, repair, expansion, and rebuilding.

In addition to the structural remains, an unusually high number of artifacts provided information as well. The abundance of artifacts in the sand is likely due to two factors. First, frequent rapid flooding from storms not only damaged buildings but also swept out everything *inside* the buildings and quickly buried those items. Second, even in dry conditions, hundreds of people walking around the small community constantly churned the loose sand one to two feet below the surface, quickly burying any dropped or misplaced

Drawing of Presidio Santa Rosa by Dominic Serres, 1743.

UNINTENDED USE OF THE 1743 SERRES DRAWING OF PRESIDIO SANTA ROSA

As was the case with the Le Moyne drawings, in the years before photography, governments employed artists to make official drawings of settlements, people, and events in distant colonies. The Havana Company hired Dominic Serres, a well-known French marine artist, to make an image of Presidio Santa Rosa in 1743. It was published *twenty years later* in a British natural history book, and soon afterward, it appeared in several popular magazines as an enticement for people to settle in the new fourteenth American colony called British West Florida. By then, however, the Santa Rosa Island community had been destroyed by a hurricane. This might be one of the first instances of false advertising of Florida real estate! It can be considered a predecessor of the infamous Florida "land boom" of the 1920s, where speculators advertised false pictures and descriptions of property in Florida; people then bought the property, sight unseen, and it usually turned out to be swampy land, far from any beach or desirable land.

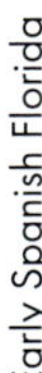

FIGURE 6.20. Excavations in the residential areas of Presidio Santa Rosa.

FIGURE 6.21. Dark linear stains from decayed timber foundations of several buildings, Presidio Santa Rosa.

item. These factors resulted in a high number of artifacts and many unusual artifacts that are rarely lost, especially small items such as clothing hooks, sewing needles, straight pins, tiny tacks, beads, jewelry, religious medallions, a music box key, a trade axe, small ceramic figurines, finger rings, and tens of thousands of other remnants of daily life (figure 6.22 and figure 6.23).

Archaeologists also excavated the area near where the Serres drawing depicted a large cross erected in the sand. There, they uncovered the foundations of a series of three buildings built on the same spot, all uniquely oriented to the cardinal directions. The scores of other buildings in the residential areas were *all* oriented northeast–southwest. Catholic churches, however, were then and still are built facing east, where local geography permits. An abundance of ceramic figurines was associated with these three unique buildings (figure 6.24). Of the 138 figurine fragments found at Santa Rosa, 80 percent (110) were in and around the foundations of the three north–south structures. In Hispanic culture, figurines are associated with the church, women, and children. These lines of evidence suggest that the foundations of the three superimposed buildings oriented to the cardinal directions must be those of the

FIGURE 6.22. Examples of the thousands of tiny artifacts caught in the sand at Presidio Santa Rosa.

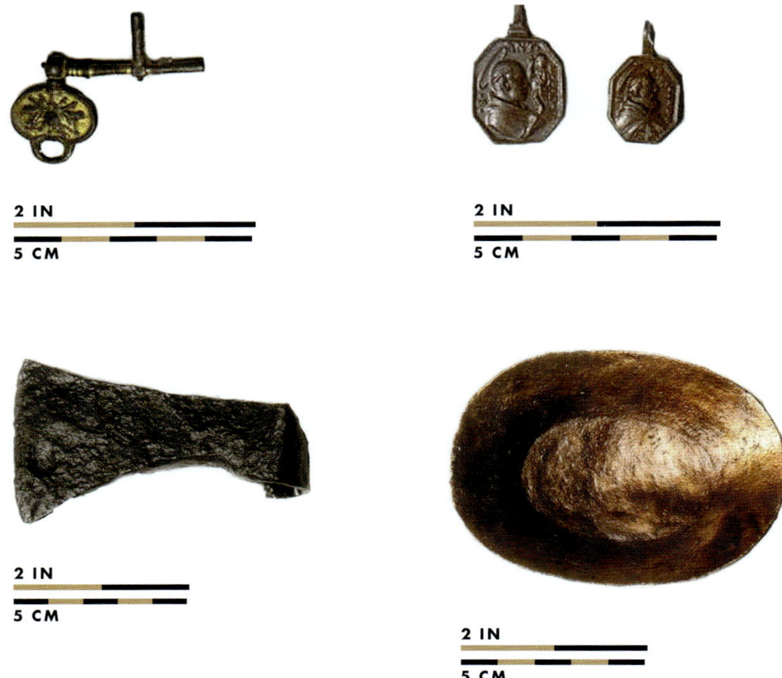

FIGURE 6.23. Examples of rare metal artifacts from Presidio Santa Rosa: (*a*) music box key, (*b*) religious medallions, (*c*) iron trade axe, and (*d*) shallow copper bowl, perhaps for baptisms.

three churches described in the documents, which were built and rebuilt on the same consecrated ground after the two devastating hurricanes.

In sum, the community outside the small fort at Presidio Santa Rosa lived in scores of wooden buildings along the shore and down a few streets. Because the community was on a thin, low barrier island of coarse sand, storms repeatedly damaged the structures with heavy rains, winds, and tidal surges. Buildings poorly anchored in the loose sand continually had to be repaired and rebuilt. Constant flooding also washed out and covered materials from inside the buildings, burying many diverse artifacts in the sand. Historical and archaeological records have revealed that hundreds of people lived in flimsy wooden buildings and had their settlement wholly destroyed twice. After those catastrophes, the people escaped only with their lives, leaving everything behind.

After the 1752 hurricane, the barrier island was declared uninhabitable, and most people moved across the bay to the mainland, where a large ware-

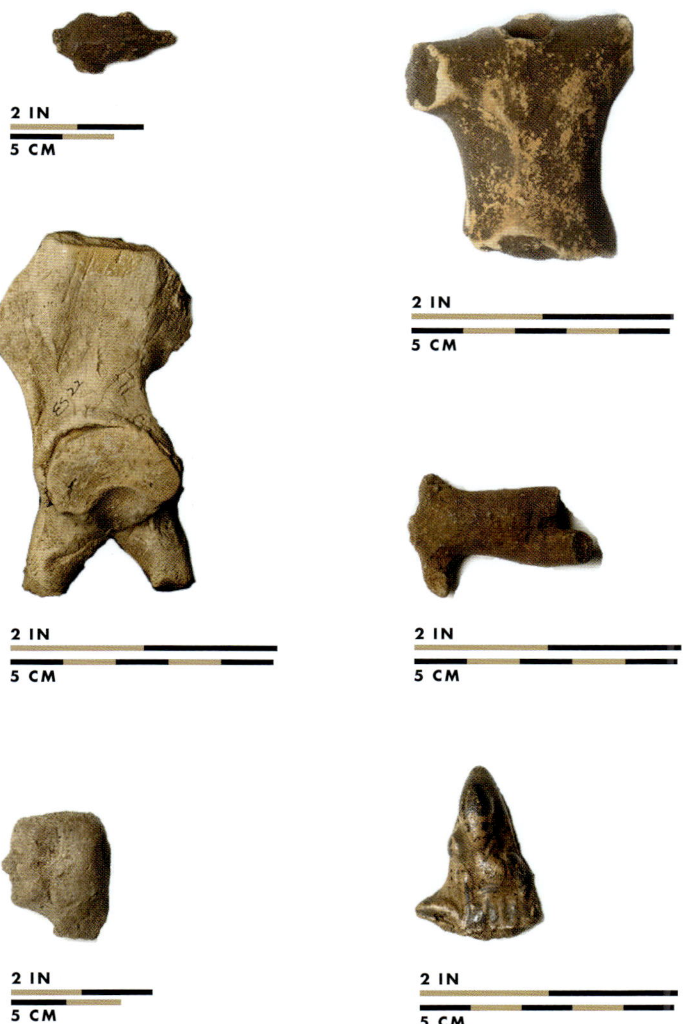

FIGURE 6.24.
Small ceramic figurines from Presidio Santa Rosa.

house had been built after the 1740 hurricane. By 1757, they had built a new fort, Fort San Miguel, and the population lived within its walls and in nine residential compounds just outside their protection (figure 6.25). Elizabeth Benchley of UWF has studied one of the residential compounds. It was near the fort's west gate and was likely owned and occupied by Carlos Antonio Ricardo, a wealthy trader, and his family. A historical map shows that the compound had a large residence, two outbuildings, and a well. The archaeologists realized the foundations of the large house were unique. The house was supported by a series of vertical squared posts set in large, earth-filled

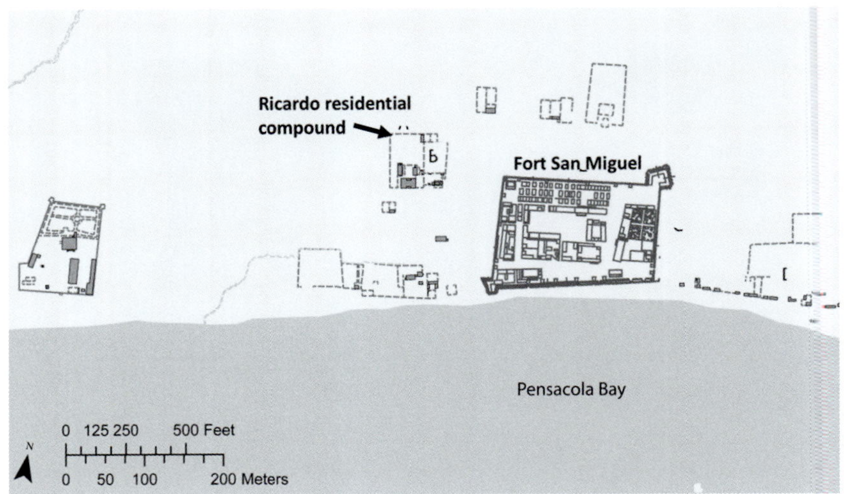

FIGURE 6.25. Map of Spanish residences outside Fort San Miguel.

FIGURE 6.26. Foundations of the Ricardo house, dating to about 1760.

trenches (figure 6.26). Construction debris in and around the foundation trenches included bricks and pieces of limestone, probably used for insulation between the wall studs. The archaeologists also found plaster, indicating the exterior walls had a whitewashed stucco appearance. The front of the house had a porch or open gallery. Refuse from inside the home contained pieces of tiles, plaster, and windowpane glass, indicating an upscale interior. Surprisingly, the house garbage contained a high number of British-made ceramics. Trade with the British was illegal in Spanish Pensacola then, but documents reveal that Ricardo was known for dealing in British contraband.

In general, on the mainland, few people lived outside of fort walls for safety from attacks by British- and French-allied Indians. There was a short-lived village at Presidio Santa María, but after a few years, living there was just too dangerous, and everyone moved into the fort. At Presidio San Miguel, a large community developed without a fort for five years, but once one was built, the threat of violence meant that only a few people lived outside the walls. At Santa Rosa, everyone lived outside the fort walls, because the water protected them from the British-led Native attacks. However, the harsh environment on the barrier island and destructive storms made the settlement unsustainable. Our information about daily life outside the forts varies from one location to another. At Santa María and Santa Rosa, researchers have studied the residence of a military officer and an Indian woman, and at San Miguel, they examined the residential compound of a wealthy Spanish trader dealing in illegal British contraband. At Santa Rosa, scholars have studied two crowded residential areas and a church. As it turned out, the fort was the only safe place at both the mainland presidios; and at the island presidio, there was no safe place from Mother Nature.

The *Rosario* Shipwreck

Ships of the Windward Fleet supplied the West Florida presidios throughout their existence. Usually, a fleet from Veracruz serviced several coastal installations on one voyage, dropping off supplies, payroll, soldiers, and convict laborers at several places along the Gulf and Caribbean coasts. The fleet also performed other tasks, such as reconnoitering, escorting ships, and picking up materials and people on return trips.

One such fleet arrived at Presidio Santa María in 1705, bringing needed supplies and dropping off a crew of ten skilled carpenters. They were to cut one hundred previously marked tall pine trees on Santa Rosa Island and

FIGURE 6.27. Excavating the *Rosario*'s hull in Pensacola Bay.

prepare them for masts, spars, and topmasts to be used in the shipyard at Veracruz. On the return trip, the ship *Nuestra Señora del Rosario y Santiago Apóstol,* commanded by Admiral Antonio de Landeche, stopped at Santa Rosa Island to pick up the prepared poles and carpentry crew and take them to the Veracruz shipyard. He anchored off Santa Rosa Island near a temporary warehouse, but a hurricane struck the next day. The *Rosario* was driven into the shallows, hit the bottom, keeled over, lost her rudder, and broke apart. After the storm, the crew salvaged what they could and burned the vessel to the waterline, presumably to salvage the iron fasteners and other useful metal. While no one was killed, two hundred members of the ship's crew and the carpenters were stranded for a time at Presidio Santa María, along with ninety other shipwreck victims from a passing French vessel that sank nearby in the same hurricane.

The wreck of the *Rosario* was found in shallow water just off Santa Rosa Island in Pensacola Bay by the Florida Bureau of Archaeological Research. UWF maritime archaeologists and students investigated the shipwreck, exposing a substantial portion of the hull and recovering more than a thousand artifacts (figure 6.27). The hull is well preserved, including the stem, frame, and support timbers as well as the keel (figure 6.28). Archaeologists determined that the ship was built in Campeche and was made primarily of the mahogany and Spanish cedar that grows in that region. One of the most unusual features about the shipwreck is the preservation of artifacts

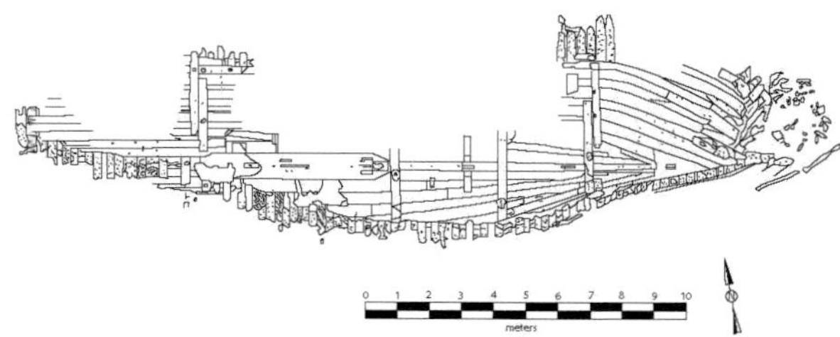

FIGURE 6.28.
Scale drawing of the remains of the *Rosario*'s hull.

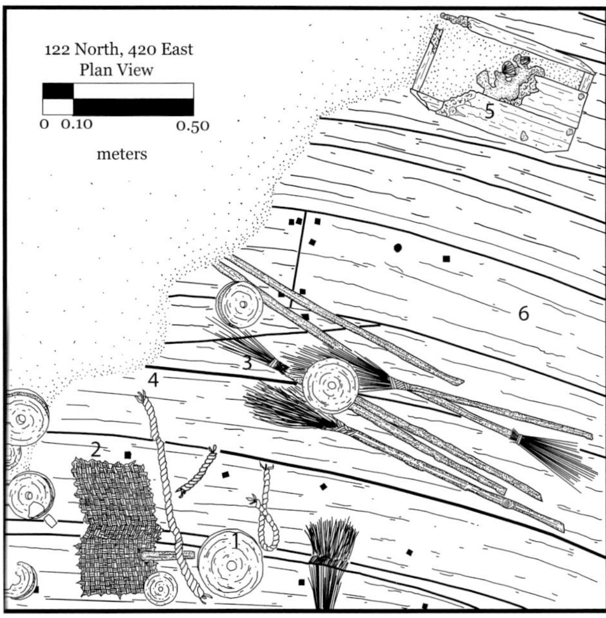

FIGURE 6.29.
Materials found on the *Rosario*'s hull: pulley parts, straw brooms, rope, deck mats, and a wooden box of nails.

made from organic materials. Even the smallest organic items do not decay in the bay's muddy bottom because there is no oxygen in the mud for the organisms that cause decomposition, like shipworms. Lying on the hull were woven deck mats, wooden pulley parts, straw brooms, a triangular wooden wedge for aiming cannons, leather shoes, and a wooden box of nails (figure 6.29). The pulley parts probably were used for the ship's rigging and to pull the extremely heavy pine poles into the ship through temporary openings in the vessel's bow. Other unusual artifacts on the *Rosario* include personal items such as a razor blade handle, wooden and bone rosary beads, a gaming piece, wooden buttons, a possible leather button, and a finger ring. The 1705 wreck of the *Rosario* provides a window into shipboard life and activities and offers unique evidence of the fragile straw brooms, shoes, or woven deck mats that rarely get preserved.

The People

Two groups of people with very different cultures moved into West Florida between 1698 and 1763: a Spanish military community from New Spain and refugee Native Americans from various parts of the Southeast. At first, the two groups lived together at Santa María, but after 1718, they lived apart; the military community lived along the coastal strip, and the Natives lived in mission villages across the bay and up the rivers. However, even during the time the two groups lived apart, they were intertwined and interdependent. Their experiences, perspectives, and objectives evolved in West Florida over their sixty-five years together. Both groups of people were far from their homelands and endured hardships on the frontier.

SPANISH MILITARY COMMUNITY

People with Spanish ancestry were at the top of hierarchical Spanish colonial society. Those born in Spain were called *peninsulares,* those born into high positions in Spain or the colonies were *españoles,* and those born in the colonies but in lower positions than españoles were *criollos.* The term *casta* had both the general meaning of caste and the designation of a dark-skinned person of mixed race. The majority of the colonial population sent to West Florida had mixed-race ancestry from interracial marriages and relationships that were accepted in New Spain and elsewhere in Latin America. By the eighteenth century, the Spanish colonial government had imposed a classification system based on ancestry, called the *casta* system, to differentiate the wide variety of mixed-race people. It was a formal legal and social hierarchy based on a person's racial makeup, skin color, and assumed personality traits (figure 6.30). A person's casta category greatly influenced their social status, rights, opportunities, and possible occupations. At the top of the casta hierarchy were *mestizos* (children of a white Spaniard father and Indian mother), and at the bottom were *torna atrás* (children of a dark-skinned, mixed-race father and an Indian mother). There were many casta categories in between, and there was no set number—they could range from eight to one hundred. While a person's casta designation was an actual legal status, it also was flexible. It could change during one's lifetime for various reasons, such as the accumulation or loss of wealth, marriage, immigration, or misfortunes.

Almost everyone sent to the West Florida presidio were castas from central New Spain, specifically Mexico City and Veracruz. Military recruits were volunteers and conscripts from the poorest neighborhoods and jails

FIGURE 6.30.
Painting illustrating the castas (castes) in New Spain.

Krista Eschbach's studies of the presidio population revealed that the military was not especially concerned about the specific casta categories of the people sent to the West Florida presidio. At the top of the military hierarchy were people with Spanish ancestry, usually españoles or criollos, who served as officers and senior administrators. Craftsmen were either criollos from the craft guilds in New Spain or casta soldiers locally trained through apprenticeships. Soldiers came from many castas (usually lower ones), and they were treated as social peers regardless of differences in caste. At the bottom of the hierarchy, laborers and prisoners were also from many castes but were treated equally. The Spanish considered Native Americans to be a different race, called indios; they were not part of the casta system. When an indio married a person of Spanish or mixed-race descent, their children were placed in the casta category of the father. The Spanish considered indios to be outsiders, and the military often hired them as laborers, hunters, fishers, cooks, or skilled laborers, especially carpenters.

The military used rank to segregate living quarters at the presidios. Officers lived in the highest-quality barracks in the most favorable locations and, along with administrators, often had separate houses or private residential compounds with several structures. Soldiers' barracks were adequate, and married soldiers had separate small cabins at the last two presidios. Convicts and laborers lived in poor-quality sleeping sheds or large rooms in multipurpose buildings. Craftspeople, servants, and enslaved people resided throughout the community, often living either where they worked or in the residential compound of the person they served. Segregation notwithstanding, the reality of living in a small community meant that people of every social, economic, and military rank interacted much more frequently than they would have done in the larger towns and cities of New Spain. The reduced importance of one's assigned casta at home and the grouping of multiple castas into one military rank provided an opportunity for individuals to upgrade their casta or improve their reputation. Despite the dangers and difficult conditions of the West Florida frontier, enlisting in the military enabled people to escape the more rigid social structure elsewhere in New Spain and provided opportunities to improve their social standing and income.

The size of the military population at the West Florida presidio varied considerably, ranging from a low of 80 to a high of 1,200. Sometimes, the population numbers spiked temporarily, such as when the Crown sent 1,200 soldiers to Presidio Santa María in 1719 for added protection during the violent attacks. After the French took that presidio, the military sent those additional troops to San Joseph to construct the second presidio there. However, the average Spanish military population at the presidio at any one time was between three hundred and five hundred.

Although the majority of residents at the presidios were military men, a number of civilian Spanish families also lived in West Florida. The first arrived in 1704 from Mission San Luis and nearby ranches and farms; they were escaping the destruction of the missions, the flight of the mission Indians, and constant British attacks. Some members of the criollo Florencia family settled in West Florida, while others went to New Spain or Cuba. The Florencia clan became powerful while at San Luis, where Juan Fernández de Florencia was the deputy governor of Florida and turned his ranching business into a fiefdom of sorts in the last quarter of the seventeenth century. His extended family filled most of the administrative posts in the Apalachee province. Magdalena de Florencia, wife of Diego Ximénez de Alfonso, and her five children arrived at Santa María in 1704 as refugees following the burning and abandonment of Mission San Luis. After assignments in Cuba and San Agustín, the military family returned to Santa María in 1713, and Diego Ximénez de Alfonso served as an adjutant there. Diego was captured by the French forces who took over Presidio Santa María 1719. After being released, he was assigned to Presidio San Joseph, where his family joined him. Diego and his family were then transferred to the Santa Rosa presidio, where Diego served as the first captain of an infantry unit. In 1733, Diego's sons, Nicolás and Pedro Ximénez de Florencia, born at San Luis, were captains of the two infantry companies at Presidio Santa Rosa. Nicolás Ximénez de Florencia also served as acting governor of the West Florida presidio three different times. In 1752, their sister Petrona Ximénez was one of ten women attached to the second infantry unit who received rations, which any woman born at the presidio had a legal right to receive. Petrona was living at San Miguel in 1756 and is thought to have been evacuated in 1763 by the British. This branch of the Florencia family can truly be called the first family of Spanish West Florida.

Another Spanish criollo family with multigenerational roots in the West Florida presidio community was that of Ygnacio de Soliz y Cárcamo. He and his wife, Doña Magdalena García, served at San Joseph and had two sons there. In 1741, Ygnacio and Magdalena were documented at Santa Rosa, living with their now-adult children and the rest of their family. In addition to these two families, other multigenerational families settled in Presidio Santa Rosa, later moving to the mainland at San Miguel.

The number of Spanish criollo and casta military families increased over time, especially because active and retired military men were encouraged with incentives of free land to settle in West Florida after their service ended instead of returning to New Spain. Many retired military personnel started farms and small businesses in the Pensacola area. As in St. Augustine, some military men also married local Indian women. Although the number of women and families increased over time, by 1740, the military needed additional members. They specifically recruited married men in New Spain for the Pensacola presidio and sent their families with them. As an added incentive, their wives were eligible for paid jobs at the presidio, such as laundresses, increasing the family income. In addition, the military recruited at least two groups of young single women, totaling 128, to go to Pensacola as potential wives for the single soldiers. The presidio provided them with transportation, food, clothing, and rations. By 1763, some families had lived in Pensacola for three generations. When the British evacuated the population in 1763, the number of Spanish families living in Pensacola had increased to 68, comprising 172 people.

Thus, despite having to relocate the presidio three times after its initial founding, the Spanish military and civilian population remained culturally cohesive for more than six decades. This cohesiveness was due primarily to the population's transfer from one installation to the next and the consistent selection of people from the same areas and social ranks in central New Spain.

While the Spanish populations of Pensacola and St. Augustine in the eighteenth century shared a language, religion, and many traditions, the people themselves differed. In St. Augustine, people of Spanish descent were always the majority, and many were born in Spain, including the soldiers and officers. In Pensacola, almost all the people were from the mixed-race lower castas of New Spain. The few people of Spanish descent in Pensacola were españoles and criollos from New Spain. St. Augustine was a royal colony, administratively and militarily connected to Havana and Spain, while Pensacola was served by the Windward Fleet, connected to Veracruz and Mexico City. If you were to stroll down the street of each community, you would see noticeable differences in the population's size and ethnicity, and the quality of the forts and housing. Regardless of their differences, though, the two military presidios and settlements anchored the borders of Spanish Florida on the Atlantic and the Gulf of Mexico.

NATIVE AMERICANS

Throughout the Presidio Period in West Florida, the few Native Americans who lived there came from somewhere else, since the original Natives had been killed, had died from diseases, or had fled conflict and attack. The first Native people to arrive were Apalachee carpenters sent from Mission San Luis to Pensacola to help build Presidio Santa María. From their perspective, this was just another work assignment to fulfill their chief's labor obligation to the Spanish. Only six years later, after the mission system was destroyed, most of Florida's Natives, missionized or not, fled Spanish Florida in fear of the British. Many stopped at the presidio in Pensacola but moved on because the Spanish could not support them. Some Natives stayed and worked at Santa María, receiving rations, Catholic services, and protection. The perspective of the refugee Natives toward the Spanish at Santa María had shifted from one of confidence and support to wariness and dependence for jobs and security. Throughout the Presidio Period, scores of Indians worked there, and many groups of diverse refugees stopped and requested support but moved on. In 1718, a group of Apalachee arrived and negotiated an alliance with the presidio leaders for rations, a resident priest, and military protection in return for their trade (especially food) and settlement in the area. Two decades later, a group of Yamasee negotiated a similar alliance and started a separate village. The refugee mission villages were quasi-independent, and both relocated at least once to keep their distance from the Spanish when the presidio was moved to the mainland. Throughout the Presidio Period, however, Natives from many groups regularly traded, visited, and worked at the presidio. While mission villagers continued to be somewhat wary of the Spanish, the two groups had a mutually beneficial alliance for jobs, trade, labor, and protection.

Toward the end of the Presidio Period, however, events took a disastrous turn. In 1761, British-allied Creeks attacked and destroyed the Yamasee mission village on Escambia Bay, killing three presidio soldiers, a soldier's pregnant wife, and a five-year-old child. Two months later, Creek raiders attacked and destroyed the Apalachee mission village on the Escambia River. Following these attacks, the Spanish abandoned and burned both villages, and all the Indians retreated to Presidio San Miguel. At least seven more violent raids followed, resulting in the deaths of eleven Indians and soldiers and many more wounded. The Pensacola area had become a war zone, and Fort San Miguel was the only safe refuge. The interaction of the Indians with the Spanish changed yet again, shifting this time to complete dependency. Living adjacent to the fort in "Indian Town," the Natives helped defend the presidio and, in return, received rations from the Spanish. But in 1763, all were evacuated by the triumphant British, who sent them to New Spain.

It is clear that the Native American experience in West Florida underwent dramatic changes during the Presidio Period and ended badly. At first, missionized Apalachee chiefs who were allied with the Spanish sent their villagers to Pensacola to help construct Fort San Carlos. When the British-led Creek forces began attacking the mission system, killing and capturing thousands of Natives, the Spanish shut down the missions, leaving the missionized Indians on their own. Now distrustful of the Spanish, almost all the surviving Natives fled Florida. A few refugee groups made new alliance agreements with the Spanish at the presidios and settled nearby, and they were quasi-independent, not subservient. Some Natives still worked, received rations, and lived at the West Florida presidio, hoping the Spanish could protect them. They were once again disappointed as the British-allied Creeks destroyed their villages and killed or captured them. Fleeing to the presidio, they lived next to the fort. In the end, however, the British won the Seven Years' War, were awarded Spanish Florida, and everyone was forcibly evacuated. We can only imagine what sadness and disappointment in the Spanish the Native Americans in West Florida must have felt. Their experience with them was disastrous, ending with death or evacuation to Mexico.

Summary of Spanish West Florida, 1698–1763

West Florida was serviced by the Windward Fleet that patrolled the Caribbean and Gulf of Mexico, which brought supplies and people to and from the presidio. Archaeologists have discovered and studied the wreck of one of those ships, the *Rosario,* which has given us a unique view of and information about the ships and life aboard them. The Presidio Period was tumultuous for everyone living there. All the residents—both Spanish and Native American—were new to the region, as the original local Indigenous groups were gone, having either fled or fallen victim to disease. At the start, the mission system to the east was still operating, and Apalachee laborers were sent from Mission San Luis to help build the presidio. The presidio was forced to relocate three times due to a French attack, a treaty agreement, and catastrophic hurricanes. Fortunately for us, each relocation produced a wealth of informative documents and archaeological remains. The documents and materials spanned sixty-five years in four distinct episodes, enabling archaeologists and historians to track this community closely. Native refugee mission villages also moved at least once, and their remains and traces of them in the Spanish documents likewise allow us to follow them through time.

Forts were absolutely essential for the military's survival, and six presidio forts were built. The mainland forts were large and well built, while the one documented island fort was tiny. British- and French-led attacks were almost constant throughout this period, and the installations on the mainland were more vulnerable to attack than those on the islands or spits. While presidios on the islands were safe from attack, they were vulnerable to natural disasters, especially hurricanes.

The archaeological remains reveal that life at the presidios was driven by military rank and income. While the installation was administered and operated by Spaniards born in New Spain, the formal social category, or casta, of the mixed-race soldiers and laborers was of lesser importance than their rank and income in determining their status. People of many castas were lumped together as soldiers and laborers/convicts, which provided them with opportunities to improve their social position that were unavailable in New Spain. At first, the Hispanic population was primarily men rotating through on military service, but the number of families increased, especially after 1740, and eventually, the communities included civilian settlers and merchants.

In addition, Natives of many ethnicities came to West Florida as refugees during the Presidio Period, but the Spanish could not afford to support them, and most moved on. Groups from two ethnic groups, Apalachee and Yamasee, did stay. They entered into alliances with the Spanish, agreeing to settle in the area and trade their goods, especially food, in return for a priest, a church, and rations. The groups were small, each with probably nine or ten families and a leader or chief. British-led Creeks attacked and destroyed the Native villages, and by 1761, the region became a war zone, forcing everyone to live in or adjacent to the presidio fort. Finally, the British were awarded Spanish Florida by the treaty ending the Seven Years' War in 1763. The British forcibly evacuated all the Spanish and their Native allies, ending the Presidio Period in West Florida.

Suggested Readings

Judith A. Bense. *Presidios of Spanish West Florida.* Gainesville: University Press of Florida, 2022.

Judith A. Bense. *Presidio Santa María de Galve.* Gainesville: University Press of Florida, 2003.

James Hunter. "Leaden Logs and Broken Ships: Pensacola's First Timber Industry." *Gulf South Historical Review* 15, no. 2 (2000): 6–20.

Places to Visit

Archaeology Institute Museum. Building 89, University of West Florida, 11000 University Parkway, Pensacola, Florida.

Destination Archaeology Museum. Florida Public Archaeology Network headquarters, 207 East Main Street, Pensacola, Florida.

Pensacola Museum of History. 330 South Jefferson Street, Pensacola, Florida.

Website to Visit

Florida Public Archaeology Network: https://www.fpan.us/

SEVEN

SUMMARY

The first people to find Florida arrived about twelve thousand years ago, and they experienced a vastly different landscape and climate than today. Sea level was several hundred feet lower, exposing a peninsula twice the width of what it is today. Giant Ice Age animals roamed the region, including mammoths, mastodons, and their predators, such as saber-toothed tigers and dire wolves. Over the millennia, the world's climate changed, and the first Floridians adapted to the significant changes in shoreline, climate, and environment. Native Floridians developed new technologies for hunting, fishing, and gathering food, and in some areas, agriculture and aquaculture developed, supporting large, complex populations. People lived in villages, towns, and rural hamlets; harvested seasonal plants; cultivated gardens and fields; and hunted. When the Spanish arrived in 1513, most Indigenous Floridians were organized politically under local chiefs and were often part of a larger political entity called a chiefdom. Chiefdoms usually competed with their neighbors for land, resources, and people to pay tribute, and fighting between them was frequent.

What happened in the 250 years following the Spanish arrival is a tale of the interactions of three groups of people from very different cultures: Native Americans; Europeans, especially the Spanish; and Africans. It was a classic clash of cultures in violent competition for the same land. Members of each society experienced turbulence and were affected by it differently. Native Americans wanted to preserve their homelands and cultures. Europeans wanted the new land and resources, particularly in response to competition from other European powers. Although the Spanish brought a few Africans with them, both free and enslaved, the British brought many more into the region as chattel slaves. In the end, the Native Americans and Spanish in La Florida never found a path to coexistence or colonial success. However, the Spanish did provide freedom, safety, and humane treatment for fugitive Africans who could make it to La Florida, primarily to St. Augustine. When the slave-owning British took over Florida in 1763, the Africans left with their Spanish allies.

FIGURE 7.1. Painting of Hernando de Soto landing on Tampa Bay.

The original Spanish province of La Florida included most of what is the Southeastern United States. The first Spaniards to encounter Indigenous Floridians were slavers seeking to capture and sell them to colonists in Hispaniola and Cuba. Soon, Spanish armies arrived, led by veteran military officers who had dreams of conquering the Indigenous people, taking their resources, enslaving them, and becoming wealthy lords of vast, rich estates (figure 7.1). These first encounters were full of violence, as egotistical, greedy, self-centered leaders brutalized Indigenous people and took what they wanted from them. Spain had developed this approach during their seven-hundred-year-long civil war to take their country back from the Muslims (Moors) that ended in 1492. The accidental discovery of the Western Hemisphere and its people by a Spanish expedition seeking a new and quicker trade route to Asia was a shocking surprise. In response, the Spanish began a typical empire-building approach developed by the Persians, Greeks, and Romans: Conquer the population militarily, subjugate them, and take their resources. For more than three centuries (1450 to 1750), the Spanish Empire stretched worldwide, including parts of Europe, Africa, North and South America, and the western Pacific (figure 7.2). The discovery of precious metals, timber, and dense agricultural populations the Spanish could control made their empire the largest and richest up to that time.

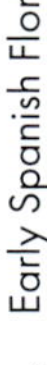

Spanish slave raids immediately spread fear and hatred of the Spanish among Florida's Native societies, and word of the new enemy quickly spread throughout the region. After the discovery of precious metals and large agricultural populations in Mexico and Peru in the mid-sixteenth century, the Crown sent military leaders and their armies to La Florida in search of similar resources there. The first two exploratory armies landed at Tampa Bay eleven years apart, Narváez in 1528 and de Soto in 1539. Both marched north, fighting through ambushes and other forms of resistance from Indians furious at the invasion and mistreatment by the Spanish. Historians and archaeologists have seen the result of these military campaigns on the Indigenous people they encountered, and it was not pleasant. Always outnumbered but armed with superior metal weapons, armor, war horses, and dogs, the Spaniards compensated for their small numbers by terrorizing everyone they found and taking Native leaders and their families hostage for protection. In this way, the explorers waged war on the Natives, forcing hundreds to assist them by providing food and laborers as porters, guides, and female sex slaves. On hearing of the Spanish army's approach, most people fled their villages to avoid trouble and waged a guerrilla war of ambushes and raids.

Historical archaeologists have reconstructed the explorers' trails, such as de Soto's first winter camp of 1539–1540 in Tallahassee, where the Spanish took over the capital town of the Apalachee Indians. Spanish materials recovered from de Soto's five-month stay there were largely utilitarian and

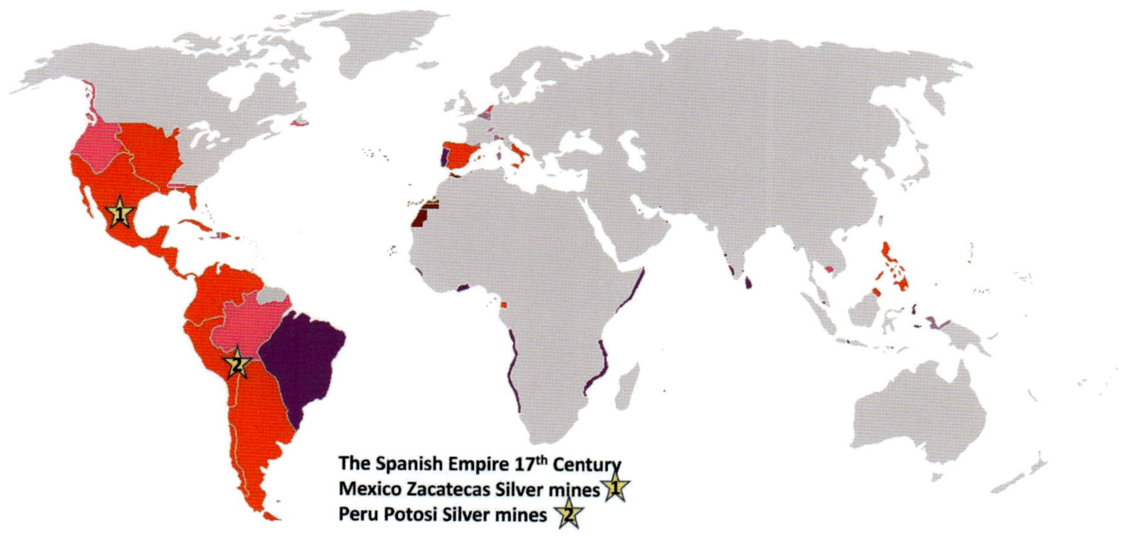

FIGURE 7.2. Map of the Spanish Empire in the seventeenth century.

reflected the soldiers' daily life inside their fort. The local Apalachee resisted the invaders with attacks and harassment, eventually driving the Spanish away. The expensive Narváez and de Soto military expeditions through La Florida failed to find gems, precious metals, or large agricultural populations that could be conquered militarily. These findings and the strong resistance from the Natives everywhere they went forced the Spanish to change their policy from trying to defeat the Indigenous peoples to a more peaceful approach. The Spanish decided to establish traditional colonies of settlers brought from Spain and protect them with military units. The colonists and military were not to force Native people to assist them but to request their support and trade. Up to this point, the Natives had successfully defended their homelands and defeated vast armies with superior weapons.

Tristán de Luna led the first expedition to peacefully colonize Spanish Florida in 1559. He was charged with establishing two new port settlements on Pensacola Bay and Port Royal Sound, South Carolina, founding a new town at Coosa in the interior, and building new roads connecting the towns and the silver mines in Zacatecas, Mexico. The expedition included 1,500 people with supplies and food for a year. Unfortunately, five weeks after they landed on Pensacola Bay, a massive hurricane struck Pensacola, sinking six of their ships, ruining a seventh, and destroying their food supply for the year. Doomed to seek food from hostile Native groups, the expedition searched for Native people to help them, but most did not and fled, burning their own fields and taking their stored food. In 1561, after two years of unsuccessfully searching for support from Native groups, the Crown terminated the Luna colonization effort and declared it another very costly failure.

Archaeologists have found the site of the Luna settlement in Pensacola and three of their sunken ships. The planned town at Pensacola became instead a base camp for rescue and relief supplies from Mexico, while large groups went into the interior to search in vain for food and support. Archaeology has revealed evidence of their stay on Pensacola Bay, including imported ceramics from Spain and Mexico, glass beads from Europe, and metal artifacts such as horseshoe nails, musket parts, lead shot, clothing fasteners, and crossbow tips. Archaeologists have also found traces of their structures. The three Luna shipwrecks also revealed a wealth of material entombed in the muddy bottom of Pensacola Bay. The materials include the ships themselves, a huge iron anchor, munitions such as stone cannonballs, a complete front of an iron breastplate, galley cooking pots, ceramic plates, and many personal items from shipboard life.

After the Luna colonial attempt failed in 1561, the Spanish king was reluctant to try again to colonize La Florida. Immediately, the French pounced on an opportunity to take Florida, starting a new chapter in Florida's early history. The French secretly built two forts, one on Parris Island in Port Royal Sound (Charlesfort) in 1562 and another at the mouth of the St. Johns River (Fort Caroline) in 1564. Alarmed, the Spanish immediately launched a military campaign under Pedro Menéndez de Avilés to drive the French out and colonize La Florida. Menéndez found Charlesfort abandoned and took Fort Caroline. He established the first capital of Florida, Santa Elena, in 1566 on the ruins of Charlesfort and erected a new military installation at what is now St. Augustine. He also established fourteen outpost forts and missions on large coastal bays of the peninsula and Atlantic, plus a string of forts into the interior from Santa Elena across the Appalachians. Historians and archaeologists have been fascinated with these earliest French and Spanish settlements, and many have been found and studied: Charlesfort and Santa Elena in South Carolina, Fort San Juan in North Carolina, and Mission/Fort San Antón and San Gregorio de Tocobaga on the Florida Gulf Coast. Local Native Americans fiercely attacked every installation and town, resisting the constant demands for support from the Spaniards and their insistence on imposing Catholic beliefs and European ways of life on them. Within two years, Native groups destroyed every fort and mission, killing all the Spaniards except those at Santa Elena and San Agustín (St. Augustine). They constantly attacked Santa Elena and forced its abandonment in 1587. While hostile local Indians also attacked St. Augustine, it survived because of a relatively large military force and constant assistance from the Crown. The Spanish needed to protect the treasure fleets along the Atlantic and maintain at least one foothold in their colony.

It is important to recognize and appreciate the success of Florida's Native Americans in stopping Spanish efforts to conquer or colonize them for almost a century. Some groups had been informed ahead of time that the Spanish were not to be trusted, and they fled before the armies arrived. To thwart the Spanish, Natives often would destroy their own houses, take all their food supplies, and burn their agricultural fields. Whenever the Spanish arrived, Native groups ambushed, attacked, and killed them until they left. Other Native groups farther north initially welcomed the Spanish, letting them stay in their villages, building them forts and housing, and providing food for the soldiers. But within a few months, the same pattern occurred. The Spanish became increasingly imperious and violent toward the local

FIGURE 7.3. Depiction of Menéndez's army arriving at Seloy's village in 1565.

people, demanded more food, and abused their women. The Natives did not tolerate this treatment and destroyed the Spanish settlements. Every military expedition, installation, mission, and town, save one, was attacked and destroyed by the local Indian group despite violent revenge assaults by the Spanish military. In short, Native Americans won the Spanish war against them for 150 years.

In St. Augustine, historical archaeologists have found Menéndez's 1565 first encampment inside the remains of Chief Seloy's village (figure 7.3). It had a defensive wall, warehouse, munitions building, and housing for the colonists. The villagers grew hostile over Spanish demands and harsh treatment, and within a few months, Menéndez moved his settlement to nearby Anastasia Island, which they heavily fortified. Although always small, St. Augustine had high strategic and political value due to the continual sailing by of the Spanish fleet just off the Florida peninsula in the Atlantic. It was also paramount that the Spanish have a permanent settlement in La Florida to protect their claim to it. As a result of these critical issues, St. Augustine was supported, defended, and maintained despite being a financial loss. Early Spanish Florida had no valuable resources, but its location was strategic in the larger picture of Spain's North American empire to protect their treasure fleets, drive off pirates, and block access to the silver mines of central Mexico.

After the failure of the Luna and Menéndez efforts to colonize La Florida, the Spanish developed a third strategy to pacify the Indigenous people of

La Florida through missionization. A network of Franciscan missions based in St. Augustine started in 1587, and at first, the strategy seemed successful. Thousands of Native people were baptized and became subservient to the Catholic cross and Spanish flag (figure 7.4). The missionization process developed by colonial administrators was to work through the existing Native political system, with participation to be voluntary and rewarded. There were two critical features of the Franciscan mission system: voluntary acceptance of resident missionaries by Native political leaders and the presence of nearby but nonresident military forces. The chiefs continued to govern their villages and agreed to build a mission church for missionaries and send food and laborers annually to St. Augustine. At least seventy missions were established between 1587 and 1706. Ultimately, the mission system became a labor pool and breadbasket for the St. Augustine presidio, providing more than a million pounds of corn annually from fields around St. Augustine by the mid-seventeenth century, and the mission provinces sent an additional 125,000 pounds of surplus corn each year.

Archaeologists and historians have found and investigated scores of missions. They found that most missions were in small villages with small churches. Friars ate a Native diet provided by the converts, and there were usually few Spanish artifacts associated with the church and friary. Converted villagers stayed in their home villages and farmed corn, beans, and squash. But one mission was different: San Luis de Apalachee. This mission was voluntarily moved at Spanish request and with the chief's agreement to a militarily strategic point on the road to St. Augustine, the Camino Real. Eventually, it transitioned into a Spanish town of Hispanic families who owned cattle ranches and farms in the region, and the Apalachee moved out of Mission San Luis into farming hamlets.

FIGURE 7.4. Drawing of a typical Franciscan priest, Friar Francisco Pareja.

Pacification through missionization was implemented for more than a century. It was headquartered in St. Augustine and extended up the Georgia coast and into the interior to Tallahassee. Rebellions occurred in all missionized Native provinces: Guale, Mocama, Timucua, and Apalachee.

As the friars' demands intensified, each group resisted, and the Spanish military brutally suppressed these rebellions. However, the missions were doomed due to population collapse from epidemics of European diseases, and the British-led slave raids finished them off. By 1706, all the missions were either destroyed or abandoned, and missionized Indians were left on their own. The Spanish retreated to St. Augustine, having established no lasting mission settlements. Fearing the British, Florida's Native Americans became homeless refugees. Some fled to St. Augustine and Pensacola, seeking protection from the presidios there, but others fled to various areas of the Southeast. Florida became virtually vacant of its Indigenous people.

At the end of the seventeenth century, Presidio San Agustín was still the only Spanish settlement in Florida. It was a military installation with a garrison and an adjacent military town. Throughout the Early Spanish period, it was repeatedly attacked, first by local Timucuans, then by English pirates, and finally by British-led Native armies who all burned it to the ground. A stone fortress built in the late seventeenth century saved the population many times, and the Spanish built four defensive walls in the eighteenth century to protect the town. The community and garrison depended on the Crown's support. However, St. Augustine was worth the expense for its strategic and political value: It enabled Spain to hold on to its claim to Florida, protect the treasure fleets, salvage shipwrecks, and rescue their crews. Historians and archaeologists have documented that the town was like a typical Hispanic colonial town with a central plaza, grid of residential streets, and Spanish way of life. The civilian population was initially composed of families of retired soldiers and administrators from Spain who stayed in the community, usually taking Indian or mestizo wives. The descendants of the founding families developed the hybrid Hispanic culture that flourished in many parts of the Spanish Empire. In Florida, they were called Floridanos, and they eventually owned haciendas for cattle and farming, operated businesses in town, and held senior colonial administrative posts.

Archaeology in St. Augustine initially focused on the military defenses, especially the defensive lines around the town and the Castillo. In the 1970s, the focus shifted to domestic life in the town and the development of Floridano Hispanic culture. Excavations targeted specific house lots with documented eighteenth-century ownership by a resident of a known occupation, income, and social position. A comparison of the archaeological information recovered from the house lots of families of different social statuses and incomes revealed how Hispanic culture developed from the mixing of Native,

Spanish, and African ethnicities and the distinctions in how people lived depending on their occupation and income. Archaeological research into domestic life in the town continues to the present day.

As soon as the British expanded into what was then northern Spanish Florida by erecting the town of Charleston in 1670, British planters began establishing new plantations based on enslaved labor. At first, Native Americans were captured and sold into slavery through the extensive British trade system. Soon, groups like the Yamasee and Creeks engaged in war with other Indigenous groups for captives to trade for firearms. The Indian traders then took the captives to the slave market in Charleston, where planters and slave traders purchased them. After the Indians at the Florida missions and in the rest of Florida were defeated and enslaved, planters turned to African slaves. The number of enslaved Africans quickly grew, and with it, the number of escapees. Word was sent out from St. Augustine that any fugitive slaves who could reach Spanish Florida would be freed and given employment. As a result, St. Augustine became a haven for runaway slaves, and they became an important part of the militia and society.

Spanish occupation of West Florida introduced a new wrinkle in the Spanish strategy to maintain their hold on Florida. In 1698, they extended the colony four hundred miles west to Pensacola Bay. The purposes of the West Florida presidio were to prevent colonial rivals from taking the deepwater bay and to protect the newly extended western border and northern Gulf Coast of Spanish Florida. Military attacks, natural disasters, and treaties caused three relocations of the presidio. In the end, the Spanish built four sequential presidios in this region, three on Pensacola Bay and one on St. Joseph Bay. The people sent to the West Florida presidio differed from those sent to St. Augustine. They were of mixed descent and came from central Mexico, where a Hispanic culture had existed for nearly two centuries. A few criollos of Spanish descent occupied the top positions of officers and senior administrators. The population hovered around three hundred to four hundred people, with short-term large influxes of military units, shipwreck victims, or refugee Indians.

There have been significant historical archaeological investigations of the West Florida presidio sites, a shipwreck, and a Native refugee mission site that have produced a wealth of information about how the Spanish military and Native American refugees lived during this period, the facilities and defenses that were built for them, and one of the ships that supplied them (figure 7.5). There were four presidio locations, six military outposts, and

FIGURE 7.5.
Excavating the keel of the *Rosario* shipwreck in Pensacola Bay.

two allied refugee Native mission villages in the region. The archaeological remains were consistent at the four presidio sites, and each made adaptations to the natural environment through time, especially in building materials. The remains reflect differences in rank and class, seen in housing, food, amenities, clothing, and jewelry. The underfunded and understaffed presidio held its ground when attacked, and when the French attacked and took the first presidio, the Spanish retook it. Their success is the reason our state today extends to the Perdido and not the Apalachicola River.

In 1763, a treaty was signed ending the Seven Years' War. Because Spain was on the losing side, as part of the agreement Britain was awarded all of Spanish Florida east of the Mississippi River. The British forcibly removed all the Spanish military, civilians, and Native allies who wanted to leave with the Spanish, including African runaways who had settled in La Florida. The St. Augustine population was sent to Cuba, and the Pensacola population was sent to Veracruz. This ended the first Spanish occupation of Florida. Even though Florida was returned to Spain eighteen years later, in 1781, few of the original population returned since they had put down roots in their new homes.

Knowing the details of what happened in Spanish Florida during those first 250 years, it is interesting to step back and see how it all fits into the more extensive colonial Spanish Empire. The most critical resources in their vast empire were the silver mines in Mexico and Peru (now Bolivia). These mines were the source of unimaginable wealth and were protected at all costs. The Potosí mine in Peru is high up in the Andes, three hundred miles inland from the Pacific coast across rugged terrain, so it was well protected from any takeover by rivals. The Zacatecas silver mines in Mexico were about 250 miles from the Gulf Coast, but the terrain was much easier to cross, and the mines were accessible from the north by land. The vulnerability of the Zacatecas mines and the proximity of the shipping lanes to the Florida peninsula were why Spanish Florida was important to the Spanish Empire. Therefore, despite the lack of valuable resources, resistance of the Indigenous people, and eventual Indigenous population collapse, the Florida colony was indispensable. This explains why the Spanish government kept trying new

policies to pacify the Native groups time after time and why, in 1763, there were still two active presidios on the Atlantic and Gulf Coasts, protecting shipping along the Atlantic and the silver shipments bound for Spain.

The story of Early Spanish Florida is a difficult one for all three groups who lived there. For the Spanish, their Florida colony was a failure. After 250 years of colonization attempts, all that was left of the once-vast province was a vacant area between two small, subsidized presidios, Pensacola and San Agustín. The Indigenous Floridians had been able to drive off the Spanish attempts to conquer them militarily for 150 years. However, the effects of missionization, population collapses from epidemics of European diseases, and undefended British slave raids spelled their end. As a result, the Indian groups in Florida vanished, with only a few survivors fleeing to safety. This was a complicated chapter in Florida history with no winners. The problems that European invasions caused for the Indigenous peoples in Florida occurred throughout the colonial world, not just in Spanish Florida.

Today, Florida has more than twenty-two million residents, with one hundred million plus visitors coming to the state annually. Our warm winters and entertainment complexes are increasingly desirable. Florida is a tremendous success and an important part of the United States. Nearly three centuries have passed since the Early Spanish period, and Florida is thriving, thanks to the hard work and accomplishments of the following generations who figured out the paths to the success that we enjoy today.

ACKNOWLEDGMENTS

It took a village to create and publish this book, and at the top of the list are Mary G. Puckett, acquisitions editor at the University Press of Florida, and Nashid Madyun, executive director of Florida Humanities. Ms. Puckett provided personal support during this book's developmental and writing stages. She agreed to important requests of mine to make the book affordable, distribute it widely, and include 150-plus illustrations. Mr. Madyun and Florida Humanities supported the illustrations and an artist to create several new important scenes. Without the assistance and support of these two professionals, this book would not have been written.

I also want to acknowledge the editor of my first-draft manuscript, Elizabeth Scott. She turned my many run-on sentences, redundancies, inconsistencies, and complex wordings into easy-to-read English. Her diligence and hard work made the Press's editing and publication process go smoothly. I also want to acknowledge Jennifer Melcher, research associate in the Archaeology Institute, and Professor John Worth in the Department of Anthropology at the University of West Florida. Ms. Melcher assisted with the frequent maps in this book, and Professor Worth answered many detailed questions and provided several of the images and maps used in this book. The two archaeological reviewers of the manuscript selected by the press offered invaluable suggestions. They pointed out I needed to bring to light the viewpoints and histories of the underrepresented groups in Early Spanish Florida, especially the Natives and Africans. I agreed, and implementing their recommendations made this book better.

Illustrations are a very important part of this book, and I spent as much time assembling and obtaining permission to use them as I did writing the text. I discovered many talented artists who have created spectacular images of scenes from the past, images that have captured the human elements of this time of violent cultural contact. The artists were supportive and helpful in bringing the past to life, and I thank them. They are Calvin Bryant, Merald Clark, Dave Edwards, George Gibbs, Nathan Glick (deceased), John Klausmeyer, Jacques Le Moyne (deceased), John LoCastro, Albert Manucy (deceased), Steve Patricia, Dan Quigley, Herb Roe, Christopher Still, Richard Thornton, and Jackson Walker.

Many archaeologists were also very generous and helpful in providing access to illustrations and clarification of details, especially Robin Beck, Christopher Rodning, David Moore, Thomas Whyte, John Worth, and Kathleen Deagan. I requested and was granted reprint permission and high-resolution images for many illustrations from the Florida Museum of Natural History, Mission San Luis, the Archaeology Institute at UWF, and the Florida Division of Historical Resources. I am grateful for their support because they helped make this book much more understandable.

The University of West Florida has been essential in facilitating my writing of this book, particularly the chair of our board of trustees, Suzanne Lewis, and President Martha D. Saunders. Thank you for your patience and support in making this book possible.

ILLUSTRATION CREDITS

Figure 1.1. "Spanish Army 1500," from Historica Wiki.
Figure 1.2. State Archives of Florida, Florida Memory.
Figure 1.3. Courtesy of Mission San Luis, Florida Department of State.
Figure 1.4. "Las Palmas Casa de Colon," from Wikimedia Commons.
Figure 1.5. Courtesy of the Archaeology Institute, University of West Florida.
Figure 2.1. Adapted from "A map of the Iberian Peninsula in 1492 highlighting the Crown of Castile," by Marnal. From Wikimedia Commons.
Figure 2.2. Del Piombo Sebastiano, "Christopher Columbus, half-length portrait, facing slightly right." Courtesy of the Library of Congress.
Figure 2.3. Map by author. Base map credit: Tomas Griger / istockphoto.
Figure 2.4. Painting by Christopher Still, courtesy of the artist.
Figure 2.5. Painting by Merald Clark, courtesy of the artist.
Figure 2.6. Map by author.
Figure 2.7. "Pánfilo de Narváez," from Wikimedia Commons.
Figure 2.8. Painting courtesy of Christopher Still.
Figure 2.9. By Carlos Múgica y Pérez, from Internet Archive. Licensed under PDM 1.0.
Figure 2.10. Courtesy of the Library of Congress.
Figure 2.11. Drawing by George Gibbs (1898). Wikimedia Commons.
Figure 2.12. Drawing from "Hernando De Soto," chapter 3 in *A History of Florida* (1904).
Figure 2.13. Map by author. Base map credit: AdobeStock.
Figure 2.14. State Archives of Florida, Florida Memory.
Figure 2.15. Courtesy of the Florida Division of Historical Resources.
Figure 2.16. Illustration by Nathan Glick, from *History of Alabama for Junior High Schools* (1938).
Figure 2.17. Art by Herb Roe, courtesy of the artist.
Figure 2.18. Map by author. Base map credit: Tomas Griger / istockphoto.
Figure 2.19. Artist unknown. Courtesy of the National Park Service.
Figure 2.20. Art by Dan Quigley, commissioned and owned by the City of Pensacola, and digitally reproduced by the UWF Historic Trust pursuant to a license from the City of Pensacola.

Figure 2.21. Map courtesy of John E. Worth.

Figure 2.22. Courtesy of the Archaeology Institute, University of West Florida.

Figure 2.23. Courtesy of the Archaeology Institute, University of West Florida.

Figure 2.24. Courtesy of the Archaeology Institute, University of West Florida.

Figure 2.25. Courtesy of the Archaeology Institute, University of West Florida.

Figure 2.26. Art by and courtesy of John LoCastro.

Figure 2.27. Courtesy of the Archaeology Institute, University of West Florida.

Figure 2.28. Courtesy of the Archaeology Institute, University of West Florida.

Figure 3.1. Pieter van der Aa, "Map of Ferdinand DeSoto's American conquests, drawn from his memoirs, 1638." Courtesy of the State Library of Florida, Florida Map Collection.

Figure 3.2. Map by author.

Figure 3.3. Courtesy of JeanRibault.org.

Figure 3.4. Engraving by Theodor de Bry. Courtesy of HathiTrust.

Figure 3.5. Engraving by Theodor de Bry after watercolor by Jacques Le Moyne. Courtesy of the Library of Congress.

Figure 3.6. Courtesy of the National Park Service, Southeast Regional Office.

Figure 3.7. Engraving by Theodor de Bry. Courtesy of HathiTrust.

Figure 3.8. Painting by Jacques Le Moyne de Morgues, engraved by Theodor de Bry. Wikimedia Commons.

Figure 3.9. Woodcut carving by José Camarón y Boronat. Wikimedia Commons.

Figure 3.10. Courtesy of JeanRibault.org

Figure 3.11. Art by Jackson Walker. Courtesy of the Florida National Guard.

Figure 3.12. Wikimedia Commons.

Figure 3.13. Photo by Christina Choe. Courtesy of Kathleen Deagan.

Figure 3.14. Courtesy of the Florida Museum of Natural History–Historical Archaeology Collections.

Figure 3.15. Art by and courtesy of Thomas Whyte.

Figure 3.16. Courtesy of the Florida Museum of Natural History–Historical Archaeology Collections.

Figure 3.17. Map by John Worth, Courtesy of the Archaeology Institute, University of West Florida.

Figure 3.18. Art by and courtesy of Merald Clark.

Figure 3.19. Courtesy of the Florida Museum of Natural History–Historical Archaeology Collections.

Figure 3.20. Courtesy of the Florida Museum of Natural History–Historical Archaeology Collections.

Figure 3.21. Art by John Klausmeyer. Courtesy of the Museum of Anthropological Archaeology, University of Michigan.

Figure 3.22. Courtesy of the Museum of Anthropological Archaeology, University of Michigan.

Figure 3.23. Courtesy of the Museum of Anthropological Archaeology, University of Michigan.

Figure 3.24. Courtesy of the Warren Wilson College Archaeology Lab.

Figure 3.25. From *Archaeology at Santa Elena: Doorway to the Past,* by Stanley South (1996). Courtesy of the University of South Carolina Libraries Scholar Commons.

Figure 3.26. Map by Stanley South. Courtesy of the National Park Service Open Parks Network.

Figure 3.27. Drawings by Stanley South. Courtesy of the National Park Service Open Parks Network.

Figure 3.28. Courtesy of the National Park Service Open Parks Network.

Figure 4.1. Art by William Celander. Courtesy of the Florida Museum of Natural History–Historical Archaeology Collections.

Figure 4.2. Courtesy of John E. Worth

Figure 4.3. Courtesy of John E. Worth

Figure 4.4. Courtesy of Robert Thornton.

Figure 4.5. Courtesy of Our Lady of the Mountains Roman Catholic Church.

Figure 4.6. Courtesy of the Division of Anthropology, American Museum of Natural History.

Figure 4.7. Courtesy of the Division of Anthropology, American Museum of Natural History.

Figure 4.8. Courtesy of Mission San Luis, Florida Department of State.

Figure 4.9. Photo by and courtesy of Austin J. Bell.

Figure 4.10. Courtesy of Mission San Luis, Florida Department of State.

Figure 4.11. Courtesy of Mission San Luis, Florida Department of State.

Figure 4.12. Courtesy of Mission San Luis, Florida Department of State.

Figure 4.13. Courtesy of Mission San Luis, Florida Department of State.
Figure 4.14. Courtesy of Mission San Luis, Florida Department of State
Figure 4.15. Courtesy of Mission San Luis, Florida Department of State.
Figure 4.16. Courtesy of Mission San Luis, Florida Department of State.
Figure 4.17. Courtesy of Mission San Luis, Florida Department of State.
Figure 4.18. Courtesy of Mission San Luis, Florida Department of State.
Figure 4.19. Courtesy of Granger Historical Picture Archive.
Figure 4.20. Art by and courtesy of Merald Clark.
Figure 5.1. Alamy.
Figure 5.2. Drawing by Jacques Le Moyne. Courtesy of HathiTrust.
Figure 5.3. Map by Baptista Boazio. State Archives of Florida, Florida Memory.
Figure 5.4. Courtesy of Carl Halbirt.
Figure 5.5. Courtesy of Carl Halbirt.
Figure 5.6. Map possibly drawn by Mestas. State Archives of Florida, Florida Memory.
Figure 5.7. Detail of map in figure 5.6. State Archives of Florida, Florida Memory.
Figure 5.8. Courtesy of the Florida Museum of Natural History–Historical Archaeology Collections.
Figure 5.9. Art by William Celander and courtesy of the Florida Museum of Natural History–Historical Archaeology Collections.
Figure 5.10. Courtesy of the Florida Museum of Natural History–Historical Archaeology Collections.
Figure 5.11. John Davis, "Stabbing the Sentry," from the *Pirates of the Spanish Main* series (N19) for Allen & Ginter Cigarettes. The Jefferson R. Burdick Collection, Gift of Jefferson R. Burdick. Metropolitan Museum of Art, New York. Licensed under CC0 1.0.
Figure 5.12. Art by William Celander. Courtesy of the Florida Museum of Natural History–Historical Archaeology Collections.
Figure 5.13. Art by and courtesy of Steve Patricia.
Figure 5.14. Wikimedia Commons.
Figure 5.15. Courtesy of City of St. Augustine Archaeology Program.
Figure 5.16. Art by Albert Manucy. From *The Houses of St. Augustine: Notes on the Architecture from 1565 to 1821,* by Albert Manucy. HathiTrust.
Figure 5.17. Art by William Celander. Courtesy of the Florida Museum of Natural History–Historical Archaeology Collections.

Figure 5.18. Art by William Celander. Courtesy of the Florida Museum of Natural History–Historical Archaeology Collections.

Figure 5.19. Courtesy of the Florida Museum of Natural History–Historical Archaeology Collections.

Figure 5.20. State Library and Archives of Florida, Florida Memory.

Figure 5.21. Art by William Celander. Courtesy of the Florida Museum of Natural History–Historical Archaeology Collections.

Figure 5.22. Wikimedia Commons.

Figure 5.23. Drawing by Albert Manucy, National Park Service. Image courtesy of the Collection of the St. Augustine Historical Society Research Library and HathiTrust.

Figure 5.24. Drawing by Albert Manucy. Image courtesy of the Collection of the St. Augustine Historical Society Research Library and Hathi Trust.

Figure 5.25 Drawing by Albert Manucy. In *The Building of Castillo de San Marcos* by Luis Rafael Arana and Albert Manucy, 1977 printing, p. 37. National Park Service Interpretive Series, History No. 1.

Figure 5.26. *Top:* National Park Service. *Bottom:* Wikimedia Commons.

Figure 5.27. Courtesy of the St. Augustine Historical Society Research Library.

Figure 5.28. Courtesy of the National Park Service.

Figure 5.29. Map by author and John Worth.

Figure 6.1. Map by author.

Figure 6.2. Courtesy of the Archaeology Institute, University of West Florida.

Figure 6.3. Art by Dave Edwards.

Figure 6.4. Painting by Dan Quigly, commissioned and owned by the City of Pensacola, and digitally reproduced by the UWF Historic Trust pursuant to a license from the City of Pensacola.

Figure 6.5. Adapted from a map by Valentin Devin. Courtesy of the Archaeology Institute, University of West Florida.

Figure 6.6. Courtesy of the Archaeology Institute, University of West Florida.

Figure 6.7. Detail of "A north view of Pensacola, on the Island of Santa Rosa." Drawing by Dominic Serres, engraved by Thomas Jefferys. Library of Congress.

Figure 6.8. Courtesy of the Archaeology Institute, University of West Florida.

Figure 6.9. Courtesy of the Archaeology Institute, University of West Florida.

Figure 6.10. Courtesy of the Archaeology Institute, University of West Florida.

Figure 6.11. Art by Dave Edwards.

Figure 6.12. Courtesy of the Archaeology Institute, University of West Florida.

Figure 6.13. Art by Dave Edwards.

Figure 6.14. Courtesy of the Archaeology Institute, University of West Florida.

Figure 6.15. Courtesy of the Archaeology Institute, University of West Florida.

Figure 6.16. Courtesy of the Archaeology Institute, University of West Florida.

Figure 6.17. Courtesy of the Archaeology Institute, University of West Florida.

Figure 6.18. Courtesy of the United States Geological Survey.

Figure 6.19. Detail of "A north view of Pensacola, on the Island of Santa Rosa." Drawing by Dominic Serres, engraved by Thomas Jefferys. Library of Congress.

Figure 6.20. Courtesy of the Archaeology Institute, University of West Florida.

Figure 6.21. Courtesy of the Archaeology Institute, University of West Florida.

Figure 6.22. Courtesy of the Archaeology Institute, University of West Florida.

Figure 6.23. Courtesy of the Archaeology Institute, University of West Florida.

Figure 6.24. Courtesy of the Archaeology Institute, University of West Florida.

Figure 6.25. Courtesy of the Archaeology Institute, University of West Florida.

Figure 6.26. Courtesy of the Archaeology Institute, University of West Florida.

Figure 6.27. Courtesy of the Archaeology Institute, University of West Florida.

Figure 6.28. Courtesy of the Archaeology Institute, University of West Florida.

Figure 6.29. Courtesy of the Archaeology Institute, University of West Florida.

Figure 6.30. *Casta painting* (anonymous). Instituto Nacional de Antropología e Historia. Wikimedia Commons.

Figure 7.1. State Library and Archives of Florida, Florida Memory.

Figure 7.2. Wikimedia Commons.

Figure 7.3. Art by Jackson Walker. Courtesy of the Florida National Guard.

Figure 7.4. Courtesy of the Florida Museum of Natural History.

Figure 7.5. Courtesy of the Archaeology Institute, University of West Florida.

Sidebar Illustration Credits

Page 13. Map courtesy of John E. Worth.

Page 26, *top*. Photo by John Worth. Courtesy of the Archaeology Institute, University of West Florida.

Page 26, *bottom*. Wikimedia Commons. Courtesy of the National Park Service.

Page 57. Engraving by Theodor de Bry. Wikimedia Commons.

Page 95, *top*. Courtesy of Mission San Luis, Florida Department of State.

Page 95, *bottom*. Wikimedia Commons.

Page 125. Courtesy of the Archaeology Institute, University of West Florida.

Page 142. Photograph by Mark A. Wilson. Wikimedia Commons.

Page 170. Drawing by Dominic Serres, engraved by Thomas Jefferys. Library of Congress.

INDEX

Page numbers in *italics* refer to illustrations.

DR. JUDY BENSE was born in Morristown, New Jersey, into a dairy farming family. She and her family moved to Panama City, Florida, where they owned and operated a small family dairy. She grew up primarily in Panama City but also lived for a few years in Lakeland and Tallahassee. She received her bachelor of science and master of science in anthropology and archaeology from Florida State University and her doctorate from Washington State University in 1972 in anthropology. After the sudden death of her parents, she returned to the farm in Panama City in 1972 and took care of the family elders and younger brothers. In 1977, she started her career at the University of Alabama, operating a large testing contract with the US Army Corps of Engineers for the Tennessee-Tombigbee Waterway in Alabama and Mississippi. Bense joined the University of West Florida (UWF) in 1980 and continued major excavation contracts on the Tenn-Tom Waterway. She founded the anthropology and archaeology programs at UWF during her forty-year tenure there, including the Department of Anthropology, the Archaeology Institute, and the Florida Public Archaeology Network. She has published more than fifty academic journal articles, reports, and five books covering a variety of topics in archaeology. Bense also served as UWF president for almost nine years, from 2008 to 2017, during which time she grew enrollment, built new dormitories, and started several new academic programs and a football team. Stepping down from the UWF presidency to return to archaeology, Bense prepared a synthesis of her primary research effort, *Presidios of Spanish West Florida,* published in 2022. Since then, she has published several academic journal articles and continues to produce research and publications. She also chairs the Florida Historical Commission, sits on the National Register of Historic Places Review Board, and has recently been inducted into the Florida Women's Hall of Fame and the Gulf South Athletic Conference Hall of Fame. Her major professional awards include the Harrington Medal for Lifetime Achievement from the Society of Historical Archaeology and the Florida Anthropological Society Lifetime Achievement Award.